Data Structure

Second Year Diploma : Semester IV

(Computer/ IT Engineering Group)

**(Strictly as per new revised 'E' Scheme
w.e.f. academic year 2010-2011)**

Dilip Kumar Sultania

B.Tech.(hons.) Computer Science and Engineering
I.I.T. ,Kharagpur.

® **Tech-Max** Publications, Pune
**Innovation Throughout
Polytechnic Division**

Data Structure

Dilip Kumar Sultania

(Semester IV – Computer/IT Engineering Group, MSBTE)

First Edition : January 2011

Printed at : Image Offset, Survey No. 10/1/1, Dhayari Gaon, Near Kailas Jeevan Factory, Pune – 41,Maharashtra State, India. Phone : 020 - 24392059

ISBN 978-81-8492-029-1

Published by
Tech-Max Publications
Head Office : B/5, First floor, Maniratna Complex, Taware Colony, Aranyeshwar Corner, Pune - 411 009. Maharashtra State, India
Ph : 91-20-24225065, 91-20-24217965. Fax 020-24228978.
Email : info@techmaxbooks.com,
Website : www.techmaxbooks.com

(Tech Max Book Code : MD225)
Price Rs. 195/-

Preface

My dear students,

I am extremely happy to come out with this edition of **"Data Structure"** for you, the Computer/IT Engineering students. I have divided the subject into small chapters so that the topics can be arranged and understood properly. The topics within the chapters have been arranged in a proper sequence to ensure smooth flow of the subject.

A large number of programs and functions have been included. So, that this book will cater for all your needs.

I am thankful to Shri. Sachin Shah and Shri. Arunoday Kumar for the encouragement and support that they have extended. I am also thankful to all members of Tech-Max Publications and others for their efforts to make this book as good as it is. We have jointly made every possible effort to eliminate all the errors in this book. However if you find any, please let us know, because that will help me to improve further.

I am also thankful to my family members and friends for patience and encouragement.

- Dilip Kumar Sultania

Syllabus

Chapter	Name of Topics	Hours	Marks
01	Introduction to data structure: 1.1 Data Representation • Abstract data Types • Data Structures (Linear and Non-Linear) • Atomic Type 1.2 Data Types • Primitive data type • Derived data type 1.3 Operations on data structures • Traversing, Inserting, Deleting • Searching and sorting **(Refer chapter 1)**	02	08
02	Principles of programming and Analysis of Algorithms: 2.1 Algorithms • Different approaches for designing an algorithm • Complexity in terms of time and space • Big 'O' Notation **(Refer chapter 2)**	02	06
03	Searching & Sorting : 3.1 Sorting • An Introduction • Efficiency of Sorting Algorithms 3.2 Sorting Techniques • Bubble Sort • Selection Sort • Insertion Sort • Radix Sort (only algorithm) • Shell Sort (only algorithm) • Quick Sort (only algorithm) 3.3 Searching • An Introduction • Linear search • Binary Search **(Refer chapter 3)**	08	16

Chapter	Name of Topics	Hours	Marks

04	**Stacks:**
	4.1 Introduction to Stacks
	   • Stacks as an Abstract Data Type
	   • Primitive operations of stacks
	4.2 Representation of Stacks through Arrays
	4.3 Application of Stacks
	   • Stack machines
	   • Recursion
	   • Arithmetic expression: Polish Notation **(Refer chapter 4)**
		06	12

05	**Queues:**
	5.1 Introduction
	   • Queue as an Abstract Data Type
	   • Representation of Queues
	5.2 Operations on queue : Searching, Insertion, Deletion.
	5.3 Types of queues
	   • Circular Queues
	   • Priority Queue
	   • Dequeues
	5.4 Application of Queues **(Refer chapter 5)**
		06	12

06	**Linked List:**
	6.1 Introduction
	   • Terminologies Node, Address, Pointer, Information,
	   • Next, Null pointer, Empty list etc.
	6.2 Operations on list Searching, Insertion and Deletion
	6.3 Types of lists
	   • Linear list
	   • Circular list
	   • Doubly list
	6.4 Array, stacks, queues, implementation using list. **(Refer chapter 6)**
		06	12

Chapter	Name of Topics	Hours	Marks
07	Trees: 7.1 Introduction to Trees 7.2 Types of Trees • General tree • Binary tree • Height balanced • Weight balanced • Binary search tree 7.3 Operations on Binary Search Tree • Insertion of node • Deletion of node • Traversal—Inorder, Preorder and Postorder • Searching-- Depth-first search and Breadth-first • Search **(Refer chapter 7)**	10	18
08	Graphs: 8.1 Introduction • Terminology graph, node (vertices), arcs (edge), directed • graph, in-degree, out-degree, adjacent, successor, • predecessor, relation, weight, path, length 8.2 Sequential Representation of Graphs 8.3 Linked Representation of Graphs 8.4 Traversal of Graphs • Depth-first search • Breadth-first search 8.5 Shortest Path algorithm for graph 8.6 Application of Graph **(Refer chapter 8)**	06	12
09	Hashing 9.1 Hash functions 9.2 Deleting items from hash tables **(Refer chapter 9)**	02	04
	Total	**48**	**100**

❑❑❑

Introduction to Data Structure

Statistical Analysis

Year	Marks
Summer - 2008	08 Marks
Winter - 2008	06 Marks
Summer - 2009	06 Marks
Winter - 2009	02 Marks
Summer - 2010	10 Marks

1.1 Data Representation

Data is a collection of numbers, alphabets and symbols combined to represent information. A computer takes raw data as input and after processing of data it produces refined data as output. We might say that computer science is the study of data.

Binary system of representation is used in computer.

- An integer number is represented by its binary equivalent

- A negative number is represented using 2's complement representation

- A character is represented using its ASCII code.

- A real number is represented using IEEE representation format.

1.1.1 Data :

Data is a collection of numbers, alphabets and symbols combined to represent information. A computer takes raw data as input and after processing of data it produces refined data as output. We might say that computer science is the study of data.

Atomic data are non-decomposible entity. For example, an integer value 523 or a character value 'A' cannot be further divided. If we further divide the value 523 in three digits '5', '2' and '3' then the meaning may be lost.

Composite data : It is a composition of several atomic data and hence it can be further divided into atomic data.

For example, date of birth (say 15/3/1984) can be separated into three atomic values. First one gives the day of the month, second one gives the month and the last one is the year.

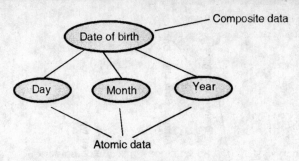

Fig. 1.1.1

1.1.2 Data Types :

A data type is a term which refers to the kind of data that variables may hold in a programming language.

Ex. : int x ; [x can hold, integer type data]

Every programming language has a method for declaring a set of variable of a particular type. A value stored in a variable can not be interpreted properly without knowing its type. A byte of information stored in computer memory may represent an integer value, a character value, a BCD (Binary Coded Decimal) value or a Boolean value. Therefore, it is necessary that the value stored in memory must be treated as of a particular type and interpreted accordingly.

1.1.3 Data Types in 'C' :

In every programming language there is set of built-in data types. Language allows variables to name data of that type. It also allows a set of operations (through operators like +, −, /, % etc) for manipulation of these values. Every programming language has its own representation for primitive data types.

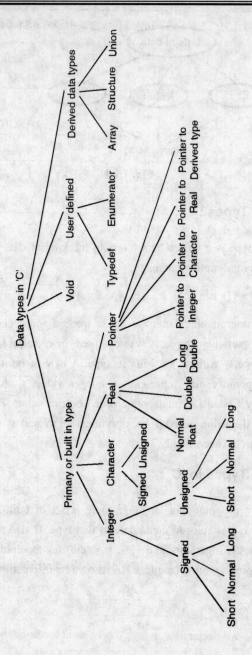

Fig. 1.1.2 : Data types in 'C'

Table 1.1.1 : Size and range of data types on a 16-bit m/c

Type	Size (bits)	Range	Representation
Char or signed char	8	– 128 to 127	2's complement ASCII
Unsigned char	8	0 to 255	Binary ASCII
int or signed int	16	– 32,768 to 32,767	2's complement
Unsigned int	16	0 to 65535	Binary
Short int or signed short int	8	– 128 to 127	2's complement
Unsigned short int	8	0 to 255	Binary
Long int or signed long int	32	– 2, 147, 483, 648 to 2, 147, 483, 647	2's complement
Unsigned long int	32	0 to 4, 294, 967, 295	Binary
Float	32	3.4E – 38 to 3.4E + 38	IEEE
Double	64	1.7E – 308 to 1.7E + 308	IEEE
Long double	80	3.4E – 4932 to 1.1E + 4932	IEEE

1.1.4   User-defined Type :

"type definition" allows user to define an identifier that will represent an existing data type.

For example : | typedef float marks ; |

After above declaration, marks can be used for float.

| marks phy, che, math; |

Here, marks is another name for float. Marks can be used to declare variables of the type float. This approach, enhances **readability** of a program.

Another user-defined data type is **enumerated data** type.

An example :

enum day (Mon, Tue, Wed, Thu, Fri, Sat, Sun);

enum day today ;

Variable today, which is declared of enum day type can be assigned a value from the set (Mon, Tue, Wed, Thu, Fri, Sat, Sun).

today = Thu ;   /* A valid statement */

if (today == Mon)   /* A valid statement */

today = Fri ;   /* A valid statement */

1.1.5 Derived Data Types :

Array : A group of similar elements is stored in contiguous memory.

Ex. int a[6] ; /* defining an array of size 6 */

a[0]	a[1]	a[2]	a[3]	a[4]	a[5]

int a[6] defines an integer array of six elements. These elements are stored in contiguous memory locations. An element of the array is accessed as "a[i] " where a is name of the array and i is index.

1.1.6 Structure :

It allows, one to group non-homogeneous elements. It becomes necessary to group all attributes of an entity or properties of an object in a single cell. Without structure, it becomes extremely difficult to handle a complex data structure.

For example :

struct student

{

      char name [35];

      int rollno;

      char address [120];

      int gender;

} ;

struct student S1, S2 ;

Elements of a structure type variable can be accessed through dot (·) operator.

S1.name;   /* name of student s / */

S1.rollno;

S1.address;

S1.gender;

Array is used for storing of homogeneous elements, structure can be used for storing of non-homogeneous elements.

1.1.7 Union :

Unions are a concept borrowed from structures and therefore follow the same syntax as structures.

However, there is major distinction between them in terms of storage. In structures, each member has its own storage location, whereas all the members of a union share the same memory locations.

Example :

Union item

    {   int m;

        float x ;

        char c ;

    } item_cd ;

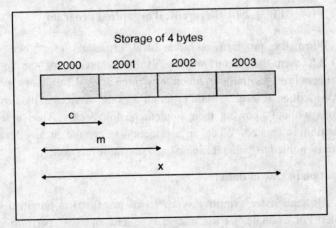

Fig. 1.1.3 : Sharing of storage locations by the members of union

To access a union member, we can use the same syntax that we use for structure members.

i.e. item_cd.m

item_cd.x

item_cd.c

1.2 Abstract Data Types (ADT)

The concept at abstraction is commonly found in computer science. A big program is never written as a monolithic piece of program, instead it is broken down in smaller modules (may be called a function or procedure) and each module is developed independently.

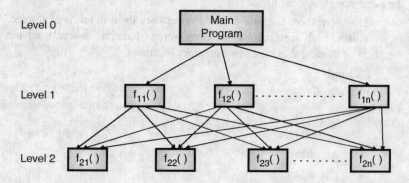

Fig. 1.2.1 : Hierarchical organized program

When the program is hierarchical organized as shown in the Fig. 1.2.1, then the "main program" utilizes services of the functions appearing at level 1. Similarly, functions written at level 1 utilizes services of functions written at level 2. Main program uses the services at the next level functions without knowing their implementation details. Thus a level of **abstraction** is created. When an abstraction is created at any level, our concern is limited to "what it can do" and not "how it is done".

Abstraction in case of data :

Abstraction for primitive types (char, int, float) is provided by the compiler. For example, we use integer type data and also, perform various operations on them without knowing :

(1)   Representation

(2)   How various operations are performed on them.

Example :

>   int x, y, z ;
>
>   x = -13 ;

Constant -13 is converted to 2's complement and then stored in x. Representation is handled by the compiler

>   x = y + z ;

Meaning of the operation '+' is defined by the compiler and its implementation details remain hidden from the user.

Implementation details (representation) and how various operations are implemented remain hidden from the user. User is only concerned about, how to use these operations.

Objects such as lists, sets and graphs along with associated operations, can be viewed as abstract data type. Integer, char, real are primitive data types and there are set of operations associated with them. For the 'set' ADT (Abstract Data Type),

We might have operations like union, intersection, size and complement. Once the data type set is defined (representation and associated functions) then the ADT set can be used in any application program.

The Abstract Data Type "List" :

A list is a sequence of 0 or more elements of a given type (element type could be integer, float etc.). Such a list is often represented as :

$a_1, a_2 \ldots \ldots \ldots a_n$

- n = Number of elements in the list

- $a_i = i^{th}$ element of the list

- When n = 0, the list is empty having no element.

- Each element other than a_1 has a predecessor

- Each element, other than a_n has a successor.

In order to form an ADT from the mathematical notation of a list, we must represent the list and define a set of operations on objects of type List.

Representation of a List :

A List can be represented in 'C' using a structure.

```
typedef struct List
{  int data[50] ;
   int n ;
}  List ;
```

- A List of maximum of 50 integer type elements
- n is the actual number of elements in the List.

A set of representative operations on a List :

1. Insert(L, X, P) : insert X at position P in List L
2. Locate(X, L) : This function returns the position of element X on List L
3. Retrieve(L, P) : This function returns the element at position P on list L
4. Delete(L, P) : Delete the element at position P of the List L.
5. MAKENULL(L) : Creates an empty List L
6. PrintList(L) : Print the elements of L in the order of occurrence.

1.3 Data Structures

Q. What is data structure ? Why do we need data structure ?
S - 08

The data structure is concerned with the following things :

1. Organization of data
2. Associativity among data elements
3. Accessing methods
4. Operations on data
5. Processing alternatives for data

While representing data, relationship between individual elements of the data should be considered. The data structure deals with representation of data considering not only the elements stored but also their relationship to each other.

For writing an efficient program, a proper data structure should be selected.

- A proper data structure should be selected so that the relationship between data elements can be expressed.
- Processing and accessing of data should be efficient.

A data structure can also be defined as an instance of ADT. A data structure is formally defined to be a triplet (D,F,A) where

D stands for a set of domains

F stands for a set of operations

A stands for a set of axioms

Q.   State the need of Data Structure.   W - 08

Need of data structure :

There is a close connection between the structuring of data and the synthesis of algorithm. For each data item, there are number of operations. Data should be represented in a way that makes efficient implementation of operation.

If a linear data is represented using linked organization then modification is less time consuming whereas accessing a large list becomes inefficient. In sequential organization, accessing is efficient but modifications are costly.

1.3.1   Linear and Non-Linear :

Q.   What are linear and non-linear data structures ? Give two example of each.   S - 09

Linear :

Elements are arranged in a Linear fashion (one dimension). All one-one relation can be handled through Linear data structures. Lists, stacks and queues are examples of linear data structure.

Representation of Linear data structures in an array :

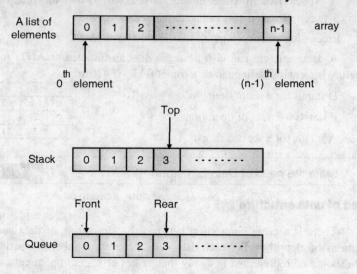

Representation of Linear data structures through Linked structure :

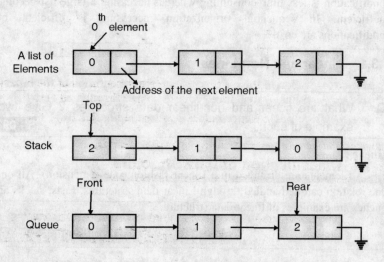

Non-Linear :

All one-many, many-one or many–many relations are handled through non-linear data structures. Every data element can have a number of predecessors as well as successors. Tree graphs and tables are examples of non-linear data structures.

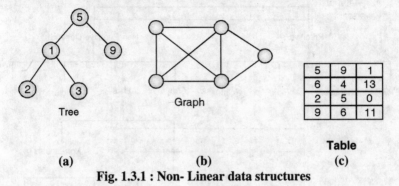

Fig. 1.3.1 : Non- Linear data structures

(a) Representation of the binary
tree through linked structure

(b) Representation of the binary
tree through an array

Fig. 1.3.2 : Representation of tree of Fig. 1.3.1(a)

1.4 Classification of Data Structure

Q. Give classification of data structure and give two examples of each.　　S - 08, W - 08, S - 09, W - 09, S - 2010

Data structures are normally divided into two categories :

1. Primitive data structure
2. Non – Primitive data structure (derived)

Classification of data structure is shown in Figure 1.4.1

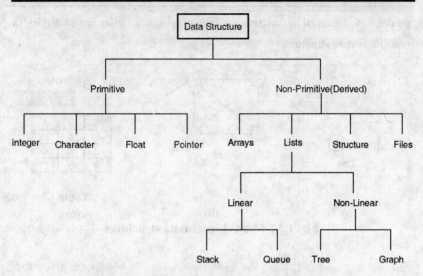

Fig. 1.4.1 : Classification of data structure

1.4.1 Primitive and Non-Primitive :

Primitive :

The integers, reals, logical data, character data, pointers and reference are primitive data structures. These data types are available in most programming languages as built in type. Data objects of primitive data types can be operated upon by machine level instructions.

Non-Primitive :

These data structures are derived from primitive data structures. A set of homogeneous and heterogeneous data elements are stored together.

Examples of Non-primitive data structures : Array, structure, union, linked-list, stack, queue, tree, graph.

Some of the most commonly used operations that can be performed on data structures are shown in Fig. 1.4.2.

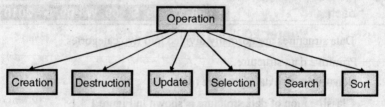

Fig. 1.4.2 : Data structure operations

1.5 Operations on Data Structures

Q. Describe various types of operation that can be performed on data structure.　　　　　　　　　　　　　**S - 2010**

Many operations are performed on a data structure. Typical operations on a data structure are :

1. Traversing
2. Searching
3. Inserting
4. Deleting
5. Sorting

Traversing a data structure is accessing each data and accessing only once.

Searching is finding the location of a data in within the given data structure.

Inserting is adding a new data in the data structure.

Deleting is removing a data from the data structure.

Sorting is arranging of data in some logical order.

1.6 MSBTE Questions and Answers

Summer 2008 – Total Marks 08

Q. 1 What is a data structure ? Why do we need data structure ?
(Section 1.3)　　　　　　　　　　　　　　　　**(4 Marks)**

Q. 2 Give classification of data structure and give two examples of each.
(Section 1.4)　　　　　　　　　　　　　　　　**(4 Marks)**

Winter 2008 – Total Marks 06

Q. 3 Define primitive Data Structure. Give 4 operations of Data structure.
(Section 1.4)　　　　　　　　　　　　　　　　**(2 Marks)**

Q. 4 State the need of data structure. Give classification of Data Structure.
(Sections 1.3 and 1.4)   (4 Marks)

Summer 2009 – Total Marks 06

Q. 5 State different types of Data Types. (Section 1.4)   (2 Marks)

Q. 6 What are linear and non linear data structures ? Give two examples of each. (Section 1.3.1)   (4 Marks)

Winter 2009 – Total Marks 02

Q. 7 Describe the term "Primitive data structures" Enlist four types of primitive data structure. (Section 1.4)   (2 Marks)

Summer 2010 – Total Marks 10

Q. 8 Describe various types of operation that can be performed on data structure. (Section 1.5)   (6 Marks)

Q. 9 What is data structure? Explain classification of data structure.
(Section 1.4)   (4 Marks)

❑❑❑

Principles of Programming and Analysis of Algorithms

Syllabus

Algorithms

- Different approaches for designing an Algorithm
- Complexity in terms of time and space
- Big 'O' notation

Statistical Analysis

Year	Marks
Summer - 2008	06 Marks
Winter - 2008	06 Marks
Summer - 2009	06 Marks
Winter - 2009	14 Marks
Summer - 2010	08 Marks

2.1 Introduction to Algorithm

Q. Define Algorithm with example.   S - 09

The field of Computer Science revolves around writing of programs for several problems for various domains. A program consists of data structures and algorithms. An algorithm is a set of steps required to solve a problem. These steps are performed on a sample data representing an instance of the problem. Thus an algorithm maps a set of input data (from input domain) to a set of output data (in output domain) through a sequence of operations. An algorithm must have the following properties :

(1) **Input :** Input data, supplied externally (zero or more).

(2) **Output :** Result of the program.

(3) **Finiteness :** In every case, algorithm terminates after a finite number of steps.

(4) **Definiteness :** The steps should be clear and unambiguous.

(5) **Effectiveness :** An algorithm should be written using basic instructions. It should be feasible to convert the algorithm in a computer program.

Take the problem of finding the GCD (Greatest Common Divisor) of two positive integers an example.

Inputs to the algorithm are two positive integers. Output is a positive integer which is GCD of two positive integers given as input.

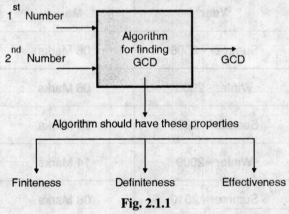

Fig. 2.1.1

The algorithm is described as a series of steps of basic operations. These steps must be performed in a sequence. Each step of the algorithm is labeled.

Step 1 : Read two positive integers and store them in x and y.

Step 2 : Divide x by y. Let the remainder be r and the quotient be q.

Step 3 : If r is zero then go to step 7.

Step 4 : Assign y to x.

Step 5 : Assign r to y.

Step 6 : goto step 2.

Step 7 : Print y (the required GCD)

Step 8 : stop

The steps mentioned in the above algorithm are simple and unambiguous. Anybody, carrying out these steps will clearly know what to do in each step. Hence, the above algorithm satisfies the **definiteness** property of an algorithm.

Table 2.1.1 depicts step-wise execution of the above algorithm on two input numbers 15 and 9.

Table 2.1.1

Steps performed	Value of the variables				
	x	y	r	q	
Step 1	15	9	–	–	Input data supplied externally
Step 2	15	9	6	1	
Step 3	15	9	6	1	
Step 4	9	9	6	1	
Step 5	9	6	6	1	
Step 6	9	6	6	1	
Step 2	9	6	3	1	
Step 3	9	6	3	1	
Step 4	6	6	3	1	
Step 5	6	3	3	1	
Step 6	6	3	3	1	
Step 2	6	3	0	2	

Steps performed	Value of the variables				
	x	y	r	q	
Step 3	6	3	0	2	
Step 7	⟶ Print the output (GCD) as 3.				

Algorithm terminates after a finite number of steps. It is easy to prove that the algorithm will terminate for any two given integer numbers. Thus the above algorithm satisfies the **finiteness** property of the algorithm. Every programming language has input statement, output statement, assignment statement, conditional branching statement, unconditional branching statement and hence the above algorithm can easily be converted to a program. Thus the above algorithm satisfies the **effectiveness** property of the algorithm.

An algorithm can be described in many ways. A language like English can be used but it should be free from any ambiguity. Flowcharts, consisting of graphical symbols like :

Table 2.1.2 : Symbols used in flowcharts

Symbol	Purpose
⬭	Terminal Symbol (Start / Stop)
▭	Assignment Statements, expression etc.
▱	Read / Print
◇→	Decision making
◯	Connector
⟶	Flow indication

Example : Write an algorithm for adding 10 numbers.

Solution : flow chart

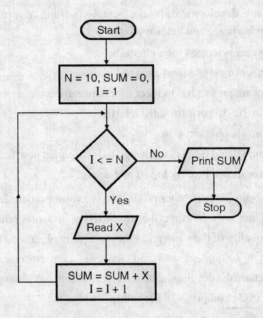

Fig. 2.1.2 : Flowchart for adding 10 numbers

Algorithm as a series as steps :

Step 1 : Assign 10 to N

Step 2 : Assign 0 to SUM

Step 3 : Assign 1 to I

Step 4 : if (I > N) go to step 9

Step 5 : read x

Step 6 : Assign SUM + X To SUM

Step 7 : Assign I + 1 to I

Step 8 : Go to step 4

Step 9 : Print SUM

Step 10 : Stop

2.2 Program Development

Program development is not simply writing a program in any programming language and get it working.

- A program is written for a client.
- A number of people work on a s/w project.
- A software project has to meet user requirements.
- Program has to perform satisfactorily.
- Program should be robust.
- Program should be easy to change to incorporate new features.
- Program should be easy to test and debug.

A program like any other product has to follow a definite sequence of steps. It will not only improve the productivity of a programmer but also improve the quality of the software. From inception of an idea for a software system, until it is implemented and delivered to a customer, the system undergoes gradual development and evolution. A sample software development cycle comprises of the following phases :

(1) Requirements

(2) Design

(3) Analysis

(4) Refinement and coding

(5) Verification and testing

Requirements :

The purpose of this phase is to identify and document the exact requirements of the program. Requirements of the program written down in terms of end-user requirements.

- Input/output requirement for each case must be written down.
- Facts about the business process must be collected.
- Data must be collected on available files, decision points and how transactions are handled by the current system.

At the end of the requirements phase, programmer has a firm understanding of what is to be done.

Design :

Design of a program produces the details that clearly describes how a software will meet the requirements identified during previous phase.

There may be several data objects (like a list, a polynomial, a matrix etc.). We may have to perform several operations on these objects. These objects may be interrelated. Design of these objects should permit efficient implementation of algorithms for various operation.

Analysis :

There may be many ways of meeting user requirements. There could be several algorithms for meeting a requirement. These alternate algorithms should be analyzed and the best performing one should be selected.

Refinement and coding :

In this phase, the programmer produces the actual code that will be delivered to the customer as the running program. Each data object must be represented using the programming language. Each algorithm must be coded. A large program should have.

(1)　*Modularity* : Program modules should perform independent tasks. Interaction among them should be implemented properly.

(2)　*Abstraction* : Low level details of a program module should remain hidden and should provide an abstract interface.

(3)　*Usability* : A software program is usable if its users find it easy to use. The user interface is an important component of user friendliness.

(4)　*Verifiability* : A software system is verifiable if its properties can be verified easily. It is important to verify correctness or the performance of a software system. Verification can be performed by formal or informal analysis methods or through testing.

(5)　*Maintainability* : Software maintainability, commonly refers to the modifications that are made to a program. These modifications can be made for fixing of bugs.

(6)　*Evolvability* : Like other engineering products, software products are modified over time to provide new functions or to change existing functions.

Verification and testing :

It is important that program gives correct output for all possible input combination. It may be possible to prove that a program is correct. Proof's about programs are similar to other proofs. Testing is an art of creating a set of sample test patterns. Program is run on the sample data and its output is compared with expected output. If the program fails to respond correctly then debugging is needed to determine what went wrong and how to correct it.

2.2.1 Refining An Algorithm :

Q. Explain level of refinement stages.   **W - 09**

After obtaining a suitable mathematical model of a problem, we can write an algorithm in terms of that model. The initial version of the algorithm is expressed using general statements. These statements are subsequently refined into smaller, more definite instructions.

Refinement involves :

1. Choosing representation for each data objects.
2. Writing of algorithm for each of the operations on these objects.

- Algorithms are written in two levels. Data independent part of the algorithm should be written first. Data dependent part of the algorithm will depend on the choice of data representation.

- Different design alternatives should be considered and analyzed before producing the final version of algorithm

2.3 Different Approaches for designing an Algorithm

Q. Explain different approaches to design an algorithm.   **S - 08, W - 09, S - 2010**

Design of an algorithm is an important issue. There are several approaches for designing an algorithm. These approaches include :

1. Greedy Algorithm
2. Divide and Conquer
3. Dynamic Programming
4. Backtracking

2.3.1 Greedy Algorithm :

The greedy method is a very simple technique and it can be applied to a wide variety of problems. Greedy algorithms work in phases in each phase, a decision is made that appears to be good, without regard for future consequences.

- At each stage, we select an input.
- Input selected is added to the set of optimal solution.
- Selection is made on the basis of some selection procedure.
- Inclusion of next input into the partially constructed optimal solution should result in a feasible solution.

2.3.2 Divide and Conquer :

In divide and conquer strategy, we split a problem into sub problems. Sub problems resulting from divide and conquer are of the same type as the original problem. These sub problems are solved recursively. Recursion will eventually terminate when the sub problem to be solved is small enough to be solved without further splitting. Now, there must be a method to combine sub solutions into a solution of the whole.

Thus, divide and conquer algorithms consist of two parts :

1. Divide : smaller problems are solved recursively.
2. The solution to the original problem is then formed form the solutions to the sub problems.

2.3.3 Dynamic Programming :

Dynamic programming is based on non-recursive approach. In this approach, answers to the sub problems are recorded.

We can understand the concept of dynamic programming with the help of Fibonacci numbers.

We know that the natural recursive program to compute Fibonacci numbers is very inefficient. To compute Fibonacci F_N ' there is one call to F_{N-1} and F_{N-2}. However, since F_{N-1} recursively makes a call to F_{N-2} and F_{N-3}, there are actually two separate calls to F_{N-2}. If we trace our algorithm then we can see that :

F_{N-2} is computed two times

F_{N-3} is computed three times

F_{N-4} is computed four times and so on.

We can avoid computation of same number again and again by recorded the value. i.e. if F_{N-3} is computed once, it is recorded and subsequently, recursive calls are not made.

For Example :

$F_2 = F_1 + F_0 = 1 + 0 = 1$

F_2, is recorded and it can be used for computation of F_3

$F_3 = F_2 + F_2 = 1 + 1 = 2$

2.3.4 Backtracking :

In many problems, there may not be any known algorithm for finding optimal solution. In such cases, we have to resort to exhaustive search to locate the optimal solution. Backtracking is an exhaustive search technique.

2.4 Complexity in terms of Time and Space

2.4.1 Algorithm Analysis :

Q.	Explain different ways of analyzing algorithms.	**W - 08**
Q.	Compare Time Complexity and Space Complexity with respect to algorithm.	**W - 08**
Q.	Explain time and space complexity related to algorithms and also state their importance.	**S - 09**
Q.	Enlist different ways of analyzing algorithm.	**W - 09**
Q.	Explain the time and space complexity of an algorithm.	**W - 09**

Most often there are many algorithms for solving a problem. On what basis should we choose an algorithm ? There are often two contradictory goals.

(i)　Algorithm should be easy to understand, write and debug.

(ii)   Algorithm should make efficient use of computer resources like CPU, memory etc.

When we write a program to be used a few times, goal (1) is most important. Cost of writing the program will have an upper hand over the cost of running the program, when the program is to be used many times, the cost of running the program and hence the goal (2) should be given more weightage.

Analyzing a program should quantify the requirement of computing resources during execution. Most important of these resources are computer time and memory. Analysis of algorithms focuses on computation of space and time complexity. Space requirement means the space required to store input data either static or dynamic. Space required on top of the system stack to handle recursion/function Call should also be considered. Computing time, an algorithm might require for its execution, would normally depend on the size of the input.

```c
#include <stdio.h>
void main( )
{
    int i, n, sum, x ;
    sum = 0 ;
    printf("\n enter no of data to be added");
    scanf("%d",&n) ;
    for (i =1 ; i<= n ; i++)
    {
        scanf("%d", &x) ;
        sum = sum + x ;
    }
    printf("\n sum = %d", sum) ;
}
```

Space requirement = Space required to store the variables i, n, sum and x = 2 + 2+ 2 +2 =8

[an integer requires 2 bytes of memory space.]

Calculation of computation time :

Statement	Frequency	Computation time
sum = 0	1	t_1
printf ("\n Enter no of data to be added");	1	t_2
scanf ("%d", & n)	1	t_3
for (i = 1 ; i <=n ; i++)	n + 1	$(n + 1) t_4$
scanf ("%d", &x)	n	nt_5
sum = sum + x	n	nt_6
printf("\n sum = %d", sum)	1	t_7

$$\text{Total computation time } = t_1 + t_2 + t_3 + n (t_4 + t_5 + t_6) + t_4 + t_7$$
$$T = n (t_4 + t_5 + t_6) + (t_1 + t_2 + t_3 + t_4 + t_7)$$

For large n, T can be approximated to

$$T \approx n (t_4 + t_5 + t_6) = kn$$

where

$$k = t_4 + t_5 + t_6, \dots\dots \text{ a constant value.}$$

Thus, $T = kn$

or $T \propto n$

(i) t_1 , t_2 ......t_7 are computer dependent, on a faster computer, the execution time of an instruction will be less.

(ii) for (i = 1;i <= n ; i++), will be executed n + 1 times and not n times. For all values of i between 1 and n, the condition i < = n will evaluate to true and when i becomes n+1, the condition i < = n will evaluate to false. Thus the above instruction will be executed n + 1 times.

Example 2.4.1 :   Determine the frequency count for all statements in the following program segment

```
1.  i = 1;
2.  while ( i <= n)
    {
3.      x = x + 1;
4.      i = i + 1 ;
    }
```

Solution :

Statement No.	Frequency
1	1
2	$n + 1$
3	n
4	n.

2.4.2 Measuring the Running Time of a Program (Time Complexity) :

Running time of a program can be judged on the basis of factors such as :

1. Input to the program.
2. Size of the program.
3. Machine language instruction set.
4. The machine we are executing on.
5. Time required to execute each machine instruction.
6. The time complexity of the algorithm of the program.

2.4.3 Measurement of Growth Rate (Asymptotic Growth Rate) :

2.4.3.1 Asymptotic Consideration :

When considering time complexities $f_1(n)$ and $f_2(n)$ of two different algorithms for a given problem of size n, we need to consider and compare the behaviour of the two functions only for large n. If the relative behaviour of two functions for smaller values conflict with the relative behaviour for larger values, then we ignore the conflicting behaviour for smaller values. For example, consider the following functions.

$$f_1(n) = 100n^2$$

$$f_2(n) = 5n^3$$

Representing time complexities of two solutions of a problem.

n	$f_1(n)$	$f_2(n)$
1	100	5
5	2500	625

n	$f_1(n)$	$f_2(n)$
10	10000	5000
20	40000	40000

$f_1(n) \geq f_2(n)$ for $n \leq 20$

We would still prefer the solution having $f_1(n)$ as time complexity because

$f_1(n) \leq f_2(n)$ for all $n \geq 20$

2.4.3.2　The Constant Factor in Complexity Measure :

Let us consider an algorithm having a timing complexity given by the function $f(n) = 100\, n^2$

Where [100 – a constant, n – size of the problem].

The time required for solving a problem, depends not only on the size of the problem but also, on the hardware and software used to execute the solution. The effect of hardware and software on the time required may closely be approximated by a constant.

Suppose, a new computer executes a program two times faster than another computer. Then irrespective of the size of the problem, the new computer solves the problem roughly two times faster than the computer. Thus we conclude that the time requirement for execution of a solution, changes by a constant factor on change in hardware or software.

An important consequence of the above discussion is that if the time taken by one machine in executing a solution is of the order of n^2 (say), then time take by every machine is of the order of n^2. Thus, function different from each other by constant factor, when treated as time complexities, should not be treated as different. i.e. should be treated as complexity wise same.

Following functions have the same time complexities :

$f_1(n) = 5n^2$

$f_2(n) = 100n^2$

$f_3(n) = 1000n^2$

$f_4(n) = n^2$

Time complexity of $f_1(n)$ = Time complexity of $f_2(n)$

= Time complexity of $f_3(n)$

= Time complexity of $f_4(n)$

2.5 The Notation O : (pronounced as big-oh), ($O(n^2)$ is pronounced as big-oh of n^2)

Q. Describe Big 'O' notation used in algorithms.   S - 08

Q. Describe Big 'O' notation used in algorithms. Give time complexity of any four sorting algorithms.   S - 2010

Provides asymptotic upper bound for a given functions. Let $f(x)$ and $g(x)$ be two functions then $f(x)$ is said to be $O(g(x))$ if there exist two positive integer/real number constants c and k such that

$$f(x) \leq cg(x) \text{ for all } x \geq k$$

The constant k is due to asymptotic consideration and the constant c for hardware/software environment.

Example 2.5.1 : $f(x) = x^2 + 5x$
$g(x) = x^2$ let us take c = 2

Solution :

x	$x^2 + 5x$	$2x^2$	
1	5	2	
2	14	8	$f(x) \leq c x^2$
5	50	50	For $x \geq 5$
			(asymptotic behavior)

$f(x) \leq cg(x)$ for all $x \geq k$ where c =2 and k = 5

Example 2.5.2 :   For the function defined by
$f(x) = 5x^3 + 6x^2 + 1$ show that $f(x) = O(x^3)$

Solution :

$f(x) = 5x^3 + 6x^2 + 1 \leq 5x^3 + 6x^3 + 1x^3$ for all $x \geq 1$

or, $f(x) \leq 12x^3$ for $x \geq 1$

(by replacing each term of x by the highest degree term x^3)

there exist c =12 and k = 1 such that

$f(x) \leq c x^3$ for all $x \geq k$

Hence $f(x)$ is $O(x^3)$

> **Note :** Time complexity of a polynomial is same as the time complexity of the highest degree term.

Calculating the running time of a program :

Example 2.5.3 : [A program fragment without a loop]

$$x = x + 1$$

The timing complexity is of constant order and it is represented by O(1).

Example 2.5.4 :   1 :   for (i = 1 ; i < = n ; i++)
                              2 :   x = x + 1;

Solution :

Step no. 1 will be executed $n + 1$ times whereas the step no. 2 will be executed n time. With the assumption that each step requires a constant time, the time required to execute the above program will be of the order of $2n + 1 = O(n)$.

$$f(n) = 2n + 1$$
$$f(n) \leq cn \ \text{for} \ c = 3 \ \text{and}$$
$$n \geq 1$$

Conclusion : A loop without nesting has a timing complexity O(n).

Example 2.5.5 :   for (i = 1 ; i < = n ; i++)
                              for (j = 1 ; j < = n ; j++)
                                 x = x + 1 ;

Solution : Since, the statement $x = x + 1$ will be executed n^2 times, the timing complexity of the above program segment is $O(n^2)$.

Example 2.5.6 :

A large program $\Big\}$
n = 500 ; $\Big\}$ O (1)   Timing Complexity
x = 1 ; $\Big\}$ O (1)
y = 2 ; $\Big\}$ O (1)

for (i = 1 ; i < = n ; i++) $\Big\}$ O(n)
   x = x + 1 ;

for (j = 1 ; j < = n ; j++) $\Big\}$ O(n)
   y = y + 1 ;

$$\left.\begin{array}{l} \text{for } (i = 1 \; ; \; i <= n \; ; \; i{+}{+}) \\ \quad \text{for } (j = 1 \; ; \; j <= n \; ; \; j{+}{+}) \\ \qquad x = y + 1 \; ; \end{array}\right\} \; O(n^2)$$

Hence, the combined time complexity is

$O(\max(O(1), O(1), O(1), O(n), O(n), O(n^2))) = O(n^2)$

| if $f(x) = 5x^3 + 6x^2 + 1$ |
| $O(f(x)) = x^3$ .... proved earlier |

Conclusion :

If $T_1(n)$ and $T_2(n)$ are the running times of two program fragments P1 and P2 and that $T_1(n)$ is $O(f(n))$ and $T_2(n)$ is $O(g(n))$. Then the running time of the complete program P1 followed by P2 is $O(\max(f(n), g(n)))$. For finding the timing complexity of a program, consider the program fragment having the highest timing complexity.

Example 2.5.7 : Calculate the time complexity for the following program segment

```
for ( i = 1; i < n; i++)
    for ( j = 0; j < n-i; j ++)
        if (a [ j ] > a [ j + 1])
        {       temp = a [ j];        ⎤  Statements
                a [ j ] = a [ j+1];   ⎬  for interchange
                a [ j + 1] = temp;    ⎦  of a [ j ] and a [ j +1]
        }
```

Solution : For calculation of timing complexity, it is sufficient to express number of interchanges in terms of n (number of data)

Program trace	Number of interchanges
$i = 1$, j varies from 0 to $n - 2$	$n - 1$
$i = 2$, j varies from 0 to $n - 3$	$n - 2$
.	.
.	.
.	.
.	.
$i = n - 1$, j varies from $n - 1$ to $n - 1$	1

Total number of interchanges $= 1 + 2 + \ldots + (n-2) + (n-1)$

$$= \frac{n(n-1)}{2} = \frac{1}{2}(n^2 - n) = O(n^2)$$

[Consider, the most significant term]

Example 2.5.8 : Calculate the time complexity for the following program segment

```
int A (int n)
{
        if (n < = 1)
        return (1);
    else
        return (A (n - 1) + A (n - 1));
}
```

Solution :

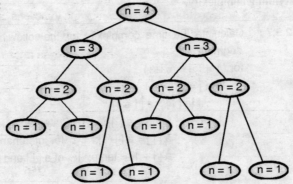

recursion tree for n = 4

Fig. Ex. 2.5.8

When the function A is called with the initial value of n = 4, it calls the same function recursively twice with n = 3

Thus, $f(n) = 2\,f(n-1)$ if $n > 1$

$f(n) = 1$ if $n < = 1$ (Best case)

Since $f(n) = 2\,f(n-1) = 2^2\,f(n-2) = 2^{n-1}\,f(n-(n-1))$

$$= 2^{n-1}\,f(1) = 2^{n-1} = O(2^n)$$

2.5.1 Best Case, Worst Case and the Average Case Behaviour :

Many programs do not produce same timing complexity in every case. Consider the problem of searching an element in an array with 10 elements.

5	1	9	6	2	11	13	6	7	16

Element 5 will be found in one attempt

Element 16 will require 10 comparisons to locate

Best case behavior = 1 comparison (when the element to be searched is in the beginning)

Worst case behavior = n comparisons (where n is the number of elements and the element to be searched is at the end of the array)

Average case behavior = number of comparisons will be n/2 (from probability).

Example 2.5.9 : Arrange the following computing functions as per their growth rate. $\log_2 n$, n, $n \log_2 n$, n^2, n^3, 2^n

Solution : Common computing functions and their growth rates :

$\log_2 n$	n	$n \log_2 n$	n^2	n^3	2^n
0	1	0	1	1	2
1	2	2	4	8	4
2	4	8	16	64	16
3	8	24	64	512	256
4	16	64	256	4096	65536
5	32	160	1024	32768	2, 147, 483, 648

Thus $O(2^n) > O(n^3) > O(n^2) > O(n \log_2 n) > O(n) > O(\log_2 n)$

Example 2.5.10 : Give time complexity of any four sorting algorithms.

S - 2010

Solution :

1.　Bubble sort – $O(n^2)$

2.　Selection sort – $O(n^2)$

3.　Insertion sort – $O(n^2)$

4.　Merge sort – $O(n \log n)$

Example 2.5.11 : What do you mean by frequency count ? Why only frequency count is important in deciding the time complexity of an algorithm ?

Solution :

Total time taken by a statement in execution depends on :

(i)   The amount of time a single execution will take.

(ii)   Number of times the given statement will be executed.

The product of these numbers will be the total time taken by the statement. Number of times a statement will be executed is called its frequency count. Frequency count may vary from data set to data set.

The constant factor in complexity measure :

Let us consider an algorithm having a timing complexity given by the function $f(n) = 100\, n^2$

Where,   [100 – a constant, n – size of the problem].

The time required for solving a problem, depends not only on the size of the problem but also on the hardware and software used to execute the solution. The effect of hardware and software on the time required may closely be approximated by a constant.

Suppose, a new computer executes a program two times faster than another computer. Then irrespective of the size of the problem, the new computer solves the problem roughly two times faster than the computer. Thus we conclude that the time requirement for execution of a solution, changes by a constant factor on change in hardware or software.

An important consequence of the above discussion is that if the time taken by one machine in executing a solution is of the order of n^2 (say), then time take by every machine is of the order of n^2. Thus, function different from each other by constant factor, when treated as time complexities, should not be treated as different. i.e. should be treated as complexity wise same.

Following functions have the same time complexities :

$$f_1(n) = 5n^2$$

$$f_2(n) = 100n^2$$

$$f_3(n) = 1000n^2$$

$$f_4(n) = n^2$$

Time complexity of $f_1(n)$ = Time complexity of $f_2(n)$

    = Time complexity of $f_3(n)$

    = Time complexity of $f_4(n)$

2.6 MSBTE Questions and Answers

Summer 2008 – Total Marks 06

Q. 1 Describe Big 'O' notation used in algorithms. **(Section 2.5)** **(2 Marks)**

Q. 2 Explain different approaches to design an algorithm.
(Section 2.3)   **(4 Marks)**

Winter 2008 – Total Marks 06

Q. 3 Compare Time Complexity and Space Complexity with respect to algorithm. **(Section 2.4.1)**   **(2 Marks)**

Q. 4 Explain different way of analyzing algorithms.
(Section 2.4.1)   **(4 Marks)**

Summer 2009 – Total Marks 06

Q. 5 Define Algorithm with example. **(Section 2.1)** **(2 Marks)**

Q. 6 Explain time and space complexity related to algorithms and also state their importance. **(Section 2.4.1)**   **(4 Marks)**

Winter 2009 – Total Marks 14

Q. 7 Enlist different ways of analyzing algorithm. **(Section 2.4.1)** **(2 Marks)**

Q. 8 Explain the time and space complexity of an algorithm.
(Section 2.4.1)   **(4 Marks)**

Q. 9 Explain level of refinement stages. **(Section 2.2.1)** **(4 Marks)**

Q. 10　Explain different approaches for designing algorithm.

　　　　(Section 2.3)　　　　　　　　　　　　　　　　　**(4 Marks)**

Summer 2010 – Total Marks 08

Q. 11　Describe Big 'O' notation used in algorithms. Give time complexity of any four sorting algorithms.

　　　　(Section 2.5 and Example 2.5.10)　　　　　　　**(4 Marks)**

Q. 12　Explain different approaches to design an algorithm.

　　　　(Section 2.3)　　　　　　　　　　　　　　　　　**(4 Marks)**

□□□

Searching and Sorting

Sorting : An introduction, Efficiency of Sorting algorithm

Sorting Techniques : Bubble sort, Selection sort, Insertion sort, Merge sort, Radix sort (only algorithm), Shell sort (only algorithm), Quick sort (only algorithm)

Searching : An introduction, Linear Search, Binary Search.

Statistical Analysis

Year	Marks
Summer - 2008	24 Marks
Winter - 2008	26 Marks
Summer - 2009	20 Marks
Winter - 2009	22 Marks
Summer - 2010	22 Marks

3.1 Sorting

Q. What is searching and sorting ? Enlist different methods.
W - 09

Sorting is a process of ordering a list of elements in either ascending or descending order. Sorting can be divided into two categories :

(a)　　Internal sorting　　　　(b)　　External sorting

Internal sorting takes place in the main memory of the computer. Internal sorting can take advantage of the random access nature of the main memory. Elements to be sorted are stored in an integer array. These elements can be sorted using one of the various algorithms discussed in this chapter.

External sorting is carried on secondary storage. External sorting becomes a necessity if the number of elements to be sorted is too large to fit in main memory. External sorting algorithms should always take into account that movement of data between secondary storage and main memory is best done by moving a block of contiguous elements.

- Simple sorting algorithms like bubble sort, insertion sort take $O(n^2)$ time sort n elements.

- More complicated algorithms like quick sort, merge sort, heap sort take $O(n \log n)$ time to sort n elements.

- Sorting algorithms like bubble sort, insertion sort, merge sort are stable. Whereas quick sort and heap sort are unstable. A sorting algorithm is said to be **stable** if after sorting, identical elements appear in the same sequence as in the original unsorted list.

3.1.1　Sort Stability :

Let us try to understand the concept of sort stability with the help of an example.

Name	Subject	Marks
Mohan	Phy	65
Sohan	Che	70
Mohan	Che	68
Amit	Che	74
Sohan	Phy	75

Name	Subject	Marks
Amit	Che	74
Mohan	Phy	65
Mohan	Che	68
Sohan	Che	70
Sohan	Phy	75

(a) Unsorted list　　　　**Fig. 3.1.1**　　　　**(b) Sorted list (stable)**

Name	Subject	Marks
Amit	Che	74
Mohan	Che	68
Mohan	Phy	65
Sohan	Che	70
Sohan	Phy	75

Fig. 3.1.1(c) : Sorted list (not stable)

Fig. 3.1.1(a) gives a list of unsorted records. These records are to be sorted on name.

Two records appear with the name 'Mohan'. Similarly there are two records with name 'Sohan'. Any sorting method will place the records with non-distinct keys in consecutive locations. If the original ordering among the records with non-distinct keys is preserved in sorted file then such a sorting method is known as stable.

Sorted list of Fig. 3.1.1(b) has been produced using a stable sorting method. Relative ordering of two records of 'Mohan' and two records of 'Sohan' is preserved in sorted list.

Sorted list of Fig. 3.1.1(c) has been produced using a sorting method which is not stable. Relative ordering of two records of 'Mohan' is not preserved in sorted list.

Some examples of stable sorting algorithms are :

Bubble sort

Selection sort

Insertion sort

Merge sort

Some examples of unstable sorting algorithms are :

Quick sort

Heap sort

Shell sort

3.1.2　Sort Efficiency :

In order to find the amount of time required to sort a list of n elements by a particular method, we must find the number of comparisons required to sort. Some methods are data sensitive and for such methods finding of exact number of comparisons become difficult. Usually, data sensitive algorithms are analyzed for various cases.

(1)   Best case

(2)   Worst case

(3)   Average case

Average case of an algorithm is calculated with an assumption that data distribution is random. Most of the primitive sorting algorithms like bubble sort, selection sort and insertion sort are not suited for sorting a large file. These algorithms have a timing requirement of $0(n^2)$. On the contrary, these sorting algorithms require hardly any additional memory space for sorting. A list with few records should preferably be sorted using these algorithms. Advance sorting algorithms like quick sort, merge sort and heap sort have a timing requirement of $0(n \log n)$ but they too have some additional problems as :

(1)   Complex algorithm

(2)   Complex data structure

(3)   Unstable sorting algorithm

(4)   Additional memory requirement

(5)   Data sensitivity

These algorithms should be used when the list to be sorted contains considerably large number of records.

3.1.3 Passes :

Most of the sorting algorithms work in passes. In every pass, a number is placed at position where it will appear in the sorted list. Inside a pass, numbers are compared and exchanged as required by the algorithm.

For example, if a list of a n elements is to be sorted using bubble sort then sorting of n elements will require n − 1 passes. If the elements are stored in an array from a [0] to a [n − 1] then at the end of pass 1, largest element will be in a [n − 1] at the end of pass 2, second largest element will be in a [n − 2].

at the end of pass n − 1, the smallest element will be in a [0].

In the loop of bubble sort, given below

for (i = 1; i < n; i++)

  for (j = 0, j < n – i; j++)

  {

  }

Outer loop on i is for passes. Inner loop is for comparison and exchange (if required) of two adjacent elements.

3.2 Bubble Sort

Q. Describe bubble sort with the help of example. Take minimum four values. **W - 09**

Bubble sort is one of the simplest and the most popular sorting method. The basic idea behind bubble sort is as a bubble rises up in water, the smallest element goes to the beginning. This method is based on successive selecting the smallest element through exchange of adjacent element.

5 2 1   out of sequence, hence exchange

5 1 2 out of sequence, hence exchange

1 5 2 after two exchanges, the smallest
                  element has come to the beginning

First pass of the bubble sort

Let n be the number of elements in an array a[ ]. The first pass begins with the comparison of a[n – 1] and a[n – 2]. If a[n – 2] is larger than a[n – 1], the two elements are exchanged. The smaller elements, now at a[n – 2] is compared with a[n – 3] and if necessary the elements are exchanged to place the smaller one in a[n – 3]. Comparison progresses backward and after the last comparison of A[1] and A[0] and possible exchange the smallest element will be placed at a[0].

As a variation, the first pass could begin comparison with a[0] and a[1]. If a[0] is larger than a[1], the two elements are exchanged. Larger one will be placed in a[1] after the first comparison. Comparison can work forward and after the last comparison of a[n – 2] and a[n – 1], the larger element will be placed in a[n –1]

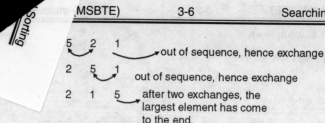

Fist pass of the bubble sort with comparison in the forward direction.

The **second pass** is an exact replica of the first pass except that this time, the pass ends with the comparison and possible exchange of a[n − 3] and a[n − 2]. After the end of second pass, the second largest element will be placed at a[n − 2].

Bubble sort requires a total of n − 1 passes. If n − 1 elements are arranged (one element each pass) in ascending order from a[1] to a[n − 1], smallest element will finally left at a[0].

Loop for sorting an array a[ ] having n elements :

```
for(i = 1; i < n; i ++)

   for(j = 0; j < n − 2i; j ++)

      if(a[j] > a[j + 1])

         exchange a[j] and a[j + 1]
```
Outer loop is for passes and the inner loop is for comparisons.

In pass 1 (i = 1), there will be n − 1 comparisons (j = 0 to n − 2)

In pass 2 (i = 2), there will be n − 2 comparisons (j = 0 to n − 3)

:

:

In pass n − 1 (i = n − 1), there will be 1 comparison (j = 0 to 0)

Original array with n = 6 5 9 6 2 8 1

First pass i = 1

Comparisons
- j = 0   5   9   6   2   8   1
- j = 1   5   9   6   2   8   1
- j = 2   5   6   9   2   8   1
- j = 3   5   6   2   9   8   1
- j = 4   5   6   2   8   9   1

Second pass i = 2

Comparisons
- j = 0   5   6   2   8   1   9
- j = 1   5   6   2   8   1   9
- j = 2   5   2   6   8   1   9
- j = 3   5   2   6   8   1   9

Third pass i = 3

Comparisons
- j = 0   5   2   6   1   8   9
- j = 1   2   5   6   1   8   9
- j = 2   2   5   6   1   8   9

Fourth pass i = 4

Comparisons
- j = 0   2   5   1   6   8   9
- j = 1   2   5   1   6   8   9

Fifth pass i = 5

Comparisons
- j = 0   2   1   5   6   8   9

Sorted array a[ ] →   1   2   5   6   8   9

Illustration of bubble sort.

> **Program 3.2.1 : Program for sorting an integer array using bubble sort.**

Q. Write a program for Bubble sort in 'C/C++' language.   W - 08

Q. Write a program to sort an array of ten elements with bubble sort.   S - 2010

```c
#include<conio.h>
#include<stdio.h>
void bubble_sort(int[],int);
void main()
{
   int a[30],n,i;
   printf("\nEnter no of elements :");
   scanf("%d",&n);
   printf("\nEnter array elements :");
   for(i=0;i<n;i++)
        scanf("%d",&a[i]);
   bubble_sort(a,n);
        printf("\nSorted array is :");
   for(i=0;i<n;i++)
        printf("%d",a[i]);
   getch();
}
void bubble_sort(int a[],int n)
{
   int i,j,temp;
   for(i=1;i<n;i++)
        for(j=0;j<n-i;j++)
            if(a[j]>a[j+1])
            {
               temp=a[j];
               a[j]=a[j+1];
               a[j+1]=temp;
            }
}
```

Output

Enter no of elements : 6					
Enter array elements : 57	89	64	56	77	333
Sorted array is :	56	57	64	77	89	333

Improved version of bubble sort :

In our algorithm for bubble sort, sorting algorithm requires n − 1 passes. The method may even be terminated earlier if no exchange is found necessary in an earlier pass. Absence of any exchange in a pass ensures that the elements are already sorted and there is no point in continuing further.

- Absence of any exchange in inner loop of bubble sort can be detected through a variable flag.
- Before entering the inner loop, flag is set to 0(flag = 0)
- If an exchange is required then flag is set to 1 in inner loop.
- On exiting the inner loop, if the value of the flag is found to be 0, algorithm terminates.

➢ **'C' function for improved bubble sort.**

```
void imp_bubble sort(int a[ ], int n)
{
        int i, j, temp, flag;
        flag = 1;
        for(i = 1; i < n && flag = = 1; i ++)
        {
            flag = 0
            for(j = 0; j < n – i; j ++)
            if(a[j] > a[j + 1])
            {
                flag = 1;
                temp = a[j] ;
                a[j] = a[j + 1];
                a[j + 1] = temp;
            }
        }
}
```

bubble sort :

us consider the loop for bubble sort :

Line 1　　for(i = 1; i < n; i + 1)

Line 2　　　　for(j = 0; j < n – i; j ++)

Line 3　　　　　　if(a[j] > a[j + 1])

Line 4　　　　　　　　exchange a[j] and a[j + 1];

For a fixed value of i, the loop of lines(2 – 4) runs n – i times.

Hence total number of comparisons

$$= \sum_{i=1}^{n-1} (n-i)$$

$$= (n-1) + (n-2) + \ldots \; 3 + 2 + 1$$

$$= \frac{n(n-1)}{2} = \frac{1}{2}(n^2 - n) = O(n^2)$$

3.3 Selection Sort

Q. Describe the principle of selection sort with one example.

W - 08

　　　Selection sort is a very simple sorting method. In the ith pass, we select the element with lowest value among a[i], a[i + 1] … , a[n – 1] and we swap it with a[i]. As a result, after i passes (pass number 0 to i – 1) first i elements will be in sorted order. Selection sort can be described by

```
for(i = 0; i < n – 1; i ++)
        select the smallest element among
                a[i], …. , a[n –1] and
        swap it with a[i];
```

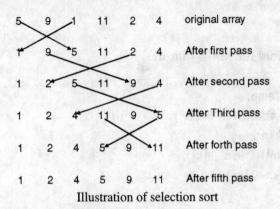

5	9	1	11	2	4	original array
1	9	5	11	2	4	After first pass
1	2	5	11	9	4	After second pass
1	2	4	11	9	5	After Third pass
1	2	4	5	9	11	After forth pass
1	2	4	5	9	11	After fifth pass

Illustration of selection sort

> **Program 3.3.1 : A sample program for selection sort.**

Q.	Write a program in 'C' language for selection sort and arrange the given numbers in ascending order using selection sort. Numbers : 16, 23, 13, 9,7,5 **S - 08**
Q.	Write a program in 'C' language for selection sort and arrange the given numbers in ascending order using selection sort number : 16, 23, 13, 9, 7, 5. **S - 2010**

```c
#include <stdio.h>
#include <conio.h>
void selection_sort(int [],int);
void main()
{
   int a[50],n,i;
   clrscr();
   printf("\nEnter no of elements :");
   scanf("%d",&n);
   printf("\nEnter array elements :");
   for(i=0;i<n;i++)
      scanf("%d",&a[i]);
   selection_sort(a,n);
   getch();
```

```
}

void selection_sort(int a[],int n)
{
    int i,j,k,temp;
    printf("\nUnsorted Data:");
    for(k=0;k<n;k++)
         printf("%5d",a[k]);
    for(i=0;i<n-1;i++)
     {
       k=i;
       for(j=i+1;j<n;j++)
          if(a[j]<a[k])
               k=j;
       if(k!=i)
        {
          temp=a[i];
          a[i]=a[k];
          a[k]=temp;
        }
     }
    printf("\nSorted data:");
    for(k=0;k<n;k++)
     printf("%5d",a[k]);

}
```

Analysis of selection sort :

Selection sort is not data sensitive. In i^{th} pass, $n - i$ comparisons will be needed to select the smallest element.

Thus, the number of comparisons needed to sort an array having n elements.

$$= (n - 1) + (n - 2) + \dots + 2 + 1$$

$$= \frac{n(n-1)}{2} = \frac{1}{2}(n^2 - n) = O(n^2)$$

Example 3.3.1 : Compare the three sorting algorithms

          (a) Bubble sort   (b) Selection sort (c) Insertion sort

Solution : A sorting algorithm can be judged on the basis of following parameters :

1.   Simplicity of algorithm :

      All the three sorting algorithms are equally simple to write.

2.   Timing complexity :

      Bubble sort and selection sort are not data sensitive. Both of them have a timing requirement of $O(n^2)$.

      Insertion sort is data sensitive. It works much faster if the data is partially sorted.

      Best case behaviour (when input data is sorted) = $O(n)$.

      Worst case behaviour (when input data is in descending order) = $O(n^2)$.

3.   Sort stability :

      All the three sorting algorithms are stable.

4.   Storage requirement :

      No additional storage is required. All of them are in-place sorting algorithms.

5.   All of them can be used for internal as well as external sorting.

Example 3.3.2 : Sort the following numbers using selection sort.

          Numbers : 16, 23, 13, 9, 7, 5   **S - 08, S - 2010**

Solution :

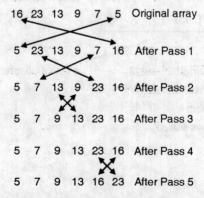

3.4 Insertion Sort

Q. Write the algorithm for Insertion sort and arrange the given numbers in ascending order using insertion sort. Numbers : 77, 33, 44, 11, 88, 22, 66, 55   **W - 08**

Q. Write an algorithm for insertion sort and arrange the given numbers in ascending order using insertion sort. Numbers 45, 22, 8, 34, 19.   **S - 09**

An element can always be placed at a right place in sorted list of element for example

List of elements(sorted) 5 9 10 15 20

Element to be placed = 6

If the element 6 is to be inserted in a sorted list of elements (5, 9, 10, 15, 20), its rightful place will be between 5 and 9. Elements with value > 6 should be moved right by one place. Thus creating a space for the incoming element.

5 | 9 10 15 20 | →   Moved right by 1 place

5   6   9   10   15   20   →   Element 6 is inserted between 5 and 9

Insertion sort is based on the principle of inserting the element at its correct place in a previously sorted list. i can be varied from 1 to n − 1 to sort the entire array.

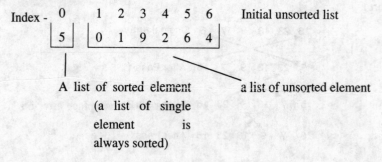

Index -   0   1   2   3   4   5   6   Initial unsorted list

     | 5 | | 0   1   9   2   6   4 |

A list of sorted element   a list of unsorted element
(a list of single
element   is
always sorted)

1ˢᵗ iteration (Place element at location '1' i.e. a[1], at its correct place)

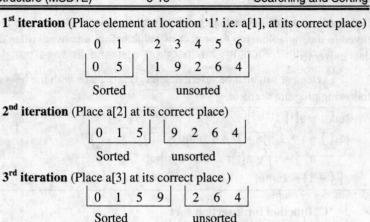

1ˢᵗ iteration (Place element at location '1' i.e. a[1], at its correct place)

0	1		2	3	4	5	6
0	5		1	9	2	6	4

Sorted　　　　unsorted

2ⁿᵈ iteration (Place a[2] at its correct place)

0	1	5		9	2	6	4

Sorted　　　unsorted

3ʳᵈ iteration (Place a[3] at its correct place)

0	1	5	9		2	6	4

Sorted　　　unsorted

4ᵗʰ iteration (Place a[4] at its correct place)

0	1	2	5	9		6	4

sorted　　　　Unsorted

5ᵗʰ iteration (Place a[5] at its correct place)

0	1	2	5	6	9		4

Sorted　　　　unsorted

6ᵗʰ iteration (Place a[6] at its correct place)

0　1　2　4　5　6　9

Fig. 3.4.1 : Sorting of elements using insertion sort

Insertion sort requires n-1 passes to sort an array having n elements. Before the ith pass starts, elements at position 0 through i-1 are already sorted.

Index →	0	1	2	3		4	5	6
a List →	1	5	9	11		6	2	5	1

↑

at the beginning of pass = 4

Element at position i = 4 can be inserted at its correct place after he following operations :

temp = a[4]

a[4] = a[3]

a[3] = a[2]

a[2] = temp

All elements larger than 6 are moved right by 1 place. i^{th} element is saved in the variable temp to protect its value before it is overwritten due to data movement.

i^{th} element can also be inserted at its correct place with the help of the following program segment.

```
temp = a[i] ;
for( j = i - 1 ; j> = 0 && temp < a[ j] ; j  - -)
     a[ j + 1] = a[j]; /*move input */
a[ j + 1] = temp;
```

➢　　**'C' function for insertion sort**

```
void insertion_sort(int a[ ], int n)
{
     int i, j, temp;
     for(i=1;i<n;i++)                    /* passes 1 through n - 1 */
     {
          temp = a[i];
          for( j = i - 1; j > = 0 && a[ j] > temp; j --)
               a[j + 1] = a[ j];
          a[ j + 1] = temp;
     }
}
```

Analysis of insertion sort :

For loop of lines (3 – 4) will be executed $\sum\limits_{i-1}^{n-1} i$ times under its worst case behaviour. If the number to be sorted are initially in descending order then the for loop of lines (3 – 4) will make i iterations during pass i.

Elements	20	10	8	6	4	2	1	–	initially	
									pass	Positions moved
	10	20	8	6	4	2	1		1	1
	8	10	20	6	4	2	1		2	2

6	8	10	20	4	2	1	3	3
4	6	8	10	20	2	1	4	4
2	4	6	8	10	20	1	5	5
1	2	4	6	8	10	20	6	6

Thus, the total number of movement of data (if the list is initially in descending order) for sorting using insertion sort $= \sum\limits_{i=1}^{n-1} i$

$$= \frac{n(n-1)}{2} = 0(n^2).$$

| Worst case behaviour $O(n^2)$ |

If the input list presented for sorting is presorted the running time will be $0(n)$, because the test a[j] > temp in the inner loop (lines 3 – 4) will fail immediately. Thus only one comparison is made in each pass.

Total number of comparisons $= n - 1$

| Best case behaviour $O(n)$ |

Insertion sort can exploit the partially sorted nature of data. Insertion sort is highly efficient if the array is already in almost sorted order.

➢ **Program 3.4.1 : A sample program for insertion sort (for an array of integers)**

| Q. | Write a program for insertion sort and shell sort. | S - 08 |

```
#include<conio.h>
#include<stdio.h>
void insertion_sort(int[],int);
void main()
{
    int a[50],n,i;
    printf("\nEnter no. of elements :");
    scanf("%d",&n);
```

```
    printf("\nEnter array elements :");
    for(i=0;i<n;i++)
        scanf("%d",&a[i]);
    insertion_sort(a,n);
    printf("\nSorted array is :");
    for(i=0;i<n;i++)
        printf("%d",a[i]);
    getch();
}
void insertion_sort(int a[],int n)
{
    int i,j,temp;
    for(i=1;i<n;i++)
    {
        temp=a[i];
        for( j=i-1;j>=0 && a[ j]>temp;j--)
            a[ j+1]=a[ j];
        a[ j+1]=temp;
    }
}
```

Output

Enter no of elements	:	6				
Enter array elements	:	57	89	64	56	77	333
Sorted array is	:	56	57	64	77	89	333

3.4.1 Sorting an Array of Strings Using Insertion Sort :

A list of strings can be represented using a two dimensional array.

For example : A list { "ABC", "INDIA", "JAPAN", "AMERICA", "UK" } of strings can be represented as given below :

char a[10][20];

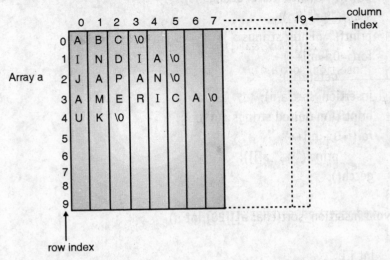

a[0] is the string "ABC"

a[1] is the string "INDIA"

a[2] is the string "JAPAN"

a[3] is the string "AMERCIA"

a[4] is the string "UK"

- Two numbers a[j] and temp are compared using the relational operation "a[j] > temp". Whereas the two string a[j] and temp should be compared using the library function strcmp(a[j], temp).

- Function strcpy(a[j+1], a[j]) should be used to move the string from location j to j+1 in the array.

➤ **Program 3.4.2 : Program showing sorting of strings using insertion sort.**

```
#include<conio.h>
#include<stdio.h>
#include<string.h>
void insertion_sort(char[][20],int);
void main()
{
    char a[10][20];
    int i,n;
```

```
    printf("\n Enter no of strings :");
    scanf("%d",&n);
    printf("\nEnter strings :");
    for(i=0;i<n;i++)
            gets(a[i]);
    insertion_sort(a,n);
    printf("\n Sorted strings :\n");
    for(i=0;i<n;i++)
            printf("%s",a[i]);
    getch();
}
void insertion_sort(char a[][20],int n)
{
    int i,j;
    char temp[20];
    for(i=0;i<n;i++)
    {
            strcpy(temp,a[i]);
            for(j=i-1;j>=0 && strcmp(a[j],temp)>0;j--)
                strcpy(a[j+1],a[j]);
            strcpy(a[j+1],temp);
    }
}
```

Output

```
Enter no of strings   : 4
Enter strings : xyz abc   ccc aaa
Sorted strings       : aaa    abc    ccc    xyz
```

3.4.2 Sorting an Array of Records on the given key Using Insertion Sort :

A company maintains record of its employees. Each record has the following format :

ENO	NAME	OCCUPATION	LOCATION

It is required to sort employee records on "ENO".

> **Program 3.4.3 : Program to sort employee records on "ENO".**

```c
#include<stdio.h>
#include<conio.h>
struct employee
{
   int ENO;
   char name[30];
   char occup[15];
   char loca[20];
};
void main()
{
   struct employee temp;
   int i,j,n;
   static struct employee
employees[]={{15,"MOHAN","PROG","DELHI"},
                {5,"RAM","ANAL","PUNE"},
                {12,"JOHN","MANA","MUMBAI"},
                {3,"SOHAN","PROG","NASIK"}
            };
   n=4;
   for(i=1;i<n;i++)
   {
        temp=employees[i];
        for(j=i-1;j>=0 && employees[j].ENO > temp.ENO;j--)
            employees[j+1]=employees[j];
        employees[j+1]=temp;
   }
```

```
    for(i=0;i<n;i++)
    {
    printf("\n%d\t%7s\t%5s\t%7s",employees[i].ENO,employees[i]
.name, employees[i].occup,employees[i].loca);
        getch();
    }
}
```

Output :

3	SOHAN	PROG	NASIK
5	RAM	ANAL	PUNE
12	JOHN	MANA	MUMBAI
15	MOHAN	PROG	DELHI

Example :

Here are five integers 1, 7, 3, 2, 0. Sort them using insertion sort.

Pass (i)	Comparisons (j)	List to sort	Remarks
		1 7 3 2 0	original list
i = 1	j = 0	1 7 3 2 0	7 > 1, therefore inner loop terminates
i = 2	j = 1	1 7 3 2 0	7 > 3, move 7 right
	j = 0	1 7 7 2 0	3 > 1, inner loop terminates
		1 3 7 2 0	insert 3
i = 3	j = 2	1 3 7 7 0	7 > 2, move 7 right
	j = 1	1 3 3 7 0	3 > 2, move 2 right
	j = 0	1 3 3 7 0	2 > 1, inner loop terminates
		1 2 3 7 0	insert 2
i = 4	j = 3	1 2 3 7 7	7 > 0
	j = 2	1 2 3 3 7	3 > 0

Pass (i)	Comparisons (j)	List to sort	Remarks
	j = 1	1 2 2 3 7	2 > 0
	j = 0	1 1 2 3 7	1 > 0
	j = – 1	1 1 2 3 7	j = – 1, inner loop terminates
		0 1 2 3 7	Insert 0

Hence the sorted list = {0, 1, 2, 3, 7}

Example :

Show that the average case running time of insertion sort is $O(n^2)$

Number of comparisons (average) required to locate the point of insertion of the ith element.

$$= \frac{1}{i}[1 + 2 + 3 + \dots + i] = \frac{1}{i} \times \frac{i[i+1]}{2} = \frac{i+1}{2}$$

Since, in the outer loop i varies from 1 to n – 1.

∴ Total number of comparisons

$$= \sum_{i=1}^{n-1} \frac{i+1}{2} = \frac{1}{2} \sum_{i=1}^{n-1} (i+1)$$

$$= \frac{1}{2}\left[(n-1) + \frac{n(n-1)}{2}\right] = \frac{1}{2}\left[\frac{2(n-1) + n(n-1)}{2}\right]$$

$$= \frac{1}{4}[(n+2)(n-1)] = \frac{1}{4}[n^2 + n - 2]$$

$$= O(n^2)$$

Example 3.4.1 : Arrange the given numbers in ascending order using insertion sort.

Numbers : 77, 33, 44, 11, 88, 22, 66, 55 W - 08

Solution :

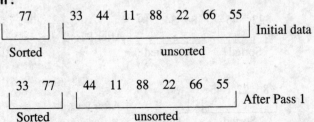

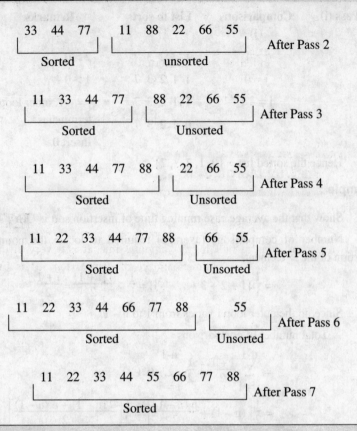

```
33   44   77      11   88   22   66   55
└─────────────┘   └─────────────────────┘   After Pass 2
     Sorted              unsorted

11   33   44   77      88   22   66   55
└──────────────────┘  └─────────────────┘   After Pass 3
        Sorted              Unsorted

11   33   44   77   88      22   66   55
└───────────────────────┘  └─────────────┘   After Pass 4
          Sorted               Unsorted

11   22   33   44   77   88      66   55
└────────────────────────────┘  └────────┘   After Pass 5
            Sorted                 Unsorted

11   22   33   44   66   77   88      55
└─────────────────────────────────┘  └───┘   After Pass 6
              Sorted                  Unsorted

11   22   33   44   55   66   77   88
└──────────────────────────────────────┘   After Pass 7
                Sorted
```

Example 3.4.2 : Arrange the given numbers in ascending order using insertion sort.

Numbers : 45, 22, 8, 34, 19　　　　S - 09

Solution :

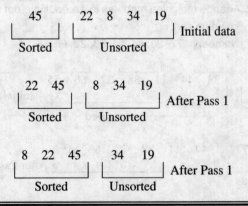

```
45      22   8   34   19
└──┘   └──────────────┘   Initial data
Sorted      Unsorted

22   45      8   34   19
└──────┘   └───────────┘   After Pass 1
 Sorted       Unsorted

8   22   45      34   19
└───────────┘   └────────┘   After Pass 1
   Sorted          Unsorted
```

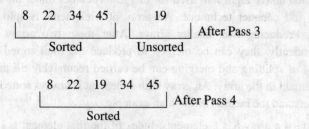

After Pass 3

After Pass 4

3.5 Two-Way Merge Sort

Q. Explain Merge sort with example program.   S - 08

Merge sort runs in O(N log N) running time. It is a very efficient sorting algorithm with near optimal number of comparisons. It is based described using a recursive algorithm. Basic operation in merge sort is that of merging of two sorted lists into one sorted list. Merging operation has a linear time complexity.

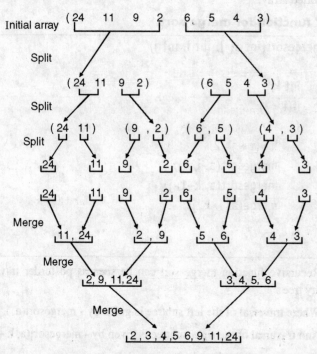

Recursive algorithm used for merge sort comes under the category of divide and conquer technique. An array of n elements is split around its centre. Producing two smaller arrays. After these two arrays are sorted independently, they can be merged to produce the final sorted array. The process of splitting and merging can be carried recursively till there is only one element in the array. An array with 1 element is always sorted. Let us try to understand the method through an example.

Given array has 8 elements. Index of the first element is i = 0, index of the last element j = 7. In order to divide the above list around the middle element, the index of the centre element $k = \dfrac{i+j}{2} = \dfrac{0+7}{2} = 3$.

- Merge sort is applied recursively to left half of the list from i = 0 to j = 3.

- After sorting of the left half of the list. Right half of the list is sorted from i = 4 to j = 7 recursively using merge sort.

- After both the lists are sorted, left list from i = 0 to j = 3 and right list from i = 4 to j = 7, these two lists are merged to produce a single sorted array.

➤ **'C' function for merge sort.**

```
void mergesort(int a[ ], int i, int j)
{
        int k;
        if(i < j)
        {
            k =(i + j)/2;
            mergesort(a, i, k);
            mergesort(a, k+1, j);
            merge(a, i, k, j);
        }
}
```

Recursive function merge sort can be seen as postorder traversal of the binary tree :

Where traversal of the left subtree is given by - mergesort(a, i, k);

And traversal of the right subtree is given by - mergesort(a, k + 1 , j);

Visiting a node is given by merge(a, i, k, j).

If the root node starts with an array (24, 11, 9, 2, 6, 5, 4, 3) having eight elements. Value of i and j for the root node will be i = 0 and j = 7 respectively. After split, value of i and j for the left child will be i = 0 and j = 3 and for the right child it will be i = 4 and j = 7. Recursion will go on expanding until the list can no longer be divided.

Post order traversal on the recursion tree will list the nodes in the following sequence :

D E B F G C A

Visit D[merge (24) (11) giving (11, 24)]

Visit E[Merge (9) (2) giving (2, 9)]

Visit B[Merge (11, 24)(2, 9) giving (2, 9, 11, 24)]

Visit F[Merge (6) (5) giving (5, 6)]

Visit G[Merge (4) (3) giving (3, 4)]

Visit C[Merge (5, 6) (3, 4) giving (3, 4, 5, 6)]

Visit A[Merge (2, 9, 11, 24), (3, 4, 5, 6) giving
(2, 3, 4, 5, 6, 9, 11, 24)]

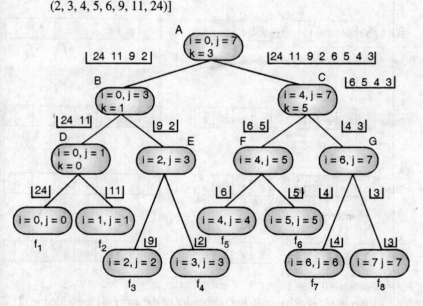

3.5.1 Merging :

The fundamental operation in merge sort algorithm is merging two sorted arrays. The merging algorithm takes two sorted arrays a[] and b[] as input and the third array c[] as output. Three variables i, j and k are initially set to the beginning of the three arrays a[], b[] and c[]. The smaller of a[i] and b[j] is copied to c[k] and appropriate variables (i, k) or (j, k) are advanced. When either of the input array a[] or b[] is exhausted, the remainder of the other array is copied to c.

Initial conditions :

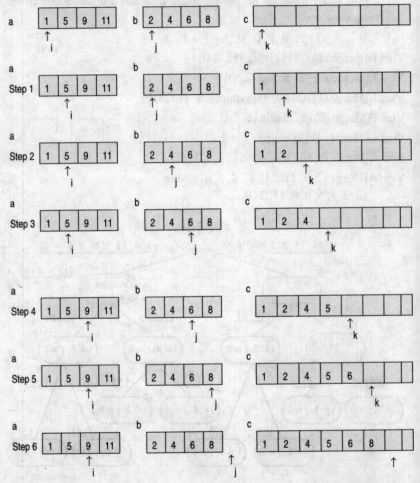

Array b[] is exhausted, the remainder of the array a[] are added to c[].

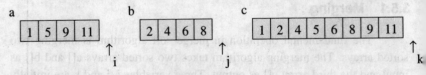

Example 3.5.1 : Sort the following list of numbers using merge sort. Show result stepwise :

50, 10, – 10, 40, 15, 25, 20, 35, 30

Solution :

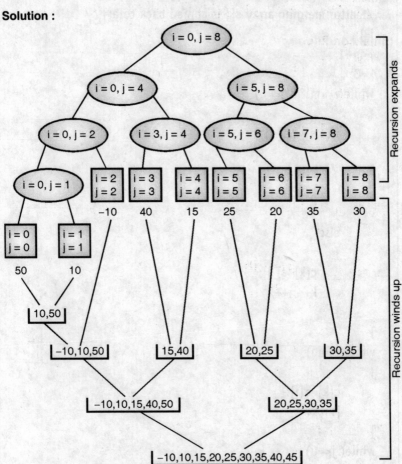

> **'C' function for merging of two sorted arrays.**

```
void merge(int a[],int l,int m,int u)
{
    int c[MAX];
    int i,j,k;
    /* First array is supposed to be
       from location l to m of array a[] */
```

```
    /* Second array is supposed to be from m+1
      to u of array a[] */
    /* Array c[] is used for merging */
    /* after merging array c[] is copied back to a[] */
    i=l;
    j=m+1;
    k=0;
    while(i<=m && j<=u)
    {
        if(a[i] < a[ j])
        {
            c[k]=a[i];
            k++;i++;
        }
        else
        {
            c[k]=a[ j];
            k++;j++;
        }
    }
    while(i<=m)
    {
        c[k]=a[i];
        i++;k++;
    }
    while( j<=u)
    {
        c[k]=a[ j];
        k++;j++;
    }
    for(i=l,j=0;i<=u;i++,j++)
        a[i]=c[ j];
}
```

> **Program 3.5.1 : Program for implementation of merge sort.**

```c
#include<stdio.h>
#include<conio.h>
#define MAX 30
void merge_sort(int[],int,int);
void merge(int[],int,int,int);
void main()
{
    int a[30],n,i;
    printf("\n No. of elements :");
    scanf("%d",&n);
    printf("Enter array elements :");
    for(i=0;i<n;i++)
            scanf("%d",&a[i] );
    merge_sort(a,0,n-1);
    printf("\n Sorted data ->\n");
    for(i=0;i<n;i++)
            printf("%d",a[i]);
    getch();
}
void merge_sort(int a[],int i,int j)
{
    int k;
    if(i<j)
    {
            k=(i+j)/2;
            merge_sort(a,i,k);
            merge_sort(a,k+1,j);
            merge(a,i,k,j);
    }
}
void merge(int a[],int l,int m,int u)
{
```

```
int c[MAX];
int i,j,k;
/* First array is supposed to be
   from location l to m of array a[] */
/* Second array is supposed to be from m+1
   to u of array a[] */
/* Array c[] is used for merging */
/* after merging array c[] is copied back to a[] */
i=l;
j=m+1;
k=0;
while(i<=m && j<=u)
{
      if(a[i] < a[ j])
      {
           c[k]=a[i];
           k++;i++;
      }
      else
      {
           c[k]=a[ j];
           k++;j++;
      }
}
while(i<=m)
{
      c[k]=a[i];
      i++;k++;
}
while( j<=u)
{
      c[k]=a[j];
      k++;j++;
```

```
    }
    for(i=l,j=0;i<=u;i++,j++)
        a[i]=c[ j];
}
```

Output

No. of elements	: 4			
Enter array elements	: 32	56	22	1
Sorted data	->	1	22	32	56

3.5.2 Analysis of Merge Sort :

Since, merge sort is a recursive program, we must write a recurrence relation for the running time.

Time to merge sort N numbers is equal to the time to merge sort left N/2 element, plus time to merge sort right N / 2 element, plus time to merge two linear lists of N/2 elements. Merging requires one pass of linear scanning of the two input arrays (each having N/2 elements). Hence the time to merge is linear.

$T(1) = 1$, since recursion terminates when $N = 1$. Time to merge sort an array having 1 element is constant.

$$T(N) = 2 T(N/2) + N$$

Or $$\frac{T(N)}{N} = \frac{T(N/2)}{N/2} + 1 \qquad \dots(1)$$

Equation (1) can be written as (expanding $T(N/2)$)

$$= \frac{T(N/4)}{N/4} + 1 + 1 = \frac{T(N/2^2)}{N/2^2} + 2$$

Let us assume, $N = 2^h$ i.e. $N/2^h = 1$

Equation (1) can be written as

$$\frac{T(N)}{N} = \frac{T(N/2^h)}{N/2^h} + h$$

$$= \frac{T(1)}{1} + h = T(1) + h \qquad \dots(2)$$

Since $$N = 2^h$$

Taking log on both sides, we have

$$\log N = \log_2 2^h = h$$

Writing h as log N in Equation (2)

$$\frac{T(N)}{N} = T(1) + \log N$$

or $\qquad T(N) = NT(1) + N \log N = \mathbf{O(N \log N)}$

Although the running time of merge sort is $O(N \log_2 N)$, it is seldom used for internal sorting. Merging of two sorted arrays require additional memory. Two sorted arrays are merged through a temporary array and the contents of the temporary array is copied back requiring additional space and time. Merge sort is found to be very effective in external sorting.

3.5.3 Non-Recursive Merge Sort :

Non-recursive merge sort uses bottom up approach.

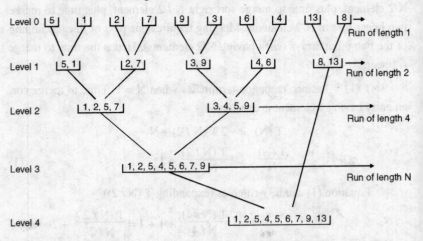

When the initial array a[] of N elements is divided into N groups (each group having 1 element), elements inside a group are sorted (a group with 1 element is always sorted). This is also called that initially, array is organized into runs of length 1.

The first pass of the algorithm merges n pair of runs of length = 1 at level 0 to create runs of length 2 at level 1.

The second pass merges a pair of runs of length = 2 at level 1 to create runs of length 4 at level 2. In every successive pass, number of runs is reduced by half and the length of runs is doubled.

If P passes are required for sorting, then $2^P >= N$.

➤ 'C' function for non-recursive merge sort.

```c
void non_recursive_mergesort(int a[],int N)
{
   int run_size,no_of_runs,i,j;
   run_size=1;                  //one element at atime at level 0
   while(run_size<N)
   {
        no_of_runs=N/run_size;
        if(no_of_runs*run_size < N)
            no_of_runs++; //last run of smaller size
        i=0; j=run_size;      /* i=beginning of the first run
                      j=beginning of the next run */
        while(no_of_runs > 1)
        {
            if(i+2*run_size > N)  //last run of smaller size
                    merge(a,i,j-1,N-1);
            else
                    merge(a,i,j-1,j+run_size-1);
            i=i+run_size;
            j=j+run_size;
            no_of_runs=no_of_runs-2;
        }
        run_size=run_size * 2;
   }
}
```

Example 3.5.2 : Sort the following numbers in ascending order using merge sort.

{15, 84, 62, 08, 41, 57, 33, 18, 51, 32} W - 09

Solution :

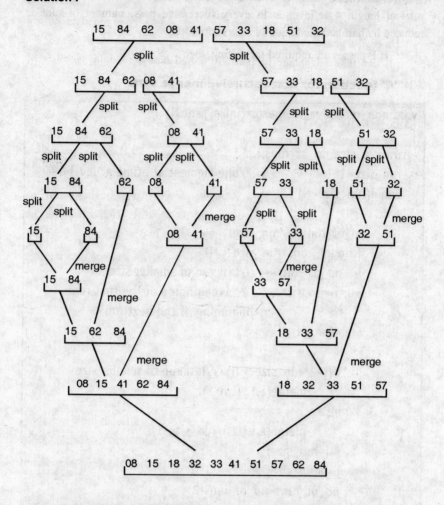

Example 3.5.3 : Explain advantages and disadvantages of merge sort.

W - 09

Solution :

Advantages :

1.   It has a timing complexity of O(n log n)
2.   It can be used both for internal as well as external sorting.
3.   It is a stable sorting algorithm.

Disadvantages :

1. It requires an additional memory for storing of merged data during merging phase.

2. It can take advantage of partially sorted nature of data. Number of passes are fixed.

3.6 Radix Sort

Q. Explain Radix sort with example.   S - 08

Radix sort is generalization of bucket sort. To sort decimal numbers, where the radix or base is 10, we need 10 buckets. These buckets are numbered 0, 1, 2, 3, 4, 5, 6, 7, 8, 9. Sorting is done in passes.

Number of passes required to sort using shell sort is equal to number of digits in the largest number in the list.

Range	Passes
0 to 99	2 passes
0 to 999	3 passes
0 to 9999	4 passes

- In the first pass, numbers are sorted on least significant digit. Numbers with the same least significant digit are stored in the same bucket.

- In the 2nd pass, numbers are sorted on the second least significant digit.

- At the end of every pass, numbers in buckets are merged to produce a common list.

- Number of passes depends on the range of numbers being sorted.

The following example shows the action of radix sort.

Initial numbers :

     10   5   99   105   55   100   135   141   137   200   199

Buckets after 1ˢᵗ pass :

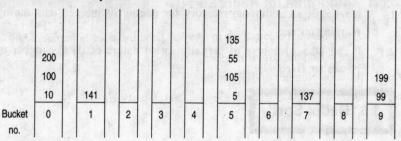

Merged 10 100 200 141 5 105 55 135 137 99 199
list =

Buckets after 2ⁿᵈ pass :

100									
5									
200			137						199
100	10		135	141	55				99
0	1	2	3	4	5	6	7	8	9

merged 100 200 5 105 10 135 137 141 55 99 199
list =

Buckets after third pass :

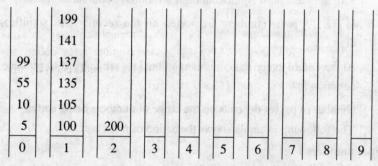

Merged 5 10 55 99 100 105 135 137 141 199 200
list =

3.6.1　Algorithm for Radix Sort :

/*numbers to be sorted are in array a[ ] and there are N numbers */
1.　　large = find the largest number in a [ ]
2.　　passes = Number of digits in large
3.　　Div = 1 /* divisor for extracting i^{th} least significant digit */
4.　　for (i = 1; i < = passes; i++)
　　　　　{
　　　　　　　1.　Initialize all buckets b0 to b9
　　　　　　　2.　for each number x from a [0] to a [N – 1]
　　　　　　　{
　　　　　　　　　1.　bucket_no = (x/div)%10
　　　　　　　　　2.　insert x in bucket with bucket_number
　　　　　　　}
3.　　Copy elements of buckets back in array a [ ]
4.　　DIV = DIV * 10
　　　　}
5.　　exit

3.6.2　C-function for Radix Sort :

Input to functions are :

n= number of elements in the array a []

a [ ] = Array holding elements.

Buckets are represented using a two dimensional array buckets [10] [10]. Each bucket can hold upto ten values. Another array count [10] gives number of elements in the corresponding bucket. If buckets [1] has five elements then the value of count [1] will be five.

Whenever, an element is inserted in i^{th} bucket, count [i] should be incremented by 1.

```
void radix (int a[ ], int n)
    {      int buckets[10][10], count[10];
           int passes, large, div, bucketno, i, j, k;
    /* find the largest number in a [ ]  */
           large = a[0];
           for (i = 1; i < n; i++)
```

```
                if (a[ i] > large)
                     large = a[i];
     /* find number of digits in large and store the count in passes
*/
     passes = 0;
     while (large > 0)
          {     passes++;
                large = large /10;
          }
     /* perform radix sort */
          div = 1;
     for (i = 1; i < = passes; i++)
     { /*initialize bucket */
          for ( j = 0; j < = 9; j++)
               count [ j] = 0;
     /* insert elements in respective buckets */
          for ( j = 0; j < n; j++)
          {     bucketno = (a[ j]/div)%10;
                buckets[bucketno][count[bucketno]]
                     = a[ j];
                count [bucketno]++;
          }
     /* merge elements of buckets and store them in a[0] ...a[n –
1] */
     j = 0;
     for (bucketno = 0; bucketno < = 9; bucketno++)
          for (k=0; k < count[bucketno]; k++)
          a [ j++] = buckets[bucketno] [k];
          div = div * 10;
     }
}
```

> **Program 3.6.1 : Program to sort elements of an array using radix Sort**

```c
#include <stdio.h>
#include <conio.h>
void radix(int a[ ], int n);
void main( )
   {      int a[30], n, i;
          printf("\n enter no. of elements");
          scanf("%d",&n);
          printf("\n enter data :");
          for (i = 0; i < n; i++)
              scanf("%d", &a[i]);
              radix (a, n);
          printf("\n sorted data :");
          for (i = 0; i < n;  i++)
              printf("%d\t", a[i]);
   }
void radix (int a[ ], int n)
   {      int buckets[10][10], count[10];
          int passes, large, div, bucketno, i, j, k;
   /* find the largest number in a [ ]  */
          large = a[0];
          for (i = 1; i < n; i++)
              if (a[ i] > large)
                    large = a[i];
   /* find number of digits in large and store the count in passes
*/
   passes = 0;
   while(large > 0)
        {    passes++;
```

```
                    large = large /10;
           }
    /* perform radix sort */
    div = 1;
    for (i = 1; i < = passes; i++)
    { /*initialize bucket */
          for ( j = 0; j < = 9; j++)
               count [j] = 0;
    /* insert elements in respective buckets */
          for ( j = 0; j < n; j++)
          {    bucketno = (a[j]/div)%10;
               buckets[bucketno][count[bucketno]]
                    = a[ j];
               count [bucketno]++;

          }
/* merge elements of buckets and store them in a[0] ...a[n – 1]*/
    j = 0;
    for (bucketno = 0; bucketno < = 9; bucketno++)
          for (k=0; k < count[bucketno]; k++)
               a [ j++] = buckets[bucketno] [k];
               div = div * 10;

    }
```

Output

enter no. of elements : 11
enter data   : 10 5   99 105 55 100 135 141 137   200 199
sorted data   : 5   10 55 99 100 105 135 137 141   199 200

3.6.3 Analysis of Radix Sort :

If the number to be sorted are k digits long then inside every pass :

* Distribution of elements among buckets take 0(n) time
* Merging of elements take 0(n) time

Number of passes = k

∴ Overall complexity is 0(kn)

if k is regarded as a constant

then

0(kn) = 0(n).

Thus, timing complexity of Radix Sort = 0(n)

Space requirement : There is additional memory requirement for buckets and storing number of elements in each bucket.

Radix sort is the most preferred algorithm for sorting of strings

---

Example 3.6.1 : Sort the given numbers in ascending order using Radix sort.
Numbers : 348, 14, 614, 5381, 47   **W - 08**

Solution :

Buckets after pass 1 :

Merged list : 5381, 14, 614, 47, 348

Buckets after pass 2 :

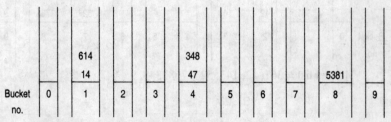

Merged list : 14, 614, 47, 348, 5381

Bucket after pass 3 :

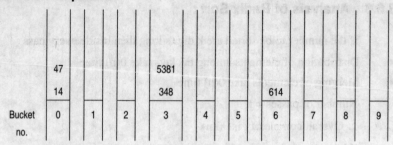

Merged list = 14, 47, 348, 5381, 614

Buckets after pass 4 :

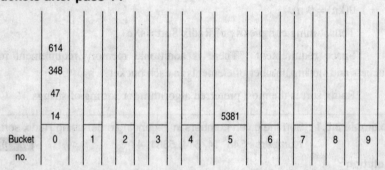

Merged list = 14, 47, 348, 614, 5381

Example 3.6.2 : Sort the given numbers in ascending order using radix sort.

361, 12, 527, 143, 9, 768, 348   S - 09

Solution :

Buckets after pass 1 :

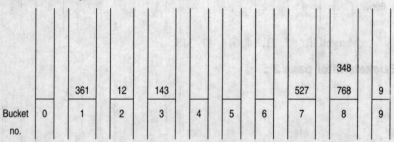

Merged list = 361, 12, 143, 527, 768, 348, 9

Buckets after pass 2 :

Merged list : 9, 12, 527, 143, 348, 361, 768

Buckets after pass 3 :

Merged list : 9, 12, 143, 348, 361, 527, 768.

3.7 Shell Sort

This method makes repeated use of insertion sort. If an array of n elements is to be sorted using shell sort then sorting requires that a number d_i called increment should be chosen before every pass. di should be less than n. d_i should diminish with every pass and for the last pass di should be 1.

Initial value of increments di can be taken as n/2 and in subsequent passes di should be halved.

i.e.

$d_1 = n/2$

$d_2 = d_1/2$

$d_3 = d_2/2$

$d_{i+1} = d_i/2$

If an array a[0] ... a[7], has 8 elements then the initial value of increment $d_1 = 8/2 = 4$ with increment as 4, original array will be divided into four sub-lists :

1st sub list : (a [0], a[0 + 4])

2nd sub list : (a [1], a[1 + 4])

3rd sub list : (a [2], a[2 + 4])

4th sub list : (a [3], a[3 + 4])

Each of these lists is sorted independently using insertion sort.

In the second pass, the value of increment d_2 is taken as

$d_2 = d_1/2 = 4/2 = 2$

Array will be divided into two sub lists :

1st sub list :   (a[0], a[0 + 2], a[0 + 4], a[0 + 6])

2nd sub list :   (a[1], a[1 + 2], a[1 + 4], a[1 + 6])

each of these lists is sorted independently using insertion sort.

In the third pass the value of increment d_3 is taken as

$d_3 = d_2/2 = 2/2 = 1$

Since, the value of increment is 1, entire array with elements

(a[0], a[1], a[2] ... a[6], a[7])

will be sorted using insertion sort.

3.7.1 C-function for Shell Sort :

Example 3.7.1 : The function shell sort, as given below, sometimes called diminishing increment sort, sorts an array a[n] of integers by sorting n / 2 pairs (a[i], a[n / 2 + i]) for $0 \leq i < n / 2$ in the first pass, n / 4 four-tuples (a[i], a[n / 4 + i] , a[n / 2 + i], a[3n / 4 + i]) for $0 \leq i < n / 4$ in the second pass, n/8 eight-tuples in the third pass and so on. In each pass the sorting is done using insertion sort in which we stop sorting once we encounter two elements in the proper order.

Solution :

```
void shellsort(int a[ ], int n)
    {
```

```
        int i, j, step;
         int temp;
        for(step = n/2; step > 0; step = step/2)
        for(i = step; i < n; i++)
        {
            temp = a[i];
            for( j = i; j > = step; j = j - step)
                if(temp < a[ j - step])
                        a[ j] = a[ j - step];
                else
                        break;
                a[ j] = temp;
            }
    }
```

➤ **Program 3.7.2 : Sorting of data using shell sort**

Q. Write a program for insertion sort and shell sort.	S - 08

```
#include <stdio.h>
#include <conio.h>
void shellsort (int a[], int n);
void main ( )
{   int a[30], i, n;
    printf("\n enter no. of elements :");
    scanf ("%d", &n);
    printf("\n enter data :");
    for (i = 0; i < n ; i++)
        scanf ("%d", &a[i]);
    shellsort (a, n);
    printf("\n sorted data :\n");
    for (i = 0; i < n; i++)
```

```
        printf("%d/t", a[i]);
}
void shellsort(int a[ ], int n)
  {
        int i, j, step;
         int temp;
        for(step = n/2; step > 0; step = step/2)
        for(i = step; i < n; i++)
        {
            temp = a[i];
            for( j = i; j > = step; j = j - step)
                if(temp < a[ j - step])
                        a[ j] = a[ j - step];
                else
                        break;
                a[ j] = temp;
            }
    }
```

Output

```
enter no. of elements : 8
enter data : 1 5 2 4 6 11 3 7
sorted data : 1 2 3 4 5 6 7 11
```

Example 3.7.2 :   Sort the following sequence of integers
                        (5 1 9 8 2 4 6 9) using shell sort

Solution :

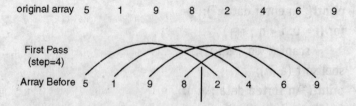

there are four groups, each group has 2 elements.

Elements of a group are sorted using insertion sort.

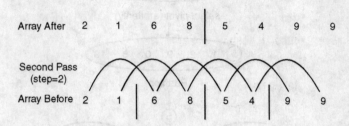

there are 2 groups, each group has 4 elements.

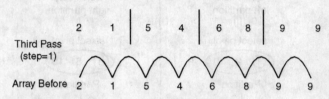

there is only one group, group has 8 elements.

elements of the group are sorted using insertion sort.

Array after 1 2 4 5 6 8 9 9

3.8 Quick Sort

Q. Write and explain the procedure for recursive quick sort. Justify the same with example. **S - 2010**

Quick sort is the fastest internal sorting algorithm with the time complexity = O(n log n). The basic algorithm to sort an array a[ ] of n elements can be described recursively as follows :

1.　If n < = 1, then return

2.　Pick any element V in a[ ]. This is called the pivot.

Rearrange elements of the array by moving all elements $x_i > V$ right of V and all elements $x_i \le V$ left of V. If the place of the V after re-arrangement is j, all elements with value less than V, appear in a[0], a[1] … a[j – 1] and all those with value greater than V appear in a[j + 1] … a[n – 1].

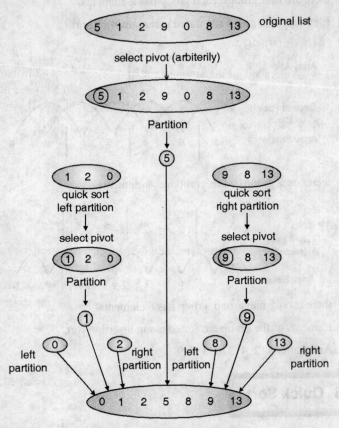

Fig. 3.8.1 : Illustration of quick sort

3. Apply quick sort recursively to a[0] ..... a[j – 1] and to a[j + 1] ... a[n – 1]

   Entire array will thus be sorted by as selecting an element V.

   (a) partitioning the array around V.

   (b) recursively, sorting the left partition.

   (c) recursively sorting the right partition.

3.8.1 Picking a Pivot :

We will choose the popular choice of the first element as the pivot. There are several strategies for pivoting. These strategies will be discussed later in the chapter.

Choose the first element as the pivot

3.8.2 Partitioning :

Let the elements of the array a[l], a[l + 1] .... a[n – 1], a[n] are to be partitioned around the pivot V = a[l]. Initial value of l will be 0 and that of n will be n – 1. As recursion proceeds, these values will change. Index of the pivot (say K) will satisfy the following conditions :

$$K \geq l$$
$$K \leq n$$

Two cursors (index variable) are initialized with

i = l + 1 and

j = n – 1

i moves towards right searching for an element greater than V. j moves towards left searching for an element smaller than V. When these elements are found they are interchanged. Again i moves towards right and j towards left and exchange is made whenever necessary. The process ends when i is equal to j or i > j.

j gives the index of the pivot element after termination of the above process.

Above procedure is explained with the help of the following example.

Let the array of number be

0	1	2	3	4	5	6	7	8	9	10	11	12
30	35	10	15	20	34	5	18	6	11	13	26	38

Initially l = 0, j = 12, V = a[l] {i.e. V = 30}

i is set to l + 1 and j is set to n – 1 as shown below

30	35	10	15	20	34	5	18	6	11	13	26	38

↑   ↑

i = 1   j = 12

Now i moves right, while a[i] < 30. Hence i does not move further to right as a[1] > 30.

Then, j moves left, while a[j] > 30.

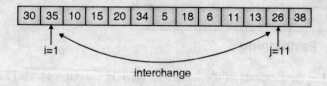

At this point a[i] and a[j] are interchanged and the movement of i and j resumes.

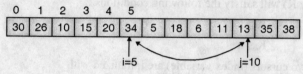

i moves right to a[5] as 34 > 30. j moves left to a[10] as 13 < 30. Once again a[i] and a[j] are swapped.

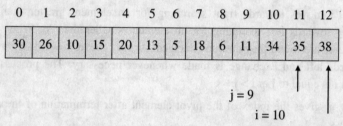

Now, i moves to a[10] as 34 > 30 and j moves to a[9] as 11 < 30.

Since, i > j, the process ends. j gives the location of the pivot element. Pivot element a[l with l = 0] is interchanged with a[i] to partition the array.

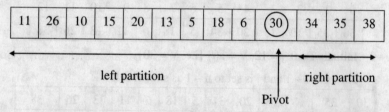

Please note that all element a[i] with $l \leq i < j$ are less than 30 and all elements a[j] with $u \geq i > j$ are greater than 30.

> **'C' function for the above partitioning algorithm.**

```
int partition(int a[],int l,int u)
{
    int v,i,j,temp;
```

```
    v=a[l];
    i=l;
    j=u+1;
    do
    {
            do
                i++;
            while(a[i]<v && i<=u);
                do
                        j--;
                while(v<a[j]);
                                if(i<j)
                {
                        temp=a[i];
                        a[i]=a[j];
                        a[j]=temp;
                }
    }while(i<j);
    a[l]=a[j];
    a[j]=v;
    return(j);
}
```

> **'C' function for sorting an array of element using quick sort.**

```
void quick_sort(int a[],int l,int u)
{
    int j;
    if(l<u)
    {
            j=partition(a,l,u);
            quick_sort(a,l,j-1);
```

```
        quick_sort(a,j+1,u);
    }
}
```

> **Program 3.8.1 : Write a program in 'C' to implement quick sort.**

```c
#include<conio.h>
#include<stdio.h>
void quick_sort(int[],int,int);
int partition(int[],int,int);
void main()
{
   int a[30],n,i;
   printf("\nEnter no of elements :");
   scanf("%d",&n);
   printf("\nEnter array elements :");
   for(i=0;i<n;i++)
        scanf("%d",&a[i]);
        quick_sort(a,0,n-1);
        printf("\nSorted array is :");
   for(i=0;i<n;i++)
        printf("%d",a[i]);
   getch();
}
void quick_sort(int a[],int l,int u)
{
   int j;
   if(l<u)
   {
        j=partition(a,l,u);
        quick_sort(a,l,j-1);
        quick_sort(a,j+1,u);
   }
```

```
}
int partition(int a[],int l,int u)
{
   int v,i,j,temp;
   v=a[l];
   i=l;
   j=u+1;
   do
   {
   do
        i++;
   while(a[i]<v && i<=u);

   do
        j--;
   while(v<a[j]);
   if(i<j)
   {
        temp=a[i];
        a[i]=a[j];
        a[j]=temp;
   }
   }while(i<j);
   a[l]=a[j];
   a[j]=v;
   return(j);
}
```

Output

| Enter no of elements :   4 |
| Enter array elements : 23   1 55   33 |
| Sorted array is   :   1   23   33   55 |

Example 3.8.1 : Here are sixteen integers : 22, 36, 6, 7, 9, 26, 45, 75, 13, 31, 62, 27, 76, 33, 16, 62, 49. Sort them using quick sort.

Solution :

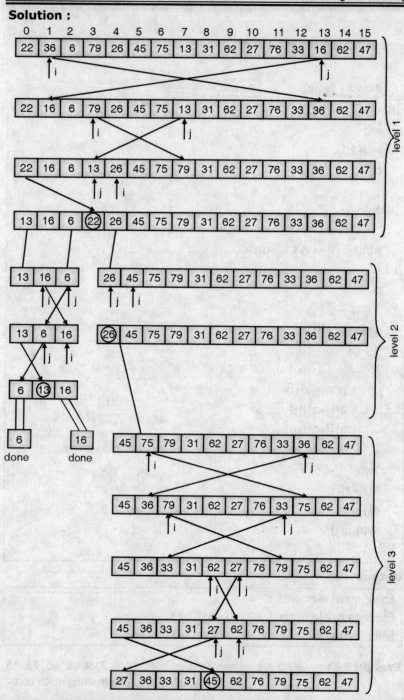

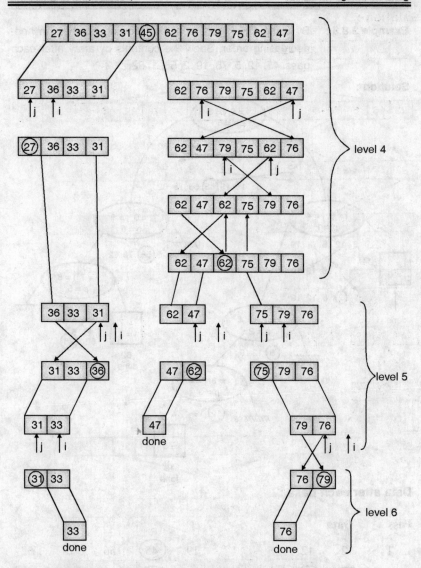

Note : *Partition point at each level is encircled.*

Example 3.8.3 : By using Quick sort, sort the following numbers in non-decreasing order. Show the contents by array after each pass. 45, 12, 5, 78, 19, 2, 56, 1, 62

Solution :

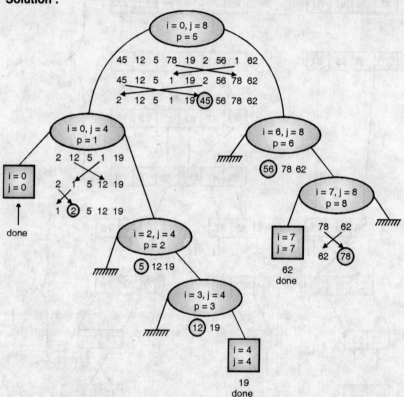

Data after each pass :

Pass	Data								
1	2	12	5	1	19	(45)	56	78	62
2	[1]	(2)	5	12	19	(45)	56	78	62
3	[1]	(2)	(5)	12	19	(45)	56	78	62
4	[1]	(2)	(5)	(12)	[19]	(45)	56	78	62
5	[1]	(2)	(5)	(12)	[19]	(45)	(56)	78	62
6	[1]	(2)	(5)	(12)	[19]	(45)	(56)	(62)	[78]

3.8.3 Running Time of Quick sort :

Quick sort takes O(n log n) time on the average to sort n elements and $O(n^2)$ time in worst case. Quick sort is a recursive algorithm. Its timing behaviour can be expressed using a recurrence formula. Solution of the recurrence formula will give its timing complexity. Since, the recursion terminates when n = 0 or 1.

We can take,

$$T(0) = 1 \qquad\qquad T(1) = 1$$

Running time of quick sort = running time of the left partition + running time of the right partition + time spent in partitioning the elements.

Since, partitioning requires scanning of the array linearly. It can be taken as cn, where c is a constant.

Running Time of the left partition = T(j), left partition contains j elements.

Running Time of the right partition = $T(n - j - 1)$

$$\therefore\ T(n) = T(j) + T(n - j - 1) + cn$$

3.8.3.1 Worst-case Analysis :

In the worst case, either j = 0 or $n - j - 1$ is equal to 0. j will always be 0 if the data presented for sorting is already sorted in ascending order. $n - j - 1$ will always be 0 if the data presented for sorting is already sorted in descending order.

Let us take the case of j = 0

$$
\begin{aligned}
T(N) &= T(0) + T(N - 1) + CN \text{ for } N > 1 \\
&\qquad\qquad \text{neglecting } T(0) \text{ being insignificant}
\end{aligned}
$$

$$
\begin{aligned}
T(N) &= T(N - 1) + CN \\
&= T(N - 2) + C(N - 1) + CN \\
&= T(N - 3) + C(N - 2) + C(N - 1) + CN \\
&\ \ \vdots \\
&\ \ \vdots \\
&= T(1) + C \cdot 2 + C \cdot 3 + \dots + C(N - 2) + C(N - 1) + CN
\end{aligned}
$$

$$= T(1) + C \cdot \sum_{i=2}^{N} i$$

$$= O(N^2)$$

3.8.3.2 Best-case Analysis :

Running time will be minimum if the pivot is always found in the middle. Left partition and the right partition will have equal number of elements.

$$\therefore T(N) = 2T(N/2) + CN$$

$$= 2^2 T(N/2^2) + 2CN$$

$$= 2^3 T(N/2^3) + 3CN$$

Let us assume that $N/2^h = 1$

$$\therefore N = 2^h \text{ or } \log_2 N = h$$

$$\therefore T(N) = 2^h T(N/2^h) + h \cdot C \cdot N$$

$$= 2^h T(1) + C h N$$

$$= N T(1) + C \cdot N \cdot \log_2 N$$

$$= O(N \log_2 N)$$

3.8.3.3 Average-case Analysis :

Let us consider the recurrence relation,

$$T(N) = T(j) + T(N - j - 1) + CN$$

Since, the variable j could take any value from 0 to $O(n-1)$ with equal probability,

The recurrence relation for average case can be written as,

$$T(N) = \frac{1}{N} \left[\sum_{j=0}^{N-1} T(j) + \sum_{j=0}^{N-1} T(N-j-1) \right] + CN$$

As j varies from 0 to $N - 1$, $N - j - 1$ varies from $N - 1$ to 0

Hence
$$\sum_{j=0}^{N-1} T(N-j-1) = \sum_{j=0}^{N-1} T(j)$$

$$\therefore T(N) = \frac{2}{N} \sum_{j=0}^{N-1} T(j) + CN \qquad \text{...(1)}$$

$$\text{Or} \quad NT(N) = 2 \sum_{j=0}^{N-1} T(j) + CN^2 \qquad \text{...(2)}$$

With N written as N – 1, equation (2) becomes

$$(N-1)\,T(N-1) = 2 \sum_{j=0}^{N-2} T(j) + C(N-1)^2 \qquad \text{...(3)}$$

If we subtract (3) from (2), we get

$$NT(N) - (N-1)\,T(N-1) = 2T(N-1) + 2CN - C$$

Dropping C being insignificant and arranging terms.

$$NT(N) = N+1)\,T(N-1) + 2CN$$

Dividing throughout by N(N + 1)

We get,

$$\frac{T(N)}{N+1} = \frac{T(N-1)}{N} + \frac{2C}{N+1}$$

$$= \frac{T(N-2)}{N-1} + \frac{2C}{N} + \frac{2C}{N+1}$$

$$= \frac{T(N-3)}{N-2} + \frac{2C}{N-1} + \frac{2C}{N} + \frac{2C}{N+1}$$

$$\vdots$$

$$= \frac{T(1)}{2} + \frac{2C}{3} + \dots + \frac{2C}{N} + \frac{2C}{N+1}$$

$$= \frac{T(1)}{2} + 2C \sum_{i=3}^{N+1} \frac{1}{i}$$

$$2C \sum_{i=3}^{N+1} \frac{1}{i} \approx \int \frac{1}{N} = \log N$$

$$\therefore \frac{T(N)}{N+1} = \frac{T(1)}{2} + \log N$$

$$\therefore T(N) = \frac{T(1)}{2} (N + 1) + (N + 1) \log N$$

$$= O(N \log N)$$

Quick sort gives its worst behavior when data presented for sorting is already sorted in either ascending or descending order.

3.9 Comparison of Sorting Algorithms

Define the following terms with respective sorting.

(i) sort stability　　　(ii) efficiency　　　(iii) passes

Sorting algorithm	Efficiency	Passes	Sort stability
Bubble sort	$O(n^2)$	$n - 1$	stable
Selection sort	$O(n^2)$	$n - 1$	stable
Insertion sort			stable
Best case	$O(n)$	$n - 1$	
Worst case	$O(n^2)$	$n - 1$	
Quick sort			unstable
Best case	$O(n \log n)$	$\log n$	
Worst case	$O(n^2)$	$n - 1$	
Merge sort	$O(n \log n)$	$\log n$	stable
Shell sort			unstable
Best case	$O(n)$	$\log n$	
Worst case	$O(n^2)$	$\log n$	
Radix sort	$O(n)$	No. of digits in the largest number	stable

3.9.1 Best-case, Worst-case and Average-case Analysis of Sorting Algorithm :

	Best-case	Worst-case	Average-case
Bubble sort	$O(n^2)$	$O(n^2)$	$O(n^2)$
Selection sort	$O(n^2)$	$O(n^2)$	$O(n^2)$

	Best-case	Worst-case	Average-case
Insertion sort	$O(n)$	$O(n^2)$	$O(n^2)$
Quick sort	$O(n \log n)$	$O(n^2)$	$O(n \log n)$
Merge sort	$O(n \log n)$	$O(n \log n)$	$O(n \log n)$
Shell sort	$O(n)$	$O(n^2)$	$O(n^2)$
Radix sort	$O(n)$	$O(n)$	$O(n)$

If the sorting algorithm is not data sensitive, its best case, worst case and average case timing behaviour will be same.

Bubble sort, selection sort, merge sort and radix sort algorithms are not data sensitive. Quick sort and shell algorithms are data sensitive.

Example 3.9.1: Sort the following numbers in ascending order using radix sort

14, 1, 66, 74, 22, 36, 41, 59, 64, 54

Buckets after 1st pass :

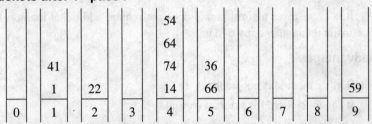

merged list =   1   41   22   14   74   64   54   66   36   59

Buckets after 2nd pass :

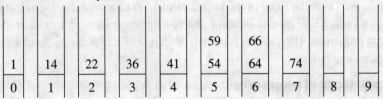

merged list =   1   14   22   36   41   54   59   64   66   74

3.9.2 Compare Quick Sort and Heap sort :

Q. Compare Quick sort and Heap sort with respect to working principle and time complexity.   **W - 08**

Quick sort is the fastest internal sorting algorithm with the time complexity = O(n logn). It is recursive algorithm. The working principle of quick sort is summarized below :

1. Select an element V as a partition element.

2. Partition the array around V such that every element in the left partition ≤ V and every element in the right partition ≥ V.

3. Left partition is subjected to quick sort recursively.

4. Right partition is subjected to quick sort recursively.

Advantages :

1. It is the fastest internal sorting algorithm with time complexity = O(n log n).

2. It is an in-place algorithm and does not require additional memory to maintain another copy of data.

Disadvantages :

1. Sorting method is not stable.

2. It cannot be used for external sorting.

3. Quick sort algorithm degenerates if the data being sorted is already sorted either in ascending or descending order.

Heap sort algorithm is based on creation of max-heap (to sort in ascending order). In a max-heap, the largest element is the root element. Thus, we know the value of the largest element in heap trivially. Heap sort is based on deletion of root element and re-adjustment of heap to restore the heap properties. This process is carried out repeatedly to generate elements in descending order.

Advantages of heap sort :

1. It has a time complexity of O(n log n).

2. It can be used to implement priority queue.

3. It is used in Kruskal's algorithm for finding minimum cost spanning tree.

Disadvantages :

1.　This algorithm is not stable.

2.　It cannot be used for external sorting.

3.　There is an additional overhead of maintaining a heap.

3.9.3　Compare Merge Sort and Quick Sort :

> **Q.**　Compare Merge sort and Quick sort with respect to working principle and time complexity.　**S - 09**

1.　Both merge sort and Quick sort have a time complexity of O (n log n).

2.　Merge sort is normally used for external sorting but quick sort is used for internal sorting.

3.　Merge sort algorithm is stable but the quick sort algorithm is not stable.

4.　Merge sort requires an additional memory for the purpose of merging. Its memory requirement is 2 times that of quick sort algorithm.

Working principle of merge sort :

1.　It is a recursive algorithm.

2.　The array of n elements to be sorted is recursively divided into two smaller arrays.

3.　Left array is sorted recursively.

4.　Right array is sorted recursively.

5.　After these two arrays are sorted, they are merged to produce the final sorted array.

Working principle of quick sort :

1.　Select an element V as a partition element.

2.　Partition the array around V such that every element in the left partition ≤ V and every element in the right partition ≥ V.

3.　Left partition is subjected to quick sort recursively.

4.　Right partition is subjected to quick sort recursively.

3.9.4　Compare Quick Sort and Radix Sort :

> **Q.**　Compare quick sort and radix sort with respect to working principle and time complexity.　**W - 09**

Radix sort is the fastest internal sorting algorithm with time complexity = O(d.n), where

$$d = \text{number of digits in the largest number in the array.}$$

$$n = \text{number of data elements to be sorted.}$$

The radix sort uses queue data structure. The working principle of radix sort is summarized below.

1. Number of passes required to sort using radix sort is equal to number of digits in the largest number in the list.

2. In the first pass, numbers are distributed among 10 queue (queue no. 0 to 09) on the basis of least significant digit.

    •   In the second pass on the basis on second digit from the right and so on.

3. At the end of every pass, number in buckets are merged to produce a common list.

•   Radix sort is widely used for sorting of strings.

•   Radix sort algorithm is stable.

•   There is an additional overhead of maintaining the queue data structure.

The working principle of quick sort is summarized below :

1. select an element V as a partition element.

2. Partition the array around V such that every element in the left partition ≤ V and every element in the right partition ≥ V.

3. Left partition is subjected to quick sort recursively.

4. Right partition is subjected to quick sort recursively.

•   Quick sort is an in-place internal sorting algorithm without any additional memory for storing data.

•   Quick sort algorithm is not stable.

•   Quick sort algorithm degenerates if the data being sorted is already sorted, either in ascending or descending order.

3.10 Searching

Q.   What is searching and sorting ? Enlist different methods.
W - 09

Q.　What is searching ? Explain linear search with example.

S- 2010

　　　Searching is a technique of finding an element in a given list of elements. List of elements could be represented using an :

(a)　Array

(b)　Linked List

(c)　A binary tree

(d)　A B-tree

(e)　Heap

　　　Elements could also be stored in file. Searching technique should be able to locate the element to be searched as quickly as possible. Many a time, it is necessary to search a list of records to identify a particular record. Usually, each record is uniquely identified by its key field and searching is carried out on the basis of key field. If search results in locating the desired record then the search is said to be successful. Otherwise, the search operation is said to be unsuccessful. The complexity of any searching algorithm depends on number of comparisons required to find the element. Performance of searching algorithm can be found by counting the number of comparisons in order to find the given element.

2.10.1 Sequential Search :

Q.　What is searching ? Explain linear search with example.

S - 2010

　　　In sequential search elements are examined sequentially starting from the first element. The process of searching terminates when the list is exhausted or a comparison results in success.

　　　Algorithm for searching an element 'key' in an array 'a[ ]' having n elements :

　　　The search algorithm starts comparison between the first element of a[ ] and "key". As long as a comparison does not result in success, the algorithm proceeds to compare the next element of "a[ ] with "key". The process terminates when the list is exhausted or the element is found.

> ➤ **'C' function for sequential search.**

```c
int sequential (int a[ ] , int key, int n)
{
    int i = 0 ;
    while (i < n)
    {
        if (a[i] == key)
            return (i) ;
        i++ ;
    }
    return (- 1) ;
}
```

The function returns the index of the element in 'a[ ]' for successful search. A value –1 is returned if the element is not found.

Analysis of sequential search algorithm :

Number of comparisons required for a successful search is not fixed. It depends on the location (place) being occupied by the key element. An element at i^{th} location can be searched after i-comparisons. Number of comparisons required is probabilistic in nature. We could best calculate the average number of comparisons required for searching an element.

Let P_i is the probability that the element to be searched will be found at i^{th} position. i number of comparisons will be required to search the ith element.

∴ Expected number of comparisons for a successful search

$$C = 1.P_1 + 2.P_2 + \ldots + nPn$$

Since the element could be found at any location with equal probability.

$$P_1 = P_2 \ldots = P_n = 1/n$$

∴ $$C = \frac{1}{n} + \frac{2}{n} + \ldots + \frac{n}{n} = \frac{1}{n}(1 + 2 + . + n) = \frac{n(n+1)}{2n} = \frac{n+1}{2}$$

Time complexity of sequential search = O(n).

Limitations of sequential search :

1. Its time complexity is of the order of O(n). It should not be used for a long list.

> **Program 3.10.1 : A sample program for sequential search.**

```c
#include<stdio.h>
#include<conio.h>
int sequential_search(int a[],int key,int n);
void main()
{
    int a[50],n,key,i;
    printf("\nNo.of elements :");
    scanf("%d",&n);
    printf("\nEnter %d numbers :",n);
    for(i=0;i<n;i++)
        scanf("%d",&a[i]);
    printf("element to be searched :");
    scanf("%d",&key);
    i=sequential_search(a,key,n);
    if(i==-1)
        printf("\n Not found");
    else
        printf("\nFound at location = %d",i+1);
    getch();
}
int sequential_search(int a[],int key,int n)
{
    int i;
    i=0;
    while(i<n && key != a[i])
        i++;
    /* search terminates here */

    if(i<n)
        return(i);
    return(-1);
}
```

Output

No. of elements :4
Enter 4 numbers : 66   77   88   99
element to be searched :88
Found at location = 3

3.10.2 Sequential Search on a Sorted Array :

Expected number of comparisons required for unsuccessful search can be reduced if the array is sorted.

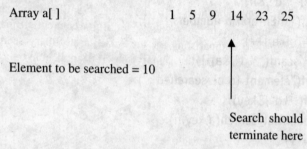

Array a[ ]   1   5   9   14   23   25

Element to be searched = 10

Search should
terminate here

Assuming elements are sorted in ascending order, the search should terminate as soon as an element with a value equal to or greater than "key" (element to be searched) is found. After termination of search, if the value of the element is equal to "key" then search is successful. If the value of the element is greater than "key" then search ends unsuccessfully.

➢ **'C' function for sequential search in a sorted array.**

```
int search_seq_sorted (int a[ ], int key, int n)
{
    int i ;
    i = 0 ;
    while (i<n && key > a[i])
        i + + ;
/* search terminates here */
    if (i < n && key == a[i])
        return (i) ;
    return (–1) ;
}
```

3.10.3 Binary Search :

Linear search has a time complexity O(n). such algorithms are not suitable for searching when number of elements is large. Binary search exhibits much better timing behaviour in case of large volume of data with timing complexity

$$O(\log_2 n)$$

Number of comparisons for n = 2^{20} (1 million)

Sequential search (in worst case) = 2^{20} comparisons.

Binary search (in worst case) = $\log_2 2^{20}$ = 20 comparisons.

Linear search (sequential search) may need 1 million comparisons for searching an element in an array having 1 million elements. Binary search will require, just 20 comparisons for the same task. Binary search uses a much better method of searching. Binary search is applicable only when the given array is sorted.

- This method makes a comparison between the "key" (element to be searched) and the middle element of the array.

- Since elements are sorted, comparisons may result in either a match or comparison could be continued with either left half of elements or right half of the elements.

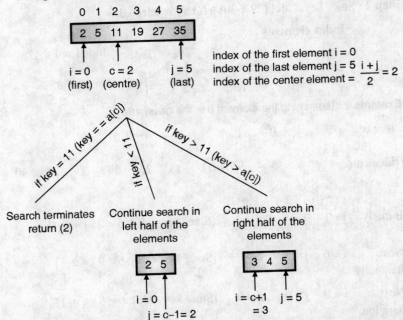

- Left half of elements could be selected by simply making j = c–1
- Right half of element could be selected by simply making i = c+1
- Process of selecting either the left half or the right half continues until the element is found or element is not there.

Example 1 : [Searching the element 29 in the given array]

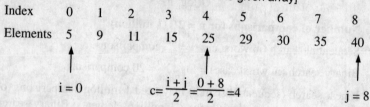

Index	0	1	2	3	4	5	6	7	8
Elements	5	9	11	15	25	29	30	35	40

$$i = 0 \qquad c = \frac{i+j}{2} = \frac{0+8}{2} = 4 \qquad j = 8$$

Element to be searched, key = 29

Step 1 : Since key > a[c] (29>25) right half is selected.

index	5	6	7	8
elements	29	30	35	40

$$i = 5 \qquad c = 6 \qquad j = 8$$

Step 2 : Since key < a[c] (29 < 30) left half is selected.

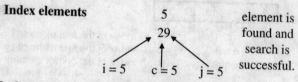

Index elements

5
29

$$i = 5 \qquad c = 5 \qquad j = 5$$

element is found and search is successful.

Example 2 : [searching the element 6 in the given array]

Index	0	1	2	3	4	5	6	7	8
Elements	5	9	11	15	25	29	30	35	40

Initially	i =0	j = 8	c = 4	[Since key <a[c]; 6 < 25 j = c–1]
Next iteration	i = 0	j = 3	c= 1	[Since key <a[c]; 6 < 9 j = c–1]
Next iteration	i = 0	j = 0	c = 0	[Since key <a[c]; 6 < 5 j = c–1]

Next   i = 1   j = 0   c = 0   Element not found.
iteration

> i > j indicates, element is not found

➢ 'C' Function for binary search (Non-recrusive)

```c
int bin_search(int a[],int i, int j, int key)
{
    int c;
    c=(i+j)/2;
    while(a[c]!=key && i<=j)
    {
    /* search as long as element is not
            found and it could be there*/
if(key>a[c])
                i=c+1; // select right half
        else
                j=c-1; //select left half
        c=(i+j)/2;
    }
    if(i<=j)
        return(c);
    return(-1);
}
```

Analysis of binary search algorithm worst case behaviour (Unsuccessful search) :

Let us assume that the array contains n elements.

$\therefore$ The maximum number of elements after 1 comparison

$$= n/2$$

The maximum number of elements after 2 comparisons

$$= n/2^2$$

The maximum number of elements after h comparisons

$$= \frac{n}{2^h}$$

For the lowest value of h[maximum number of elements left = 1]

$$\therefore \frac{n}{2^h} = 1 \text{ or } 2^h = n$$

or $$h = \text{Log}_2 n = O(\text{Log}_2 n)$$

Thus, the worst case behaviors of binary search algorithm has a timing complex $= O(\text{Log}_2 n)$

> A searching algorithm requires maximum number of comparisons in unsuccessful search.

Average case behaviour [Successful search] :

Let us try to understand the average case behaviour with the help of an array having 15 elements.

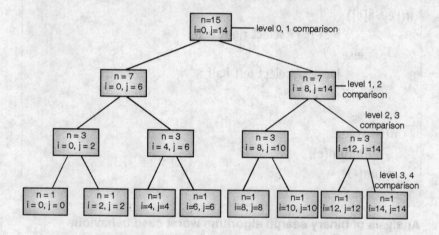

- Binary search starts with 15 elements and if the element is found at the centre, search terminates with a success with 1 comparison – i.e. success at level 0.

- At level 1, search starts with either left half of the elements or the right half of the elements. Probability of successful search at level 1 is twice that of a successful search at level 0. Level zero has one event (one node) and level 1 has 2 events (2 nodes) of success.

- Relation between last level (h = 3) and number of elements (n = 15) is given by $2^{3+1} = 15+1$

  Or $$2^{h+1} = n+1$$

Or $\qquad h+1 = \log_2(n+1)$

Or $\qquad h = [\log_2(n+1)] - 1$

$\therefore$ Total number of comparison to search every element of array is given by :

$$C = 1.2^0 + 2.2^1 + \dots + (h+1)2^h \qquad \dots(1)$$

$$2C = 1.2^1 + 2.2^2 + \dots + h2^h + (h+1)2^{h+1} \qquad \dots(2)$$

Subtracting (2) from (1)

$$-C = 1.2^0 + 2^1 + 2^2 + \dots 2^h - (h+1)2^{h+1}$$

or $\qquad C = (h+1)2^{h+1} - [2^0 + 2^1 + 2^2 + \dots + 2^h]$

$$= (h+1)2^{h+1} - (-1 + 2^{h+1})$$

$$= h.2^{h+1} + 1$$

Therefore, average number of comparisons

$$= \frac{h.2^{h+1} + 1}{n} = \frac{h.2^{h+1} + 1}{2^{h+1} - 1}$$

$$\approx h \text{ for large } n$$

$$= O \log_2(n)$$

Thus, expected number of comparisons for successful as well as unsuccessful search – $O(\log_2 n)$

> **Recursive function for binary search.**

```
int bin_search(int a[],int i,int j,int key)
{
    int c;
    if(i<=j)
    {
        c=(i+j)/2;
        if(key==a[c])
            return(c);
        / * Change it to <
        if the numbers are in descending order */
        if(key>a[c])
            return(bin_search(a,c+1,j,key));
```

```
            return(bin_search(a,i,c-1,key));
    }
    return(-1);
}
```

> **Program 3.10.2 : Program to implement binary search algorithm.**

Q. Write 'C/C++' program for Binary search.   W - 08

```
#include<stdio.h>
#include<conio.h>

void bubble_sort(int [],int);
int bin_search(int [],int,int);
void main()
{
    int a[30],n,i,key,result;
    printf("\nEnter number of elements :");
    scanf("%d",&n);
    printf("\nEnter the array elements :");
    for(i=0;i<n;i++)
        scanf("%d",&a[i]);
    printf("\nEnter the element to be searched :");
    scanf("%d",&key);
    bubble_sort(a,n);
    result=bin_search(a,key,n);
    if(result==-1)
        printf("\nElement not found :");
    else
        printf("\nElement  is found at location %d",result+1);
    getch();
}
void bubble_sort(int a[],int n)
{
    int i,j,temp;
```

```
    for(i=1;i<n;i++)
          for(j=0;j<n-i;j++)
              if(a[j]>a[j+1])
              {
                    temp=a[j];
                    a[j]=a[j+1];
                    a[j+1]=temp;
              }
}
int bin_search(int a[],int key,int n)
{
   int i,j,c;
   i=0;
   j=n-1;
   c=(i+j)/2;
   while(a[c]!=key && i<=j)
   {
          if(key>a[c])
              i=c+1;
          else
              j=c-1;
          c=(i+j)/2;
   }
   if(i<=j)
          return(c);
   return(-1);
}
```

Output

```
Enter number of elements : 6

Enter the array elements :12 34 54 23 11 90

Enter the element to be searched : 11

Element  is found at location 1
```

Example 3.10.1 : Apply binary search on the following numbers stored in array from A [0] to A [10]

9, 17, 23, 38, 45, 50, 57, 76, 79, 90, 100 to search numbers − 10 to 100.

Solution :

Searching 10 :

0	1	2	3	4	5	6	7	8	9	10	
9	17	23	38	45	50	57	76	79	90	100	i j k

i j k
0 10 5

↑ (i)　　　　↑ (k)　　　　↑ (j)

Step 1 : Since $10 < A[5]$, $j = K - 1 = 4$

0	1	2	3	4
9	17	23	38	45

0
4
2

↑ (i)　　↑ (k)　　↑ (J)

Step 2 : Since $10 < A[2]$, $j = K - 1 = 1$

0	1
9	17

↑ ↑
↑

0 1 0

i j
k

Step 3 : Since 10 > A [0], j = K + 1 = 1

                                     <u>i j k</u>

     1   1 1 1

     17

     ↑ ↑ ↑

     i j k

Step 4 : Since 10 < A [1], j = K – 1 = 0

As i becomes less than j, element 10 is not in the array A [ ]

Searching 100 :

0	1	2	3	4	5	6	7	8	9	10			
9	17	23	38	45	50	57	76	79	90	100	i	j	K
↑					↑					↑	0	10	5
i					k					j			

Step 1 : Since 100 > A [5], i = K + 1 = 6

     6   7   8   9   10

     57   76   79   90   100

     ↑   ↑   ↑   6

                                           1

                         0   8

     i   k   J

Step 2 : Since 100 > A [8], i = K + 1 = 9

     9   10

     90   100   9

     ↑   ↑

     ↑

     i   j

     k

Step 3 :　Since $100 > A[9]$, $i = K + 1 = 10$

10

100

↑　↑　↑　　　　　　　　　　　　　　　　　　　　　　10　10　10

i　j　k

　　　Since, the element to be searched is found at A [10], search terminates with a success.

3.11 MSBTE Questions and Answers

Summer 2008 – Total Marks 24

Q. 1　Explain Merge sort with example program. **(Section 3.5)**　**(4 Marks)**

Q. 2　Write a program in 'C' language for selection sort and arrange the given numbers in ascending order using selection sort.

　　　Numbers : 16, 23, 13, 9,7,5

　　　(Program 3.3.1, Example 3.3.2)　　　　　　　　　**(8 Marks)**

Q. 3　Explain Radix sort with example. **(Section 3.6)**　**(4 Marks)**

Q. 4　Write a program for insertion sort and shell sort.

　　　(Program 3.4.1, Example 3.7.2)　　　　　　　　　**(4 Marks)**

Q. 5　Explain Binary Search algorithm and also give it's advantages.

　　　(Section 3.10.2)　　　　　　　　　　　　　　　**(4 Marks)**

Winter 2008 – Total Marks 26

Q. 6　Write 'C/C++' program for Binary search. **(Program 3.10.2)**　**(3 Marks)**

Q. 7　Sort the given numbers in ascending order using Radix sort Numbers : 348, 14, 614, 5381, 47. **(Example 3.6.1)**　　　　**(3 Marks)**

Q. 8 Write the algorithm for Insertion sort and arrange the given numbers in ascending order using insertion sort.

Numbers : 77, 33, 44, 11, 88, 22, 66, 55

(Section 3.4, Example 3.4.1)   **(8 Marks)**

Q. 9 Describe the principle of selection sort with one example.

(Section 3.3)   **(4 Marks)**

Q. 10 Write a program for Bubble sort in 'C/C++' language.

(Program 3.2.1)   **(4 Marks)**

Q. 11 Compare Quick sort and Heap sort with respect to working principle and time complexity. **(Section 3.9.2)**   **(4 Marks)**

Summer 2009 – Total Marks 20

Q. 12 Explain the Linear Search Algorithm. Also give its limitations.

(Section 3.10.1)   **(4 Marks)**

Q. 13 Write an algorithm for insertion sort and arrange the given numbers in ascending order using insertion sort numbers 45, 22, 8, 34, 19.

(Section 3.4 and Example 3.4.2)   **(8 Marks)**

Q. 14 Arrange the given in ascending order using Radix sort.

361, 12, 527, 143, 9, 768, 348. **(Example 3.6.2)**   **(4 Marks)**

Q. 15 Compare Merge sort and Quick sort with respect to working principle and time complexity. **(Section 3.9.3)**   **(4 Marks)**

Winter 2009 – Total Marks 22

Q. 16 What is searching and sorting ? Enlist different methods.

(Sections 3.1 and 3.10)   **(4 Marks)**

Q. 17 Describe bubble sort with the help of example. Take minimum four values. **(Section 3.2)**   **(6 Marks)**

Q. 18 Explain Merge sort, state advantage and disadvantage. Sort the following numbers in ascending order using merge sort.

{15, 84, 62, 08, 41, 57, 33, 18, 51, 32 }

(Section 3.5 and Examples 3.5.2 and 3.5.3)　　　　　　　**(8 Marks)**

Q. 19 Compare quick sort and radix sort with respect to working principle and time complexity. **(Section 3.9.4)**　　　　　　　**(4 Marks)**

Summer 2010 – Total Marks 22

Q. 20 What is searching ? Explain linear search with example.

(Sections 3.10 and 3.10.1)　　　　　　　**(4 Marks)**

Q. 21 Write and explain the procedure for recursive quick sort. Justify the same with example. **(Section 3.8)**　　　　　　　**(6 Marks)**

Q. 22 Write a program in 'C' language for selection sort and arrange the given numbers in ascending order using selection sort number : 16, 23, 13, 9, 7, 5. **(Example 3.3.2, Program 3.3.1)**　　　　　　　**(8 Marks)**

Q. 23 Write a program to sort an array of ten elements with bubble sort.

(Program 3.2.1)　　　　　　　**(4 Marks)**

□□□

Stacks

Introduction to Stacks : Stacks as an Abstract Data type, Primitive operations of Stack; Representation of Stack through array; Application of Stack : Stack machines, Recursion, Arithmetic expression : Polish notation.

Statistical Analysis

Year	Marks
Summer - 2008	10 Marks
Winter - 2008	12 Marks
Summer - 2009	16 Marks
Winter - 2009	14 Marks
Summer - 2010	14 Marks

4.1 Introduction to Stack

Q. State the principle of stack with basic operations. `S - 09`

Q. Define stack what are the basic operations performed on it. `S - 2010`

- Stack is a LIFO (Last In First Out) structure. It is an ordered list of the same type of elements. A stack is a linear list where all insertions and deletions are permitted only at one end of the list. When elements are added to stack it grows at one end. Similarly, when elements are deleted from a stack, it shrinks at the same end.

- Fig. 4.1.1 shows expansion and shrinking of a stack. Initially stack is empty.

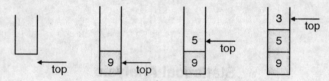

Fig. 4.1.1 : Insertion of 9,5,3 in a stack

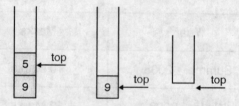

Fig. 4.1.2 : Deletion of 2 elements from the stack

- A variable top, points to the top element of the list.

4.2 Stack as an ADT

Stack is a LIFO structure. Stack can be represented using an array. A one-dimensional array can be used to hold elements of a stack. Another variable "top" is used to keep track of the index of the top most element.

Formally, a stack may be defined as follows :

typedef struct stack

```
            {
                int data[SIZE];
                int top;
            } stack;
```
/* SIZE is a constant, maximum number of elements that can be stored */

Associated with the object stack there are several operations that are necessary :

(1) void initialize (stack *p) :

It initializes a stack as an empty stack. Initial value of top is set to –1.

(2) int empty (stack *p) :

Function checks whether the stack is empty. It returns 1 or 0 depending on whether the stack is empty or not.

(3) int full (stack *p) :

The function checks whether the stack is full. A stack is said to be full when the associated array is completely filled up. Whenever the stack is full, top points to the last element (i.e. data[SIZE-1]) of the array. The function returns 1 or 0 depending on whether the stack is full or not.

(4) int pop (stack *p) :

The function deletes topmost element from the stack and also returns it to the calling program. Deletion from an empty stack will cause underflow.

(5) void push (stack *p, int x) :

The function inserts the element x onto the stack pointed by P. Insertion will cause an overflow if the stack is full.

4.3 Operations on Stacks

Q. State the principle of stack with basic operations.   S - 09

Q. Define stack what are the basic operations performed on it.
                                                                S - 2010

1.   Initialize( ) - Make a stack empty

2.　　Empty( ) - To determine if a stack is empty or not

3.　　Full( ) - To determine if a stack is full or not

4.　　Push( ) - if a stack is not full then push a new element at the top of the stack (similar to insert in a list)

5.　　Pop( ) – If a stack is not empty, then pop the element from its top(similar to delete( ) from a list)

4.4　Array Representation

A one – dimensional array can be used to hold elements of a stack. Another variable "top" is used to keep track of the index of the top most element.

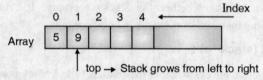

Fig. 4.4.1

Formally, a stack may be defined as follows :

typedef struct stack

{

        int data[MAX] ;

        int top ;

}stack ;

/*MAX is a constant, maximum number of elements that can be stored */

- Initially, top is set to –1

- A stack with top as –1 is an empty stack.

- When the value of top becomes MAX – 1 after a series of insertions, it is full.

- After "push" operation top = top + 1 (Stack growing)

- After "pop" operation top = top – 1 (Stack shrinking)

4.4.1 'C' functions for Primitive Operations on a Stack :

```
void initialize(stack *s)
{
    s → top = −1 ;
}
```

Initially, stack is empty.

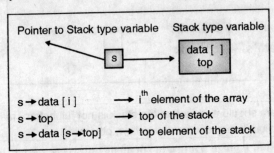

Fig. 4.4.2 : Accessing elements of a stack using a pointer

```
int empty(stack * s)
{
        if(s → top == − 1)
            return(1) ; /* stack is empty */
        return(0) ; /* stack empty condition is false*/
}
```

Above function checks whether a stack is empty [containing 0 elements]. Function returns a value 1(true) if the stack is empty. Function returns a value 0(false) if the stack is not empty (there are some elements).

```
int full(stack *s)
{
        if( s→top == MAX −1)
            return(1);
        return(0);
}
```

A stack is full, if no more elements can be added.

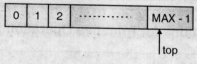

Fig. 4.4.3

Above function checks whether a stack is full (no more elements can be added). Function returns a value 1(true) if the stack is full. Function returns a value 0(false) if the stack is not full (more elements could be added).

```
void push(stack *s, int x)
{
    s → top = s → top + 1 ;
    s → data[s → top] = x;
}
```

main program should ensure that the stack is not full before making a call to push( ) function. It may cause an overflow, otherwise.

```
int pop(stack *s)
{
    int x ;
    x = s → data[s → top] ;
    s → top = s →top –1 ;
    return(x);
}
```

main program should ensure that the stack is not empty before making a call to pop( ) function. It may cause an underflow, otherwise.

The function push( ), increases the value of the top by 1 and the

n stores the element at the top location in "data" array.

The function pop( ) returns the top element from the stack. It also, reduces the value of top by 1 (one element is deleted from the stack).

4.5 Program Showing Stack Operations

Convert a decimal number to binary using a stack :

Example :

Input no = 21 (Decimal)

$21 \% 2 = 1$

| 1 |

$10 \% 2 = 0$

| 0 |
| 1 |

$5 \% 2 = 1$

| 1 |
| 0 |
| 1 |

$2 \% 2 = 0$

| 0 |
| 1 |
| 0 |
| 1 |

$1 \% 2 = 1$

| 1 |
| 0 |
| 1 |
| 0 |
| 1 |

$(21)_{10} = (1\ 0\ 1\ 0\ 1)_2$

A decimal number can be converted to binary form through repeated division of the number by 2. Remainder at each step is saved in a stack. Finally, the bits stored in stack can be printed one by one through POP( ) operation.

➤ **Program 4.5.1 : Program for conversion of decimal Number to binary form.**

```
#include<stdio.h>
```

```c
#include<conio.h>
#define MAX 20
typedef struct stack
{
   int data[MAX];
   int top;
}stack;
void init(stack *);
int empty(stack *);
int full(stack *);
int pop(stack *);
void push(stack *,int);
void main()
{
   stack s;
   int x;
   init(&s);
   printf("\nEnter decimal number:");
   scanf("%d",&x);
   while((x!=0))
   {
        if(!full(&s))
        {
            push(&s,x%2);
            x=x/2;
        }
        else
        {
            printf("\nstack overflow");
            exit(0);
        }
   }
   printf("\n");
   while(!empty(&s))
```

```
   {
        x=pop(&s);
        printf("%d",x);
   }
}
void init(stack *s)
{
   s->top= -1;
}
int empty(stack *s)
{
   if(s->top== -1)
        return(1);
   return(0);
}
int full(stack *s)
{
   if(s->top==MAX-1)
        return(1);
   return(0);
}
void push(stack *s,int x)
{
   s->top=s->top+1;
   s->data[s->top]=x;
}
int pop(stack *s)
{
   int x;
   x=s->data[s->top];
   s->top=s->top -1;
   return(x);
}
```

Output

```
Enter decimal number:12
1100
```

Example 4.5.1 : Using stack functions, write an algorithm to determine if an input character string is of the form : $a^i b^i$ where $i \geq 1$

Solution :

1.   s : stack   [s is a stack]
2.   initialize s
3.   while (! end of input)

       {

             x ← read next character

             if (x is a)

               push (s, a);

             else

               pop (s); goto step 4.

       }

4.   while (! end of input)

       {

             x ← read next character

             if (stack is empty)

             {

                  print "b's are more than a's"

                  goto step 6.

             }

             else

               pop(s)

       }

5.   if (stack is empty)

        print "a's are equal to b's"

        else

          print "a's are more than b's"

6.   End

4.5.1 Operations on Stack Considering Overflow and Underflow : [Array Implementation]

Q. Define the terms 'Overflow' and 'Underflow' with respect to stacks.   W - 08

Q. Explain the terms overflow and underflow with respect to stack. Use suitable data and diagram.   W - 09

Q. Write a procedure to push an element on stack. Also give meaning of stack overflow term.   S - 2010

Stack overflow :   Stack overflow is caused by insertion in a stack that is already full.

Stack underflow :   Deletion from an empty stack will cause a stack underflow.

➤ **'C' functions for operations on stack.**

```c
void push()
{
   if(p->top==N –1)
        printf("\noverflow !! can not be inserted");
   else
   {
        p->top=p->top+1;
        p->data[p->top]=x;
   }
}
int pop(stack *p)
{
   int x;
   if(p->top== –1)
        printf("\nUnderflow !!! can not be deleted");
   else
   {
        x=p->data[p->top];
        p->top=p->top –1;
   }
   return(x);
```

```
}
void print(stack *p)
{
   int i;
   for(i=p->top;i>=0;i--)
        printf("\n%d",p->data[i]);
}
```

> **Program 4.5.2 : C-Program for implementing stack
                          using array.**

Q. Write a menu driven 'C' program for implementing stack using
       array.   S - 08

```c
/* Simulation of stack using  an array */

#include<stdio.h>
#include<conio.h>
#define MAX 6
typedef struct stack
{
   int data[MAX];
   int top;
}stack;
void init(stack *);
int empty(stack *);
int full(stack *);
int pop(stack *);
void push(stack *,int);
void print(stack *);
void main()
{
   stack s;
   int x,op;
   init(&s);
   clrscr();
```

```c
    do {
        printf("\n\n1)Push\n2)Pop\n3)Print\n4)Quit");
        printf("\nEnter Your choice: ");
        scanf("%d",&op);
        switch(op)
        {
          case 1:printf("\n enter a number :");
                scanf("%d",&x);
                if(!full(&s))
                 push(&s,x);
                else
                 printf("\nStack is full......");
                break;
            case 2:if(!empty(&s))
                { x=pop(&s);
                  printf("\npopped value= %d",x);
                }
                 else
                printf("\nStack is empty.....");
                 break;

            case 3:print(&s);break;
          }
        }while(op!=4);
}
void init(stack *s)
{
   s->top=-1;
}
int empty(stack *s)
{
   if(s->top==-1)
         return(1);
   return(0);
```

```
}
int full(stack *s)
{
    if(s->top==MAX-1)
        return(1);
    return(0);
}

void push(stack *s,int x)
{
    s->top=s->top+1;
    s->data[s->top]=x;
}

int pop(stack *s)
{
    int x;
    x=s->data[s->top];
    s->top=s->top-1;
    return(x);
}
void print(stack *s)
{
    int i;
    printf("\n");
    for(i=s->top;i>=0;i--)
        printf("%d ",s->data[i]);
}
```

4.6 Application of Stack

Stack data structure is very useful. Few of its usages are given below :

1.   Expression conversion

     (a)   Infix to postfix

    (b)   Infix to prefix

    (c)   Postfix to infix

    (d)   Prefix to infix

2.   Expression evaluation

3.   Parsing

4.   Simulation of recursion

5.   Function call

4.6.1 Expression Representation :

There are three popular methods for representation of an expression.

    (a)   infix   x +y   operator between operands

    (b)   prefix   + x y   operator before operands

    (c)   postfix   x y +   operator after operands

Example :

Infix   x + y * z

Prefix   + x * y z

Postfix   x y z * +

(a) Evaluation of an infix expression :

Infix expressions are evaluated left to right but operator precedence must be taken into account. To evaluate x + y * z, y and z will be multiplied first and then it will be added to x.

> Infix expressions are not used for representation of an expression inside computer, due to additional complexity of handling of precedence.

(b) Evaluation of a Prefix (Polish notation) expression :

To understand the evaluation of prefix expression, let us consider an example

    + 5 * 3 2

Find an operator from right to left and perform the operation.

+ 5 * 3 2

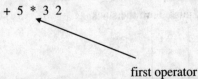

first operator

First operator is * and therefore, 3 * 2 are multiplied, expression becomes + 5 6.

First operator is + and therefore, 5 and 6 are added.

expression becomes : 11

(c) Evaluation of Postfix (Reverse polish) expression :

5 3 2 * +

1. Find the first operator from left to right and perform the operation

2. First operator is * and therefore, 3 and 2 are multiplied

expression becomes 5 6 +

3. Next operator is + and therefore, 5 and 6 are added

expression becomes : 11

Prefix and Postfix expressions are free from any precedence. They are more suited for mechanization. Computer uses Postfix form for representation of an expression.

4.6.2 Evaluation of a Postfix Expression using a Stack :

| Q. | Explain any two applications of stack. | S - 08 |
| Q. | Explain any two applications of stack. | S - 09 |

Given expression :

6 5 3 + 9 * +   stack

Initially stack is empty.

- First token is an operand, push 6 on the stack

5 3 + 9 * + | 6 |

- next token is and operand, push 5 on the stack

3 + 9 * + | 5 |
              | 6 |

- next token is and operand, push 3 on the stack

+ 9 * + | 3 |
            | 5 |
            | 6 |

- next token is an operator, pop two operands 3 and 5, add them and push the result on the stack

9 * +

```
| 8 |
| 6 |
```

- next token is an operand, push 9 on the stack

* +

```
| 9 |
| 8 |
| 6 |
```

- next token is an operator, pop two operands 9 and 8, multiply them and push the result on the stack

+

```
| 72 |
| 6  |
```

- next token is an operator, pop two operands 72 and 6, add them and push the result back on the stack

NULL

```
| 78 |
```
◄——— Final Result

➤ **Algorithm for evaluation of an expression**

```
x : tokentype
      operand1, operand2 : operand_type ;
      operator : operator_ type ;
s : stack
      Initialize(s) ;
      x = nexttoken( ) ; /* read the next token */
            while(x)
            {
                  if(x is an operator)
                  {
                        operand2 = pop(s);
                        operand1 = pop(s);
                        push(s, evaluate(x, operand1, operand2));
                  }
                  else
                        push(s, x) ;
            x = nexttoken( ) ;
```

```
                    }
        /* stack contains the evaluated value of the expression */
```

> **Program 4.6.1 : Program for evaluation of a postfix expression**

```
Assumption-- primary operators '-,+,*,/,%' operand -- a single digit
#include<stdio.h>
#include<conio.h>
#define MAX 20
typedef struct stack
{
   int data[MAX];
   int top;
}stack;
void init(stack *);
int empty(stack *);
int full(stack *);
int pop(stack *);
void push(stack *,int);
int evaluate(char x,int op1,int op2);
void main()
{
   stack s;
   char x;
   int op1,op2,val;
   init(&s);
   printf("\nEnter the expression(i.e59+3*)\nsingle digit operand and operators only:");
   while((x=getchar())!='\n')
   {
        if(isdigit(x))
```

```
                push(&s,x–48); //x-48 for removing the effect of
ASCII
        else
        {
            op2=pop(&s);
            op1=pop(&s);
            val=evaluate(x,op1,op2);
            push(&s,val);
        }
    }
    val=pop(&s);
    printf("\nvalue of expression = %d",val);
}
int evaluate(char x,int op1,int op2)
{
    if(x=='+')
        return(op1+op2);
    if(x=='–')
        return(op1–op2);
    if(x=='*')
        return(op1*op2);
    if(x=='/')
        return(op1/op2);
    if(x=='%')
        return(op1%op2);
}
void init(stack *s)
{
    s->top= –1;
}
int empty(stack *s)
```

```
{
   if(s->top== -1)
         return(1);
   return(0);
}
int full(stack *s)
{
   if(s->top==MAX -1)
         return(1);
   return(0);
}
void push(stack *s,int x)
{
   s->top=s->top+1;
   s->data[s->top]=x;
}
int pop(stack *s)
{
   int x;
   x=s->data[s->top];
   s->top=s->top -1;
   return(x);
}
```

Output

Enter the expression(i.e59+3*)

single digit operand and operators only:653+9*+

value of expression = 78

Example 4.6.1 : Evaluate the following postfix expression and show stack after every step in tabular form.

Given A = 5, B = 6, C = 2, D = 12, E = 4

ABC + *DE\–

Solution :

Input	stack
ABC + * DE/–	
BC + *DE/–	5
C + * DE/–	6 5
+ * DE/–	2 6 5
* DE/-	8 5
DE/–	40
E/–	12 40
/–	4 12 40
–	3 40
End	37

value of the expression = 37

Example 4.6.2 :   Consider the following arithmetic expression p, written in postfix notation. Translate it in infix notation and evaluate.

W - 08

Solution :

P :   12, 7, 3, –, /, 2, 1, 5, + *, +

A postfix expression can be converted to infix form by scanning it from left to right.

Step 1 :   12, $\boxed{7-3}$, /, 2, 1, 5, + *, +

Step 2 : $\boxed{12/(7-3)}$, 2, 1, 5, +, *, +

Step 3 : $\boxed{12/(7-3)}$, 2, $\boxed{1+5}$, *, +

Step 4 : $\boxed{12/(7-3)}$, $\boxed{(2*(1+5))}$ +

Step 5 :   12 / (7 – 3) + (2 * (1 + 5))

Value of the expression = 12 / (7 – 3) + (2 * (1 + 5))

= 12/4 + 2 * 6 = 3 + 2 * 6 = 15

Example 4.6.3 :   Evaluate the following postfix expressions.

(i) 5 4 6 + * 4 9 3 / + *   (ii) 7 5 2 + * 4 1 1 + / –

Solution :

(i)   5 4 6 + * 4 9 3 / + *

	Input	Stack
1.	5 4 6 + * 4 9 3 / + *	
2.	4 6 + * 4 9 3 / + *	5
3	6 + * 4 9 3 / + *	4 5
4.	+ * 4 9 3 / + *	6 4 5

	Input	**Stack**	
5.	* 4 9 3 / + *	10 5	4 + 6 = 10
6.	4 9 3 / + *	50	5 * 10 = 50
7.	9 3 / + *	4 50	
8.	3 / + *	9 4 50	
9.	/ + *	3 9 4 50	
10.	+ *	3 4 50	9/3 = 3
11.	*	7 50	4 + 3 = 7
12.	End	350	

Result = 350

(ii)   7 5 2 + * 4 1 1 + / –

	Input	**Stack**
1.	7 5 2 + * 4 1 1 + / –	

	Input	Stack
2.	5 2 + * 4 1 1 + / −	7
3	2 + * 4 1 1 + / −	5 7
4.	+ * 4 1 1 + / −	2 5 7
5.	* 4 1 1 + / −	7 7 5 + 2 = 7
6.	4 1 1 + / −	49 7 * 7 = 49
7.	1 1 + / −	4 49
8.	1 + / −	1 4 49
9.	+ / −	1 1 4 49
10.	/ −	2 4 49

	Input	Stack	
11.	–	2 49	4 / 2 = 2
12.	End	47	49 – 2 = 47

Result = 47.

Example 4.6.4 : Evaluate following postfix expression.
A : 6, 2, 3, +, –, 3, 8, 2, +, +, *, 2, ↑, 3, +   W - 09

Solution :

	Input	Stack	
1.	6, 2, 3, +, –, 3, 8, 2, +, +, *, 2, ↑, 3, +	Empty	
2.	2, 3, +, –, 3, 8, 2, +, +, *, 2, ↑, 3, +	6	
3.	3, +, –, 3, 8, 2, +, +, *, 2, ↑, 3, +	2 6	
4.	+, –, 3, 8, 2, +, +, *, 2, ↑, 3, +	3 2 6	
5.	–, 3, 8, 2, +, +, *, 2, ↑, 3, +	5 6	2 + 3 = 5
6.	3, 8, 2, +, +, *, 2, ↑, 3, +	1	6 – 5 = 1
7.	8, 2, +, +, *, 2, ↑, 3, +	3 1	

	Stack

8.　2, +, +, *, 2, ↑, 3, +

8
3
1

9.　+, +, *, 2, ↑, 3, +

2
8
3
1

10.　+, *, 2, ↑, 3, +

10	$8 + 2 = 10$
3	
1	

11.　*, 2, ↑, 3, +

13	$3 + 10 = 13$
1	

12.　2, ↑, 3, +

13	$1 \times 13 = 13$

13.　↑, 3, +

2
13

14.　3, +

169	$13^2 = 169$

15.　+

3
169

16.　End

172	$169 + 3 = 172$

∴ Result = 172

4.6.3 Evaluation of a Prefix Expression :

• A prefix expression is evaluated by scanning it from right to left.

• An operand is pushed on top of the stack.

• In case of an operator, two operands are popped from the stack, evaluated and pushed back onto the stack.

• Final result is found on top of the stack.

Example 4.6.5 : Evaluate the following prefix expression using stack for A = 16, B = 2 , C = 3, D = 10 and E = 4. Show step by step the contents of stack.

Prefix Expression = − + / A ∧ BC * DE * AC

Solution :

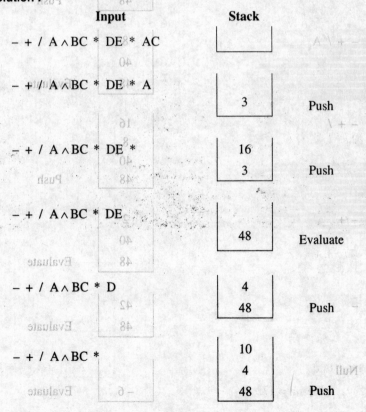

Input	Stack	
− + / A ∧ BC * DE * AC		
− + / A ∧ BC * DE * A	3	Push
− + / A ∧ BC * DE *	16 / 3	Push
− + / A ∧ BC * DE	48	Evaluate
− + / A ∧ BC * D	4 / 48	Push
− + / A ∧ BC *	10 / 4 / 48	Push

Input	Stack	
− + / A ∧ BC	40	
	48	Evaluate
− + / A ∧ B	3	
	40	
	48	Push
− + / A ∧	2	
	3	
	40	
	48	Push
− + / A	8	
	40	
	48	Evaluate
− + /	16	
	8	
	40	
	48	Push
− +	2	
	40	
	48	Evaluate
−	42	
	48	Evaluate
Null	− 6	Evaluate

Value of expression = − 6

> ## Algorithm for evaluation of a prefix expression :

```
st : stack ;
initialize st ;
Prefix ← read the prefix expression ;
for ( i ← index of the last character of prefix, down to 0 )
     {   x ← prefix[i] ;
         if ( x is an operand )
         {    push(st, char_to_int(x)) ;
         }
     else
         {    operand1 ← pop(st) ;
              operand2 ← pop(st) ;
              val ← evaluate( X, operand1 , operand2)
              push(st, val) ;
         }
     }
     val = pop(st) ;
     print val ;
```

> ## Program 4.6.2 : Evaluation of a prefix expression.

```c
/* program for Evaluation of prefix expression
   operators supported '+,-,*,/,%,∧,(,)
   operands supported -- all single character operands
*/

#include<stdio.h>
#include<conio.h>
#include<ctype.h>
#define MAX 50

typedef struct stack
{
   int data[MAX];
   int top;
}stack;
```

```c
void init(stack *);
int  empty(stack *);
int  full(stack *);
int  pop(stack *);
void push(stack *,int );
int  top(stack *); //value of the top element
void eval_prefix(char prefix[]);
int  evaluate(char x,int op1,int op2);

void main()
 { char prefix[30];
   clrscr();
   printf("\nEnter a prefix expression : ");
   gets(prefix);
   eval_prefix(prefix);
   getch();
 }
void eval_prefix(char prefix[])
 {
   stack s;
   char x;
   int op1,op2,val,i;
   init(&s);
   for(i=strlen(prefix)-1;i>=0;i--)
   {     x=prefix[i];
         if(isalpha(x))
             { printf("\nEnter the value of %c : ",x);
             scanf("%d",&val);
             push(&s,val);
             }
         else
         {     //pop two operands and evaluate
             op1=pop(&s);
             op2=pop(&s);
             val=evaluate(x,op1,op2);
```

```
              push(&s,val);
        }
   }
   val=pop(&s);
   printf("\nvalue of expression = %d",val);
}
int evaluate(char x,int op1,int op2)
{
   if(x=='+')  return(op1+op2);
   if(x=='-')  return(op1- op2);
   if(x=='*')  return(op1*op2);
   if(x=='/')  return(op1/op2);
   if(x=='%')  return(op1%op2);
}
void init(stack *s)
{
   s->top=-1;
}

int empty(stack *s)
{
   if(s->top== -1) return(1);
   return(0);
}

int full(stack *s)
{
   if(s->top==MAX -1)    return(1);
   return(0);
}

void push(stack *s,int x)
{
   s->top=s->top+1;
   s->data[s->top]=x;
}
```

```
int pop(stack *s)
{
   int x;
   x=s->data[s->top];
   s->top=s->top -1;
   return(x);
}
int top(stack * p)
{
   return(p->data[p->top]);
}
```

4.6.4 Conversion of an Expression from Infix to Postfix :

Q.	Explain any two applications of stack.	S - 08
Q.	Evaluate following PostfixExpression. A : 6, 2, 3, +, −, 3, 8, 2, 1, +, *, 2, ↑, 3, +.	S - 09

Example of an infix expression : $(A + B \wedge C) * D + E \wedge 5$ where A, B, C, D and E are integer constants and $B \wedge C$ means B^C

Manual method :

Step 1 :

In manual evaluation of the above expression, $B \wedge C$ must be calculated first. Hence, we convert $B \wedge C$ to its equivalent postfix equivalent i.e. $BC\wedge$

$(A + B \wedge C) * D + E \wedge 5$ – original expression

$(A + \underline{BC\wedge}) * D + E \wedge 5$ – $BC\wedge$ should treated as a single integer number (single token) and $A + \underline{BC\wedge}$ should be the next operation to be performed

$\underline{ABC\wedge +} * D + E \wedge 5$ —— $\underline{ABC\wedge +} * D$ is the next operation to be performed

$\underline{ABC\wedge + D*} + E \wedge 5$ —— $E \wedge 5$ is the next operation to be performed

ABC∧ + D* + E5∧ —— + is the last operation to be performed

ABC∧ + D* E5∧ + → Final expression.

Algorithmic approach :

A + B * C

- In the above example, evaluation of * precedes evaluation of + as * has higher precedence over +.

Perform an operation if the current operator has equal or higher precedence over the succeeding operator.

- Thus an operator coming on the right of the current operator will determine if the current operation should be performed.

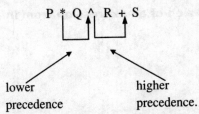

    P + Q + R

        Same precedence and hence P + Q can be performed

    P * Q + R

        Higher precedence and hence P * Q can be performed

    P * Q ∧ R + S

    lower   higher

    precedence   precedence.

Sequence in which operations will be performed

∧, *, +

- All operators must be saved on top of the stack until we get an equal or lower precedence operator

Conversion of P * Q∧R + S

Expression	Stack	Output	Remark
P*Q ∧ R + S	NULL	–	–
*Q∧R + S	NULL	P	Operand must be printed
Q∧R + S	*	P	* operation will be performed if the next operator is of lower or equal precedence.

Expression	Stack	Output	Remark
∧R + S	*	PQ	Operand must be printed
R + S	* ∧	PQ	* Can not be performed as ∧ has higher precedence
+ S	* ∧	PQR	Operand must be printed
+ S	NULL	PQR∧*	All higher precedence operators (compare to +) are popped and printed and finally the current operator is pushed on top of the stack.
S	+	PQR∧*	–
NULL	+	PQR∧* S	Operand must be printed
Null	Null	PQR∧* S +	Finally, all operators are popped and printed.

> **Algorithm for conversion of an expression from infix to postfix**

```
s : stack
while(more token)
{
        x ← next token ;
        if(x is an operand)
                print x
        else
        {
                while(precedence(x) <= precedence(top(s)))
                        print(pop(s))
                push(s,x)
        }
}
while(! empty(s))
print(pop(s)) ;
```

Example 4.6.5 : Convert the following expression from infix to postfix using a stack.

a && b ‖ c ‖ ! (e > f)

Solution :

Expression	Stack	Output	Comment
a &&b‖ c ‖ (e >f)	NULL		Initial condition
&&b ‖ c ‖ ! (e >f)	NULL	a	Print a
b ‖ c ‖ ! (e > f)	&&	a	Push &&
‖ c ‖ ! (e>f)	&&	ab	Print b
‖ c ‖ ! (e>f)	NULL	ab &&	pop and print higher precedence operators
c ‖ ! (e>f)	‖	ab &&	push the current operator
‖ ! (e>f)	‖	ab&& c	Print c
‖ ! (e>f)	NULL	ab&&c ‖	Pop and print equal or higher precedence operators
!(e > f)	‖	ab&&c ‖	Push the current operator
! (e>f)	‖	ab&&c ‖	Pop and print equal or higher precedence operators
(e > f)	‖ !	ab&&c ‖	Push the current operator
e > f	‖ ! (	ab&&c ‖	'(' should always be pushed.
> f)	‖ ! (	ab&&c ‖ e	Print e
> f)	‖ ! (	ab&&c ‖ e	Pop and print equal or higher precedence operators. Remember '(' has lowest precedence
f)	‖ ! (>	ab&&c ‖ e	Push the current operator
)	‖ ! (>	ab&&c ‖ e f	Print f
NULL	‖ !	ab&&c ‖ e f >	when the next input is')' then all operators until '(' should be popped and printed

Expression	Stack	Output	Comment
NULL	NULL	ab&&c ‖ e f >! ‖	Pop and print all operations.

Example 4.6.6 : Convert the following arithmetic expression into postfix and show stack status after every step at each step :

(i) $(A + B) * D + E / (F + A * D) + C$

(ii) $A * (B + C) / D - G$

Solution :

(i) $(A + B) * D + E / (F + A * D) + C$

Stack	Input	Output
Empty	$(A + B) * D + E / (F + A * D) + C$	–
(	$A + B) * D + E / (F + A * D) + C$	–
(	$+ B) * D + E / (F + A * D) + C$	A
(+	$B) * D + E / (F + A * D) + C$	A
(+	$) * D + E / (F + A * D) + C$	AB
Empty	$* D + E / (F + A * D) + C$	AB+
*	$D + E / (F + A * D) + C$	AB+
*	$+ E / (F + A * D) + C$	AB+D
+	$E / (F + A * D) + C$	AB+D*
+	$/ (F + A * D) + C$	AB+D*E
+/	$(F + A * D) + C$	AB+D*E
+/(	$F + A * D) + C$	AB+D*E
+/(	$+ A * D) + C$	AB+D*EF
+/(+	$A * D) + C$	AB+D*EF

Stack	Input	Output
+ / (+	* D) + C	AB+D*EFA
+ / (+ *	D) + C	AB+D*EFA
+ / (+ *	) + C	AB+D*EFAD
+ /	+ C	AB +D*EFAD*+
+	C	AB +D*EFAD*+ / +
+	End	AB +D*EFAD*+/+C
Empty	End	AB +D*EFAD*+/+C+

(ii) A * (B + C) / D – G

Stack	Input	Output
Empty	A * (B + C) / D – G	–
Empty	* (B + C) / D – G	A
*	(B + C) / D – G	A
*(	B + C) / D – G	A
*(	+ C) / D – G	AB
*(+	C) / D – G	AB
*(+	) / D – G	ABC
*	/ D – G	ABC+
/	D – G	ABC+*
/	– G	ABC+*D
–	G	ABC+*D/
–	End	ABC+*D/G
Empty	End	ABC+*D/G–

Example 4.6.7 : Trace the conversion of infix to postfix form in tabular form.
(A + B * C/D – E + F / G / (H + I))

Solution :

	Stack	Input	Output (Postfix)
1.	Empty	(A + B * C/D – E + F / G / (H + I))	–
2.	(	A + B * C/D – E + F / G / (H + I))	–
3.	(	+ B * C/D – E + F / G / (H + I))	A
4.	(+	B * C/D – E + F / G / (H + I))	A
5.	(+	* C/D – E + F / G / (H + I))	AB
6.	(+ *	C/D – E + F / G / (H + I))	AB
7.	(+ *	/D – E + F / G / (H + I))	ABC
8.	(+ /	D – E + F / G / (H + I))	ABC*
9.	(+ /	– E + F / G / (H + I))	ABC*D
10.	(–	E + F / G / (H + I))	ABC*D / +
11.	(–	+ F / G / (H + I))	ABC*D / + E
12.	(+	F / G / (H + I))	ABC*D / + E–
13.	(+	/ G / (H + I))	ABC*D / + E – F
14.	(+ /	G / (H + I))	ABC*D / + E – F
15.	(+ /	/ (H + I))	ABC*D / + E – FG
16.	(+ /	(H + I))	ABC*D / + E – FG /
17.	(+ / (	H + I))	ABC*D / + E – FG /
18.	(+ / (	+ I))	ABC*D / + E – FG / H
19.	(+ / (+	I))	ABC*D / + E – FG / H
20.	(+ / (+	))	ABC*D / + E – FG / HI

	Stack	Input	Output (Postfix)
21.	(+ /	)	ABC*D / + E – FG / HI +
22.	Empty	End	ABC*D / + E – FG / HI + / +

Postfix form :　　ABC*D / + E – FG / HI + / +

Example 4.6.8 : Convert following expression Q into postfix form.
Q = (A + B) * C – D/E * (F/G). Show stack representation.

S - 2010

Solution :

S. No.	Stack	Input	Output	Initially
1.	Empty	(A + B) * C – D/E*(F/G)	–	
2.	(	A + B) *C – D/E*(F/G)	–	
3.	(	+ B) * C – D/E * (F/G)	A	
4.	(+	B) * C – D/E *(F/G)	A	
5.	(+	) * C – D/E * (F/G)	AB	
6.	Empty	* C – D/E * (F/G)	AB+	
7.	*	C – D/E * (F/G)	AB+	
8.	*	– D/E * (F/G)	AB+C	
9.	–	D/E * (F/G)	AB+C*	
10.	–	/E * (F/G)	AB+C*D	
11.	–/	E * (F/G)	AB+C*D	
12.	–/	*(F/G)	AB+C*DE	
13.	–*	(F/G)	AB+C*DE/	
14.	–*(	F/G)	AB+C*DE/	
15.	–*(	/G)	AB+C*DE/F	
16.	–*(/	G)	AB+C*DE/F	
17.	–*(/	)	AB+C*DE/FG	
18.	–*	End	AB+C*DE/FG/	
19.	Empty	End	AB+C*DE/FG/*–	

∴ Postfix expression = AB + C * DE/ FG /*–

Example 4.6.9 : Translate the given infix expression to postfix expression using stack and show the details of stack at each step.

Expression : $((A + B) * D) \uparrow (E - F)$ S - 09

Solution :

S. No.	Stack	Input	Output
1.	Empty	$((A + B) * D) \uparrow (E - F)$	–
2.	(	$(A + B) * D) \uparrow (E - F)$	–
3.	((	$A + B) * D) \uparrow (E - F)$	–
4.	((	$+ B) * D) \uparrow (E - F)$	A
5.	((+	$B) * D) \uparrow (E - F)$	A
6.	((+	$) * D) \uparrow (E - F)$	AB
7.	(	$* D) \uparrow (E - F)$	AB+
8.	(*	$D) \uparrow (E - F)$	AB+
9.	(*	$) \uparrow (E - F)$	AB+D
10.	Empty	$\uparrow (E - F)$	AB+D*
11.	$\uparrow$	$(E - F)$	AB+D*
12.	$\uparrow$(	$E - F)$	AB+C*E
13.	$\uparrow$(	$- F)$	AB+E*E
14.	$\uparrow$(–	$F)$	AB+D*E
15.	$\uparrow$(–	$)$	AB+D*EF
16.	$\uparrow$	End	AB+D*EF–
17.	Empty	End	AB+D*EF–$\uparrow$

$\therefore$ Postfix expression = AB+D*EF–$\uparrow$

➢ **Program 4.6.8 : Program for conversion of infix to its postfix form operators supported '+,-,*,/,%,^,(,) operands supported -- all single character operands**

```
/* program for conversion of infix into its postfix form
   operators supported '+,-,*,/,%,∧,(,)
   operands supported -- all single character operands
*/
```

```c
#include<stdio.h>
#include<conio.h>
#include<ctype.h>
#define MAX 50
typedef struct stack
{
   int data[MAX];
   int top;
}stack;

int  precedence(char);
void init(stack *);
int  empty(stack *);
int  full(stack *);
int  pop(stack *);
void push(stack *,int );
int  top(stack *); //value of the top element
void infix_to_postfix(char infix[],char postfix[]);
void main()
 { char infix[30],postfix[30];
   clrscr();
   printf("\nEnter an infix expression : ");
   gets(infix);
   infix_to_postfix(infix,postfix);
   printf("\nPostfix : %s  ",postfix);
   getch();
 }
void infix_to_postfix(char infix[],char postfix[])
{ stack s;
   char x;
   int i,j;//i-index for infix[],j-index for postfix
   char token;
   init(&s);
   j=0;
```

```
    for(i=0;infix[i]!='\0';i++)
    {    token=infix[i];
        if(isalnum(token))
            postfix[j++]=token;
        else
            if(token == '(')
                push(&s,'(');
            else
                if(token == ')')
                  while((x=pop(&s))!='(')
                      postfix[j++]=x;
                else
                {

  while(precedence(token)<=precedence(top(&s)) &&
!empty(&s))
                        {
                            x=pop(&s);
                            postfix[j++]=x;
                        }
                        push(&s,token);
                }
    }
    while(!empty(&s))
    {
        x=pop(&s);
        postfix[j++]=x;
    }
postfix[j]='\0';
}
int precedence(char x)
{
    if(x == '(')                  return(0);
    f(x == '+' || x == '-')       return(1);
```

```
    if(x == '*' || x == '/' || x == '%') return(2);
    return(3);
}
void init(stack *s)
{
    s->top=-1;
}
int empty(stack *s)
{
    if(s->top==-1)  return(1);
    return(0);
}
int full(stack *s)
{
    if(s->top==MAX-1)   return(1);
    return(0);
}
void push(stack *s,int x)
{
    s->top=s->top+1;
    s->data[s->top]=x;
}
int pop(stack *s)
{
    int x;
    x=s->data[s->top];
    s->top=s->top-1;
    return(x);
}
int top(stack * p)
{
    return(p->data[p->top]);
}
```

Output

```
Enter infix expression:a*(b+c)/d+g
abc+*d/g+
```

4.6.5 Conversion of an Expression from Infix to Prefix :

Example of a infix expression : $(A + B \wedge C) * D + E \wedge 5$ where A, B, C, D and E are integer constant and $B \wedge C$ stands for B^c.

Manual method :

In manual evaluation of the above expression, B^C must be calculated first. Hence, we convert B^C to its equivalent pretfix equivalent i.e. ^BC.

$(A + B^C) * D + E^5$　　– original expression

$(A + \underline{{}^C BC}) * D + E^5$　　– $\underline{{}^C BC}$ should be treated as a single operand.

　　$\underline{+ A^C BC} * D + E^5$　　– $A + \underline{{}^C BC}$ is the next operation.

　　$\underline{* + A^C BCD} + E^5$　　– $\underline{+ A^C BC} * D$ is the next operation.

　　$\underline{* + A^C BCD} + \underline{{}^C E5}$　　– E^5 is the next operation.

　　$+ * + A^C BCD{}^C E5$　　– Addition is the last operation.

Algorithmic approach :

An infix expression can be converted into prefix form with the help of following steps :

1. Reverse the infix expression
2. Make every '(' (opening bracket) as ')' (closing bracket) and every ')' as '('
3. Convert the modified expression to postfix form. Use the algorithm given in the section 4.6.4.
4. Reverse the postfix expression.

Above algorithm can be explained by carrying out the steps from 1 to 4 on the example :

$(A + B \wedge C) * D + E \wedge 5$

Step 1 : Reverse the infix expression.

$5 \wedge E + D *) C \wedge B + A($

Step 2 :   Make every '(' as ')' and every ')' and '('

$$5^{\wedge} E + D * (C^{\wedge} B + A)$$

Step 3 :   Convert the expression to postfix form :

Expression (input)	Stack	Output	Comment
$5^{\wedge} E + D * (C^{\wedge} B + A)$	Empty	–	Initially
$^{\wedge} E + D * (C^{\wedge} B + A)$	Empty	5	Print
$E + D * (C^{\wedge} B + A)$	∧	5	Push
$+ D * (C^{\wedge} B + A)$	∧	5 E	Push
$D * (C^{\wedge} B + A)$	+	$5 E^{\wedge}$	Pop and Push
$* (C^{\wedge} B + A)$	+	$5 E^{\wedge} D$	Print
$(C^{\wedge} B + A)$	+*	$5 E^{\wedge} D$	Push
$C^{\wedge} B + A)$	+*(	$5 E^{\wedge} D$	Push
$^{\wedge} B + A)$	+*(	$5 E^{\wedge} D C$	Print
$B + A)$	+*(^	$5 E^{\wedge} D C$	Push
$+ A)$	+*(^	$5 E^{\wedge} D C B$	Print
$A)$	+*(+	$5 E^{\wedge} D C B^{\wedge}$	Pop and Push
$)$	+*(+	$5 E^{\wedge} D C B^{\wedge} A$	Print
End	+*	$5 E^{\wedge} D C B^{\wedge} A +$	Pop until '('
End	Empty	$5 E^{\wedge} D C B^{\wedge} A + * +$	Pop everything

Step 4 :   Reverse the expression

$$+ * + A^{\wedge} B C D^{\wedge} E 5$$

> **Pseudo code for conversion of an expression from infix into prefix.**

```
{
    S : stack of characters ;
    infix ← read the infix expression;
```

```
infix ← reverse the infix expression ;
infix ← reverse the direction of brackets ;
prefix ← A NULL string
i = 0 ;
while ( infix [i] is not equal to '\0)
      {   x ← infix [i] ;
          if ( x is an operand )
                add the character x at the end of prefix ;
      else
          if ( x is '(' )
                push ( S, '(')
          else
              if ( x is ')' )
                  {   while ( ( x ← pop(S)) ! = '(' )
                      prefix ← prefix + pop(S) ; //+ is for
                      concatenation
                  }
              else
                  {       while ( precedence (x) ≤ precedence
                          (top(S) )
                          {
                              prefix ← prefix + pop(S ) ;
//+ is for concatenation
                          }
                          push (S, X) ;
                  }
      i ← i + 1 ;
  }
      while ( !empty (S) )
          prefix ← prefix + pop(S) ;
      prefix ← reverse the prefix ;
      print prefix ;
  }
```

> **Program 4.6.9 : To convert infix expression to prefix expression.**

```
/* program for conversion of infix into its prefix form
   operators supported '+,-,*,/,%,∧,(,)
   operands supported -- all single character operands
*/

#include<stdio.h>
#include<conio.h>
#include<ctype.h>
#define MAX 50

typedef struct stack
{
   int data[MAX];
   int top;
}stack;
int  precedence(char);
void init(stack *);
int  empty(stack *);
int  full(stack *);
int  pop(stack *);
void push(stack *,int );
int  top(stack *); //value of the top element
void infix_to_prefix(char infix[],char prefix[]);
void infix_to_postfix(char infix[],char postfix[]);

void main()
 { char infix[30],prefix[30];
   clrscr();
   printf("\nEnter an infix expression : ");
   gets(infix);
   infix_to_prefix(infix,prefix);
   printf("\n prefix: %s  ",prefix);
   getch();
 }
```

```
void infix_to_prefix(char infix[],char prefix[])
  { int i,j;
    char temp,in1[30];
      // reverse the infix expression  and store it in in1[]
    for(i=strlen(infix)-1,j=0;i>=0;i--,j++)
    in1[j]=infix[i];
    in1[j]='\0';
    // reverse the direction of brackets
    for(i=0;in1[i]!='\0';i++)
     {
    if(in1[i]=='(')
        in1[i]=')';
     else
        if(in1[i]==')')
            in1[i]='(';
     }
    // convert from infix to postfix
    infix_to_postfix(in1,prefix);
    //reverse the final expression
    for(i=0,j=strlen(prefix)-1;i<j;i++,j--)
     {
    temp=prefix[i];
    prefix[i]=prefix[j];
    prefix[j]=temp;
     }
 }
void infix_to_postfix(char infix[],char postfix[])
{ stack s;
   char x;
   int i,j;//i-index for infix[],j-index for postfix
   char token;
   init(&s);
   j=0;
   for(i=0;infix[i]!='\0';i++)
    {    token=infix[i];
         if(isalnum(token))
             postfix[j++]=token;
```

```
            else
                if(token == '(')
                    push(&s,'(');
                else
                    if(token == ')')
                       while((x=pop(&s))!='(')
                           postfix[j++]=x;
                    else
                    {

   while(precedence(token)<=precedence(top(&s)) &&
!empty(&s))
                               {
                                    x=pop(&s);
                                    postfix[j++]=x;
                               }
                               push(&s,token);
                    }
        }
   while(!empty(&s))
{
        x=pop(&s);
        postfix[j++]=x;
   }
postfix[j]='\0';
}
int precedence(char x)
{
   if(x == '(')                  return(0);
   if(x == '+' || x == '-')        return(1);
   if(x == '*' || x == '/' || x == '%') return(2);
   return(3);
}
void init(stack *s)
{
   s->top=-1;
}
```

```
int empty(stack *s)
{
    if(s->top==-1) return(1);
    return(0);
}
int full(stack *s)
{
    if(s->top==MAX-1)    return(1);
    return(0);
}
void push(stack *s,int x)
{
    s->top=s->top+1;
    s->data[s->top]=x;
}
int pop(stack *s)
{
    int x;
    x=s->data[s->top];
    s->top=s->top-1;
    return(x);
}
int top(stack * p)
{
    return(p->data[p->top]);
}
```

4.7 Expression Conversion (A Fast Method)

4.7.1 Infix to Postfix :

1st method

Example considered for conversion is :

$$A / B^\wedge C + D*E - A*C$$

- Operands are grouped as shown below. Operator precedence and associativity rules must be followed while grouping.

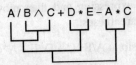

$$A / B \wedge C + D * E - A * C$$

- Operators are moved at the end of the group.

Postfix expression of the given infix expression=

$$ABC^{\wedge} / DE* + AC* -$$

2nd method

An infix expression can be converted into postfix form by fully parenthesizing the infix expression and then moving operators to replace their corresponding right parentheses.

Given infix expression : A/B^C+D*E − A*C. After fully parenthesizing the expression, we get :

$$(((A / (B \wedge C)) + (D * E)) - (A * C))$$

After moving operators to replace their corresponding right parentheses, we get :

$$ABC^{\wedge} / DE* + AC * -$$

4.7.2 Infix to Prefix :

1st method

Example considered for conversion is :

$$A/B^{\wedge}C + D*E - A*C$$

- Operators are grouped as shown below. Operator precedence and associativity rules must be followed while grouping.

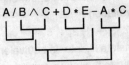

$$A / B \wedge C + D * E - A * C$$

- Operators are moved at the beginning of the group.

Prefix expression of the given infix expression = $- + /A^{\wedge}BC*DE*AC$

2nd method

An infix expression can be converted into prefix form by fully parenthesizing the infix expression and then moving operators to replace their corresponding left parentheses.

Given infix expression : $A/B^\wedge C + D*E - A*C$

After fully parenthesizing the expression, we get :

$$(((A / (B \wedge C)) + (D * E)) - (A * C))$$

After moving operators to replace their corresponding left parentheses, we get :

$+ A^\wedge BC * DE*AC$

4.7.3 Postfix to Prefix :

Postfix expression

$ABC^\wedge /DE* + AC* -$

Group the tokens as shown below

$$A B C \wedge / D E * + A C * -$$

- Grouping is done left to right
- All operators are moved at the beginning of the group.

$$- + / A \wedge BC * DE * AC$$

Postfix to Infix :

- All operators are moved between the two operands of the group

$$A / B^\wedge C + D * E - A * C$$

Example 4.7.1 :	Consider the following arithmetic expression P, written in postfix notation :
	P : 12, 7, 3, –, 1, 2, +, 5, +, *, +
	(i) Translate P, into its equivalent infix expression.
	(ii) Evaluate the infix expression. W - 08

Solution :

(i) Postfix to infix form :

Postfix expression (P) = 12, 7, 3, –, 1, 2, +, 5, +, *, +

Step 1 : Grouping of tokens as per the sequence of evaluation.

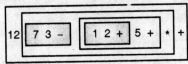

Step 2 : Operator are moved between the two operands of the group.

$$12 + (7 - 3) * (1 + 2 + 5)$$

(ii) Evaluate the infix expression

$$12 + (7 - 3) * (1 + 2 + 5)$$
$$= 12 + 4 * 8 = 12 + 32 = 44$$

Example 4.7.2 : Convert the following arithmetic expression P written in postfix notation into infix.

P : 5, 6, 2, +, *, 12, 4, /,–

Also evaluate P for final value. **S - 09**

Solution :

(i) Postfix to infix form :

Postfix expression (P) = 5, 6, 2, +, *, 12, 4, 1, /, -

Step 1 : Grouping of tokens as per the sequence of evaluation.

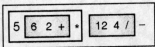

Step 2 : Operators are moved between the two operands of the group.

$$5 * (6 + 2) - 12/4$$

(ii) Evaluation of 5, 6, 2, +, *, 12, 4, /,–

	Input	Stack	Initially
1.	5, 6, 2, +, *, 12, 4, /, –		
2.	6, 2, +, *, 12, 4, /, –	5	
3.	2, +, *, 12, 4, /, –	6 5	

	Input	Stack	Initially
4.	+, *, 12, 4, /, –	2 / 6 / 5	
5.	*, 12, 4, /, –	8 / 5	6 + 2 = 8
6.	12, 4, /, –	40	5 * 8 = 40
7.	4, /, –	12 / 40	
8.	/, –	4 / 12 / 40	
9.	–	3 / 40	12/4 = 3
10.	End	37	40 – 3 = 37

∴ Result = 37

4.7.4 Prefix to Infix :

Prefix expression   – + / A^BC * DE * AC

Group the tokens as shown below

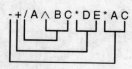

- Grouping is done right to left
- All operators are moved between the two operands of the group

    A / B^C + D *E – A * C

Prefix to Postfix :

All operators are moved at the end of the group

ABC^/ DE * + AC * /

Example 4.7.3 : Transform the expression to postfix and evaluate postfix expression by assuming A = 1, B = 2, C = 3, D = 4, E = 6, F = 6, G = 1, I = 3 and J = 3.

A + B – C * D / E + F $ G / (I + J)

Solution :

(i) Infix to postfix conversion :

1. Fully parenthesizing the expression, we get :

$$(((A + B) - ((C * D) / E)) + ((F \$ G) / (I + J)))$$

2. Moving operators to replace their corresponding right parenthesis.

AB + CD * E / – FG $ IJ + / +

(ii) Evaluation of the postfix expression :

	Input	Stack	
1.	AB + CD * E / – FG $ IJ + / +		
2.	B + CD * E / – FG $ IJ + / +	1	
3	+ CD * E / – FG $ IJ + / +	2 1	
4.	CD * E / – FG $ IJ + / +	3	1 + 2 = 3
5.	D * E / – FG $ IJ + / +	3 3	

	Input	Stack	
6.	* E / – FG $ IJ + / +	4 3 3	
7.	E / – FG $ IJ + / +	12 3	3 * 4 = 12
8.	/ – FG $ IJ + / +	6 12 3	
9.	– FG $ IJ + / +	2 3	12/6 = 2
10.	FG $ IJ + / +	1	3 – 2 = 1
11.	G $ IJ + / +	6 1	
12.	$ IJ + / +	1 6 1	
13.	IJ + / +	6 1	$6' = 6$
14.	J + / +	3 6 1	

	Input	Stack	
15.	+ / +	3 3 6 1	
16.	/ +	6 6 1	3 + 3 = 6
17.	+	1 1	6/6 = 1
18.	End	2	

Value = 2.

4.8 Introduction to Recursion

Q. What is recursion ? Write a 'C' program for multiplication of natural numbers using recursion.   **W - 09**

Recursion is a fundamental concept in mathematics. When a function is defined in terms of itself then it is called a recursive function. Consider the definition of factorial of a positive integer n.

$$\text{Factorial } (n) = \begin{cases} 1 & \text{if } (n=0) \\ n * \text{factorial } (n-1), & \text{otherwise} \end{cases}$$

Function "factorial ( )" is defined in terms of itself for n > 0. Value of the function at n = 0 is 1 and it is called the base. Recursion terminates on reaching the base.

For example :

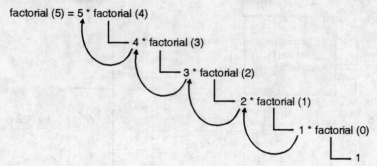

factorial (5) = 5 * factorial (4)

4 * factorial (3)

3 * factorial (2)

2 * factorial (1)

1 * factorial (0)

1

Recursion expands when n > 0 and it starts winding up on hitting the base (n = 0).

4.8.1 Converting a Recursive Function to an Equivalent C-function :

4.8.1.1 Finding Factorial of an Integer Number :

Recursive Definition of Factorial of an Integer :

$$f(n) = 1 \qquad if (n == 0)$$
$$n * f(n-1), \quad otherwise$$

➤ **'C' function for finding factorial.**

```
int factorial (int n)
{
    if (n == 0)
        return (1);
    return (n * factorial (n - 1));
}
```

Sequence of calls to be made has been shown in the Fig. 4.8.1 to give a better insight into recursion.

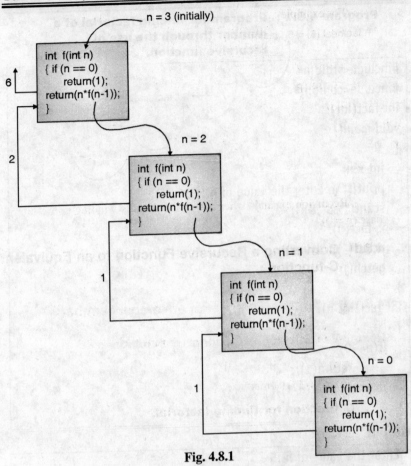

Fig. 4.8.1

Sequence of calls could also be shown through a recursion tree.

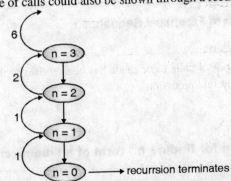

Fig. 4.8.2 : Recursion tree for finding factorial (3)

> **Program 4.8.1 : Program for finding factorial of a number through the use of recursive function.**

```c
#include<stdio.h>
#include<conio.h>
int fact(int);
void main()
{
    int x,n;
    printf("\n Enter the value of n :");
    scanf("%d",&n);
    x=fact(n);
    printf("\n %d",x);
    getch();
}
int fact(int n)
{
    if(n==0)
        return(1);
    return(n*fact(n-1));
}
```

Output

```
Enter the value of n :5
120
```

Finding n^{th} term of Fibonacci Sequence :

Recursive Definition :

$$T_n = T_{n-1} + T_{n-2} \quad \text{if } n > 1$$
$$T_1 = 1$$
$$T_0 = 0$$

> **'C' function for finding n^{th} term of a Fibonacci sequence.**

```c
int fib (int n)
```

```
{
    if (n == 0)
        return (0);
    if (n == 1)
        return (1);
    return (fib(n - 1) + fib(n - 2));
}
```

In the above example $fib(n) = fib(n - 1) + fib(n - 2)$ for $n > 1$ is a case of binary recursion. The first term on the right $fib(n - 1)$ is known as left recursion and the second term on the right $fib(n - 2)$ is known as right recursion.

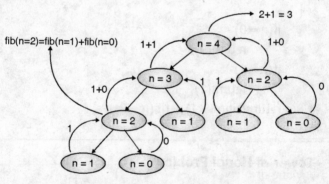

Fig. 4.8.3 : A recursion tree, showing calculation of T_4

Fibonacci series :

$$\begin{array}{ccccc} 0 & 1 & 1 & 2 & 3 \\ | & | & | & | & | \\ T_0 & T_1 & T_2 & T_3 & T_4 \end{array}$$

➤ **Program 4.8.2 : A C-program to generate Fibonacci series using recursion.**

Q. Write a 'C/C++' program to generate Fibonacci series using recursion. **W - 08**

```
#include<stdio.h>
#include<conio.h>
```

```
int fib(int);
void main()
  {
        int i, terms,val;
        printf("\n enter no. of terms:");
        scanf("%d",&terms);
        for (i = 0; i <terms; i++)
            {
                val=fib(i);
                printf("\n%d",val);
            }
  }
int fib(int n)
        {
            if(n==0)
                    return(0);
            if(n==1)
                    return(1);
            return(fib(n – 1) + fib(n – 2));
        }
```

4.8.2 Tower of Honoi Problem :

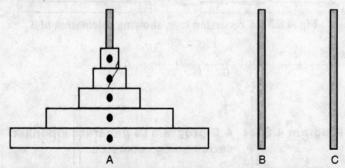

Fig. 4.8.4 : Disks are stacked on peg A in decreasing order of size

A tower of n disks is stacked in decreasing order on peg "A". These disks are to be transferred to peg "B" with the help of peg "C". Following rules must be followed while transferring disks from one peg to another peg.

(a)   Only one disk can be transferred at a time.

(b)   At no time a larger disk can be placed on a smaller disk.

In order to define the problem of Tower of Honoi recursively, We must express n disks problem in terms of a problem of n – 1 disks.

n-disks problem :

Move n disks from peg A to peg B using peg C.

Step 1 :   Move n – 1 disks from peg A to peg C.

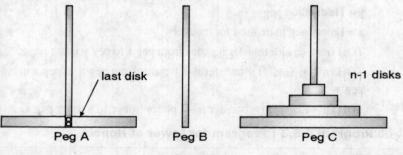

Fig. 4.8.5

Step 2 :   Move the only disk from peg A to peg B.

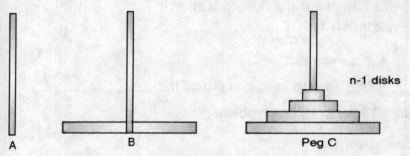

Fig. 4.8.6

Step 3 :   Move the n – 1 disks from peg C to peg B.

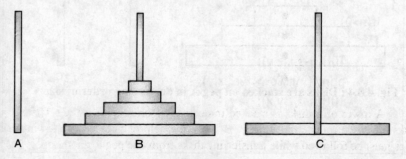

Fig. 4.8.7

Recursive definition

$$TOH(n, x, y, z) = \begin{cases} TOH(n-1, x, z, y) \\ \text{move a disk from x to y} \\ TOH(n-1, z, y, x) \end{cases} \text{ if } n \geq 1$$

n = Number of disks

x = Source peg

y = Destination peg

z = Empty peg to be used for transfer

TOH (n, x, y, z) = transfer n plates from peg x to peg y using peg z.

TOH (n – 1, x, z, y) = transfer n – 1 plates from peg x to peg z using peg y.

TOH (n – 1, z, y, x) = transfer n – 1 plates from z to y using peg x.

> **Program 4.8.3 : Program for tower of Honoi.**

```c
#include<stdio.h>
#include<conio.h>
void TOH(int n,char x,char y,char z);
void main()
{
   int n;
   printf("\n Enter number of plates:");
   scanf("%d",&n);
   TOH(n,'A','B','C');
   getch();
}
void TOH(int n,char x,char y,char z)
{
   if(n>0)
   {
        TOH(n-1,x,z,y);
        printf("\n%c -> %c",x,y);
        TOH(n-1,z,y,x);
   }
}
```

Output

```
Enter number of plates:3
A -> B
A -> C
B -> C
A -> B
C -> A
C -> B
A -> B
```

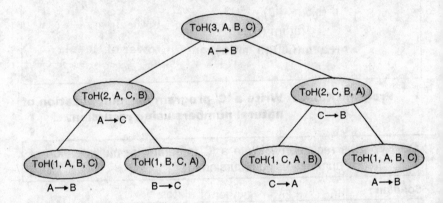

Fig. 4.8.8 : Recursion tree for the function TOH ( ) for n = 3 plates

Sequence of moves :

(1)   A → B
(2)   A → C
(3)   B → C
(4)   A → B
(5)   C → A
(6)   C → B
(7)   A → B

Sequence of moves can easily be written by making an inorder traversal on recursion tree. Concept of inorder traversal is explained in the chapter on "tree".

Example 4.8.1 : Write a C program for GCD using recursion.

Solution :

GCD of two numbers m and n can be defined as given below.

$$GCD\ (m,\ n)\ =\ \begin{cases} GCD\ (n,\ m) & \text{if m < n} \\ n & \text{if m is divisible by n} \\ GCD\ (n,\ m\ \%\ n) & \text{otherwise} \end{cases}$$

C-function for GCD :

```
int GCD (int m, int n)
  {
          if (m < n)
                  return (GCD (n, m));
          if (m%n ==0)
                  return (n);
          return (GCD (n, m%n));
  }
```

➢ **Program 4.8.4 : Write a 'C' program for multiplication of natural numbers using recursion.**

Q. What is recursion ? Write a 'C' program for multiplication of natural numbers using recursion. W - 09

Solution :

```
#include<stdio.h>
#include<conio.h>
int multiply(int, int);
void main()
  {      int x, y, result;
         printf("\n enter 2 numbers:");
         scanf("%d%d", &x, &y),
         result = multiply (x, y),
         printf("\n Product=%d", result);
         getch();
  }
  int multiply (int a, int b)
      {   if(a==0||b==0)
                  return(0);
```

```
        if(b==1)
                return(a);
        return(a + multiply(a, b – 1));
    }
```

4.9 MSBTE Questions and Answers

Summer 2008 – Total Marks 10

Q. 1   Explain any two applications of stack.

   (Sections 4.6.2 and 4.6.4)   **(4 Marks)**

Q. 2   Write a menu driven 'C' program for implementing stack using array.

   (Program 4.5.2)   **(6 Marks)**

Winter 2008 – Total Marks 12

Q. 3   Define the terms 'Overflow' and 'Underflow' with respect to stacks.

   (Section 4.5.1)   **(2 Marks)**

Q. 4   Write a 'C/C++' program to generate Fibonacci series using recursion. **(Program 4.8.2)**   **(4 Marks)**

Q. 5   Consider the following arithmetic expression P, written in Postfix notation :

   P : 12, 7, 3, –, 1, 2, 1, 5, +, *, +

   (i)   Translate P, into its equivalent Infix expression.

   (ii) Evaluate the Infix expression. **(Example 4.7.1)**   **(6 Marks)**

Summer 2009 – Total Marks 16

Q. 6   State the principle of stack with basic operations.

   (Sections 4.1 and 4.3)   **(2 Marks)**

Q. 7　Write down the applications of stacks.

(Sections 4.6.2 and 4.6.4)　　　　　　　　　　　　　(4 Marks)

Q. 8　Translate the given Infix expression to postfix expression using stack and show the details of stack at each step.

Expression : ((A + B) ∗ D) ↑ (E – F) (Example 4.6.9)　(6 Marks)

Q. 9　Convert the following arithmetic expression P written in postfix notation into infix :

P : 5, 6, 2, + , *, 12, 4, /, –

Also evaluate P for final value. (Example 4.7.2)　　　(4 Marks)

Winter 2009 – Total Marks 14

Q. 10　Evaluate following Postfix Expression.

A : 6, 2, 3, +, –, 3, 8, 2, 1, +, *, 2, ↑, 3, +. (Example 4.6.4) (6 Marks)

Q. 11　What is recursion ? Write a 'C' program for multiplication of natural numbers using recursion. (Section 4.8, Program 4.8.4)　(4 Marks)

Q. 12　Explain the terms overflow and underflow with respect to stack. Use suitable data and diagram. (Section 4.5.1)　　　　(4 Marks)

Summer 2010 – Total Marks 14

Q. 13　Define stack what are the basic operations performed on it.

(Sections 4.1 and 4.3)　　　　　　　　　　　　　(4 Marks)

Q. 14　Convert following expression Q into postfix form. Q = (A +. B) * C – D/E * (F/G) Show stack representation. (Example 4.6.8)　(6 Marks)

Q. 15　Write a procedure to push an element on stack. Also give meaning of stack overflow term. (Section 4.5.1)　　　　　(4 Marks)

□□□

Queues

Syllabus

Introduction

Queue as an Abstract Data Type, Representation of Queues.

Operations on Queue

Searching, Insertion, Deletion.

Types of queues

Circular Queues, Priority Queues, Dequeues

Application of Queues

Statistical Analysis

Year	Marks
Summer - 2008	16 Marks
Winter - 2008	12 Marks
Summer - 2009	10 Marks
Winter - 2009	10 Marks
Summer - 2010	16 Marks

5.1 Introduction

It is a special kind of list, where items are inserted at one end (the rear) and deleted from the other end (front). Queue is a FIFO (First In First Out) list.

We come across the term queue in our day to day life. We see a queue at a railway reservation counter, or a movie theatre ticket counter. Before getting the service, one has to wait in the queue. After receiving the service, one leaves the queue. Service is provided at one end (the front) and people join at the other end (rear).

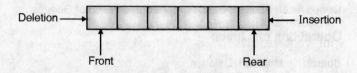

Fig. 5.1.1 : Insertion of elements is done at the rear end and deletion from the front end

5.1.1 Application of Queues :

Q.   State any two application of Queue.   W - 09

- Various features of operating system are implemented using a queue.
    a)   Scheduling of processes (Round Robin Algorithm).
    b)   Spooling (to maintain a queue of jobs to be printed).
    c)   A queue of client processes waiting to receive the service from the server process.

- Various application software using non-linear data structure tree or graph requires a queue for breadth first traversal.

- Simulation of a real life problem with the purpose of understanding its behaviour. The probable waiting time of a person at a railway reservation counter can be found through the technique of computer simulation if the following concerned factors are known :
    1)   Arrival rate
    2)   Service time
    3)   Number of service counters

5.1.2 Array Representation and Implementation of Queues :

An array representation of queue requires three entities.

a) An array to hold queue elements.

b) A variable to hold the index of the front element.

c) A variable to hold the index of the rear element.

A queue data type may be defined formally as follows :

```
# define MAX 30
typedef struct queue
{
   int data[MAX];
   int front, rear;
} queue;
```

• During initialization of a queue, its front and rear are set to –1.

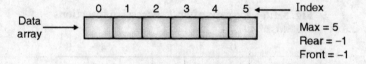

Fig. 5.1.2 : An empty queue after initialization

• Fig. 5.1.3 shows the status of an queue after insertion of the element '5'.

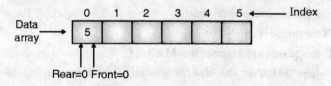

Fig. 5.1.3 : A queue after insertion of the first element '5'

• On subsequent insertions, front remains at the same place, where rear advances.

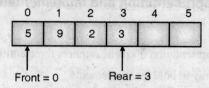

Fig. 5.1.4 : A queue after insertion of four elements

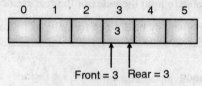

Fig. 5.1.5 : A queue after 3 successive deletions

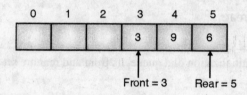

Fig. 5.1.6 : A queue after 2 successive insertions

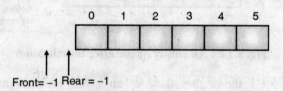

Fig. 5.1.7 : A queue after 3 successive deletions

Following points can be observed :

(1)   If the queue is empty then front = –1 and rear = –1.

(2)   If the queue is full then rear = MAX – 1.

       (where MAX is the size of the array used for storing of queue elements).

(3)   If rear = front then the queue contains just one element.

(4)   If rear > front then queue is non-empty.

       Problem with the above representation of the queue :

Problem of overflow : Refer to the Fig. 5.1.6, the queue has become full as rear = MAX –1. There are three vacant spaces (location 0, 1, 2) but these spaces cannot be utilized.

Problem of overflow can be handled by moving the queue elements to their left by number of vacant spaces. This operation could be very time consuming for a large queue.

5.1.3 Comparison between Array Representation and the Linked Representation of a Queue :

- Maximum size of the queue is fixed at the time of compilation, when the queue is represented using an array, this causes wastage of storage space. If the queue size is arbitrarily large and if less area is reserved for the queue then there will be a problem of frequent overflow.

- In case of a queue using linked structure, no memory area is reserved in advance. Memory for a node is acquired during run time, whenever a fresh insertion is to be made. There is no problem of overflow. As long as the system has free memory it can be given for a queue element.

- Array representation of a queue is simple to implement whereas the linked representation requires additional knowledge of linked list and dynamic data structure. Many programming languages do not support dynamic data structure.

- In linked representation, additional memory is required to store the address of the next element. There is no such requirement in case of array representation of a queue, as array is stored in contiguous memory locations.

5.1.4 Comparison between STACK and QUEUE :

Q. Distinguish between STACK and QUEUE.   **W - 09**

- Stack is a LIFO (Last in First Out) structure. Queue is a FIFO (First in First Out) structure.

- In a stack, all insertions and deletions are permitted only at one end of the list. In a queue, items are inserted at one end (the rear) and deleted from the other end (front).

- Stack is always implemented using a linear array but queue should preferably be implemented using a circular array.

- Stack is widely used in recursion and processing of expressions. Queue is more useful in many of the real life applications.

5.2 Operations on Queue (Implemented using Array)

Q.   Also explain any four terms in Queue.   `S - 08`

Q   Write a procedure to insert an element into a queue and to delete an element from a queue. Also explain DEQUES.   `S - 09`

Q.   Write the procedure for inserting and deleting an clement from queue.   `S - 2010`

A set of useful operations on a queue includes :

(1)   initialize( ) : Initializes a queue by setting the value of rear and front to −1.

(2)   enqueue( ) : Inserts an element at the rear end of the queue.

(3)   dequeue( ) : Deletes the front element and returns the same.

(4)   empty( ) : It returns true(1) if the queue is empty and returns false(0) if the queue is not empty.

(5)   full( ) : It return true(1) if the queue is full and returns false(0) if the queue is not full.

(6)   print( ) : Printing of queue elements.

Realization of queue operations through C-function :

(a)   Defining the maximum size of the queue.

         #define MAX 50

(b)   Data structure declaration

```
typedef struct Q
{
   int R, F;
   int data[MAX];
} Q;
```

"R" and "F" store the index of the rear and the front element respectively. "data[MAX]" is used to store the queue elements.

(c)   Declaring a queue type variable.

         Q q_1, q_2 ;

q_1 and q_2 are queue type variables

(d)   Declaring a queue type pointer variable.

Q q_1, *P;

P = &q_1

A pointer variable "P" can be used to store the address of a queue type variable.

> **'C' function to initialize( ).**

```
void initialize(Q *P)
{
    P → R = - 1;
    P → F = - 1;
}
```

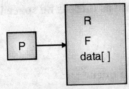

Fig. 5.2.1 : Elements of the structure 'Q' can be accessed through the pointer P (P → R, P → F, P → data[ ])

In the function "void initialize(Q *P)" a "Q" type variable is passed by address. Members of the structure type variables can be accessed through a pointer as shown in the Fig. 5.2.1. Initially the queue is empty and hence the value of the two variables "R (rear)" and "F (front)" is set to – 1.

> **'C' function to check whether queue is empty or not.**

```
int empty(Q *P)
{
    if(P → R == - 1)
            return(1);
    return(0);
}
```

Whenever the queue is empty, P → R (i.e. rear field (R) of the queue type variable whose address is stored in P) or P → F will be – 1.

➤ 'C' function to check whether queue is full or not.

```
int full(Q *P)
{
    if(P → R == MAX - 1)
          return(1);
    return(0);
}
```

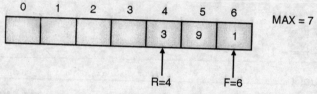

Fig. 5.2.2 : The queue is full as there is no space left for further insertion

enqueue( )

Algorithm for insertion in a queue :

(1)   Inserting in an empty queue.

    (a)   R = F = 0;

    (b)   data[R] = x /* x is the element to be inserted */

    /* Both R and F will point to the only element of the queue */

(2)   Inserting in a non-empty queue.

    (a)   R = R + 1;

        data[R] = x

/* rear is advanced by 1 and the element x is stored at the rear end of the queue */.

Note : Insertion should be carried out after it is checked that the queue is not full.

➤ 'C' function for insertion in a queue.

```
void enque(Q *P, int x)
{
    if(P → R == - 1)                    /* empty queue */
```

```
    {
            P → R = P → F = 0;
            P → data[ P→ R] = x;
    }
    else
    {
            P → R = P → R + 1;
            P → data[P → R]    = x;
    }
}
```

dequeue( )

Algorithm for deletion from a queue :

(1)　Deletion of the last element or only element($R = F$)

　　(a)　$x = data[F]$

　　(b)　$R = F = -1;$

　　(c)　$return(x)$

(2)　Deletion of the element when the queue length > 1

　　(a)　$x = data[F]$

　　(b)　$F = F + 1$

　　(c)　$return(x);$

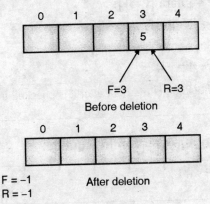

(a) Deletion of the last element

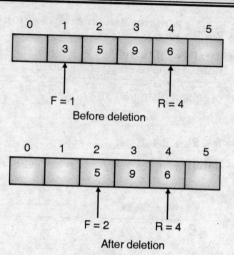

F = 1   R = 4

Before deletion

F = 2   R = 4

After deletion

(b) Deletion of an element from the queue when the queue length > 1

Fig. 5.2.3

Note : Deletion of an element from the queue should be carried out after checking that it is not empty.

➤ **'C' function for deletion from a queue**

```c
int dequeue (Q*P)
    {
        int x;
        x = P → data [P→F];
        if (P→R==P→F)
        {
            P→R= -1;
            P→F = -1;
        }
        else
            P→F=P→F+1;
        return(x);
        }
```

> **Program 5.2.1 : A menu driven program for queue.**

Q. Write a menu driven program in 'C' language for Queue having menus : Store , Retrieve and display Queue.   **S - 08**

```c
/* Simulation of  queue using an array */
#include<conio.h>
#include<stdio.h>
#define MAX 5

typedef struct Q
{
   int R,F;
   int data[MAX];
}Q;

void initialise(Q *P);
int empty(Q *P);
int full(Q *P);
void enqueue(Q *P,int x);
int dequeue(Q *P);
void print(Q *P);
void main()
{
   Q q;
   int op,x;
   initialise(&q);
   clrscr();
   do
     {
         printf("\n\n1)Insert\n2)Delete\n3)Print\n4)Quit");
         printf("\nEnter Your Choice:");
         scanf("%d",&op);
         switch(op)
             {
```

```
                case 1: printf("\n Enter a value:");
                        scanf("%d",&x);
                        if(!full(&q))
                                enqueue(&q,x);
                        else
                                printf("\nQueue is full !!!!");
                        break;
                case 2: if(!empty(&q))
                            {
                                x=dequeue(&q);
                                printf("\Deleted Data=%d",x);
                            }
                        else
                        printf("\nQueue is empty !!!!");
                        break;
                case 3: print(&q);break;
            }
    }while(op!=4);
}

void initialise(Q *P)
{
    P->R=-1;
    P->F=-1;
}

int empty(Q *P)
{
    if(P->R==-1)
            return(1);
    return(0);
}

int full(Q *P)
```

```
{
   if(P->R==MAX-1)
        return(1);
   return(0);
}

void enqueue(Q *P,int x)
{
   if(P->R==-1)
   {
        P->R=P->F=0;
        P->data[P->R]=x;
   }
   else
   {
        P->R=P->R+1%MAX;
        P->data[P->R]=x;
   }
}

int dequeue(Q *P)
{
   int x;
   x=P->data[P->F];
   if(P->R==P->F)
   {
        P->R=-1;
        P->F=-1;
   }
   else
        P->F=P->F+1;
   return(x);
}
void print(Q *P)
{
   int i;
```

```
    if(!empty(P))
    {
          printf("\n");
          for(i=P->F;i<=P->R;i++)
              printf("%d\t",P->data[i]);
    }
}
```

5.2.1 Queue as an ADT :

| **Q.** | Explain queue as an abstract data type. | S - 2010 |

(a)   Data structure declaration

        typedef struct Q

            {

                int R, F;

                int data [MAX];

            } Q;

R and F store the indices of the rear and the front element respectively. The array data[] is used to store the queue elements. MAX is a predefined constant.

Prototype of Queue functions :

1.   void initialize (Q*);
2.   int empty (Q*);
3.   int full (Q*);
4.   void enqueue(Q*, int);
5.   int dequeue(Q*);
6.   void print (Q*);

Example 5.2.1 :   Consider the following queue of characters, implemented as array of six memory locations :

Front = 2, Rear = 3

Queue : –, A, D, –, –, –

Where '–' denotes empty cell. Describe the queue as the following operations take place

(i) Add 'S'   (ii) Add 'J'

(iii) Delete two letters

(iv) Shift towards left to bring all free spaces to the right side

(v) Insert M, H, I and delete on letter.

Solution :

Initial queue :

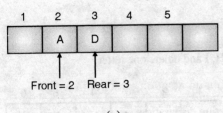

(a)

(i)   Add 'S'

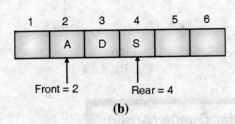

(b)

(ii) Add 'J'

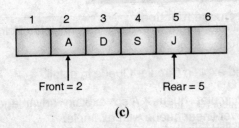

(c)

(iii) Delete two letters

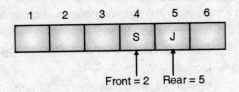

Fig. Ex. 5.2.1(d)contd..

(iv)   Shift towards left to bring all free spaces to the right.

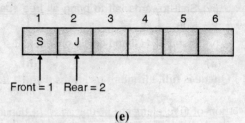

Front = 1   Rear = 2

(e)

(v)   Insert M, H, I and delete one letter.

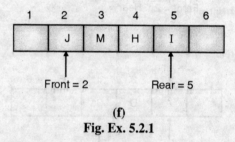

Front = 2   Rear = 5

(f)
Fig. Ex. 5.2.1

5.3 Circular Queue (Array)

> **Q.**   With suitable diagram, explain the principle of circular Queue.
> **S - 08**
>
> **Q.**   Draw and explain Circular Queue in detail.   **W- 08**
>
> **Q.**   Define circular queue. Also explain advantage of circular queue over linear queue with example.   **S - 2010**

(Advantage of circular queue)

There is one potential problem with implementation of queue using a simple array. The queue may appear to be full although there may be some space in the queue.

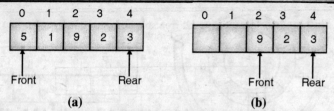

Fig. 5.3.1 : Queue is full, although locations 0 and 1 are vacant

- After insertion of five elements in the array (a queue) as shown in Fig. 5.3.1,

$$\left.\begin{array}{l} rear = 4 \\ front = 0 \end{array}\right\} \text{queue is full}$$

- After two successive deletions

$$\left.\begin{array}{l} rear = 4 \\ front = 2 \end{array}\right\} \text{queue is full}$$

queue in the Fig. 5.3.1 is full as there is no empty space ahead of rear.

The simple solution is that whenever rear gets to the end of the array, it is wrapped around to the beginning. Now, the array can be thought of as a circle. The first position follows the last element.

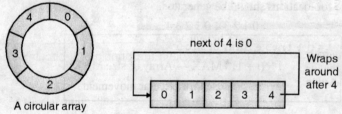

Fig. 5.3.2 : A circular array

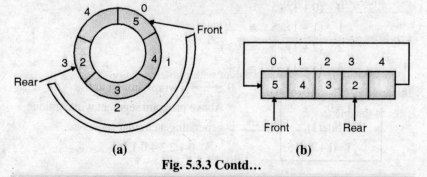

Fig. 5.3.3 Contd...

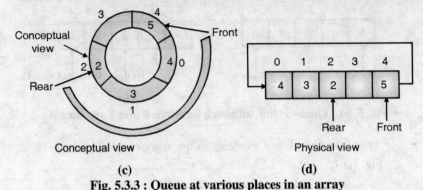

Fig. 5.3.3 : Queue at various places in an array

In a circular array, the queue is found somewhere around the circle in consecutive positions.

5.3.1 Implementation of a Circular Movement inside a Linear Array :

- To give a circular movement inside an array, whenever we go past the last element of the array, it should come back to the beginning of the array.

- Thus, when we move around an array of size five, following sequence for locations should be generated.

$$0\ 1\ 2\ 3\ 4\ 0\ 1\ 2\ 3\ 4\ \dots\dots$$

$$i = (i + 1)\%5 - \text{Array of size 5}$$
$$i = (i + 1)\%\text{MAX} \rightarrow \text{Array of size MAX}$$

expression used for circular movement

i	(i + 1)%5		
0	(0 + 1)%5	=	1
1	(1 + 1)%5	=	2
2	(2 + 1)%5	=	3
3	(3 + 1)%5	=	4
4	(4 + 1)%5	=	0 ← i wraps around to 0

```
i = 0;
while(1)
i =(i + 1)%5;
```
Above program segment will continue generating a circular sequence

$$0\ 1\ 2\ 3\ 4\ 0\ 1\ 2\ 3\ \dots..$$

> **Data type for queue in a circular array.**

```
# define MAX 30        /* A queue with maximum of 30 elements */
typedef struct queue
{
   int data[MAX];
   int front, rear;
}queue;
```

Various operation on the queue in a circular array :

> **'C' function to initialize the queue by setting values of rear and front as –1.**

```
void initialize(queue *P)
{
   P → rear = – 1;
   P → front = –1;
}
int empty(queue *P)
{
   if(P → rear == – 1)
         return(1);
   return(0);
}
int full(queue *P)
{
   if((P → rear + 1)% MAX == P → front)
         return(1);
   return(0);
}
```

Fig. 5.3.4 shows, queue is full.

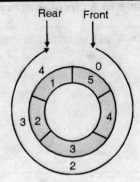

Fig. 5.3.4

When the queue becomes full, there will be no space ahead of rear in the circular array. Hence, front will be found, immediately ahead of rear in a queue that is full.

i.e. $(p \rightarrow rear + 1) \% MAX == P \rightarrow front$

```
void enqueue(queue *P, int x)
{
    if(empty(P))                        /* empty queue */
    {
        P → rear = P → front==0;    /* rear and front will point to
                                       the same element */
        P → data[P → rear] = x;
    }
    else
    {
        P → rear = (P → rear + 1)% MAX;   /* Advance P in
                                             circular array */
        P → data[P → rear] = x;
    }
}
```

```
int dequeue(queue *P)
{
        int x;
```

```
        x = P → data[P → front];
        if(P → rear == P → front)   /* deleted the last element*/

            initialize(P);
        else
            P → front =(P → front + 1)% MAX;
        /* front advances to the next position in circular array */
        return(x);
}
```

```
void print(queue *P)
{
   int i;
   i = P → front;
   while(i ! = P → rear)
   {
        printf("\n%d", P → data[i]);
        i = (i + 1) %MAX;
   }
   printf("\n%d", P → data[P → rear]);
}
```

Example 5.3.1 : Explain with suitable diagram queue full and queue empty condition for circular queue   W - 09

Solution :

When the queue becomes full, there will be no space ahead of rear end in the circular array. Hence, front will be found immediately ahead of rear in the queue that is full. The Fig. 5.3.4 shows that the queue is full. The queue full condition is given by :

(rear + 1)% MAX == front, where MAX is the size of the array.

Queue empty condition is shown in Fig. Ex. 5.3.1.

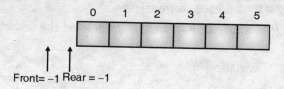

Front= -1 Rear = -1

Fig. Ex. 5.3.1 : Queue empty condition

When the queue is empty, both rear and front will be equal to -1.

> **Program 5.3.1 : Program showing various operations on a circular queue.**

```c
#include <stdio.h>
#include <conio.h>
#define MAX 30
typedef struct queue
{
    int data[MAX];
    int rear, front;
} queue;
void initialize (queue *p);
int empty (queue *p);
int full (queue *p);
void enqueue (queue *p, int x);
int dequeue (queue *p);
void print (queue *p);

void main ( )
{
    int x, op, n;
    queue q;
    initialize (&q);
    do
    {
        printf ("\n1)create \n2)insert \n3)delete \n4)print
            \n5)Quit");
        printf("\n enter your choice :");
```

```
        scanf ("%d", &op);
        switch(op)
        { case 1 : printf("\n enter no. of elements :");
                scanf("%d", &n);
                initialize (&q);
                printf("\n enter the data :");
                for(i =0; i < n; i++)
                {
                        scanf("%d", &x);
                        if (full(&q))
                        {
                            printf("\n queue is full ...");
                            exit(0);
                        }
                        enqueue (&q, x);
                }
                break;
        case 2 : printf("\n enter the element to be inserted :");
                scanf("%d", &x);
                if (full(&q))
                {
                        printf("\n queue is full ...");
                        exit(0);
                }
                enqueue (&q, x);
                break;
        case 3 : if (empty(&q))
                {
                        printf("\n queue is empty ...");
                        exit (0);
                }
                x = dequeue (&q);
                printf("\n element =%d", x);
                break;
```

```
        case 4 : print (&q);
                  break;
        default : break;
        }
   }while (op! = 5);
}
void initialize(queue *P)
{
   P → rear = − 1;
   P → front = −1;
}
int empty(queue *P)
{
   if(P → rear == − 1)
        return(1);
   return(0);
}
int full(queue *P)
{
   if((P → rear + 1)% MAX == P → front)
        return(1);
   return(0);
}
void enqueue(queue *P, int x)
{
   if(empty(P))                        /* empty queue */
   {
        P → rear = P → front==0;    /* rear and front will point to
                                        the same element */
        P → data[P → rear] = x;
   }
   else
   {
```

```
          P → rear = (P → rear + 1)% MAX;        /* Advance P in the
                                                    circular array */

          P → data[P → rear] = x;
    }
}
int dequeue(queue *P)
{
          int x;
          x = P → data[P → front];
          if(P → rear == P → front)  /* deleted the last element */
              initialize(P);
          else
              P → front =(P → front + 1)% MAX;
          /* front advances to the next position in the circular
          array */
          return(x);
}
void print(queue *P)
{
    int i;
    i = P → front;
    while(i != P → rear)
    {
          printf("\n%d", P → data[i]);
          i = (i + 1) %MAX;
    }
    printf("\n%d", P → data[P → rear]);
}
```

5.4 Dequeues

> **Q.** Write a procedure to insert an element into a queue and to delete an element from a queue. Also explain DEQUES.
>
> **S - 09**

The word **dequeue** is a short form of double ended queue. It is general representation of both stack and queue and can be used as stack and queue. In a dequeue, insertion as well deletion can be carried out either at the rear end or the front end. In practice, it becomes necessary to fix the type of operation to be performed on front and rear end. Dequeue can be classified into two types :

Input restricted dequeue :

The following operations are possible in an input restricted dequeue :

(i)　Insertion of an element at the rear and

(ii)　Deletion of an element from front end

(iii)　Deletion of an element from rear end

Output restricted dequeue :

The following operations are possible in an output restricted dequeue.

(i)　Deletion of an element from front end

(ii)　Insert ion of an element at the rear end

(iii)　Insertion of an element at the front end

There are various methods to implement a dequeue.

(a)　Using a circular array

(b)　Using a singly linked list.

(c)　Using a singly circular linked list.

(d)　Using a doubly linked list.

(e)　Using a doubly circular linked list.

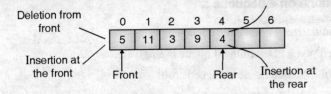

Fig. 5.4.1 : A dequeue in a circular array

Operations associated with dequeue :

(a)　empty( ) : Whether the queue is empty ?

(b)　full( ) : Whether the queue is full ?

(c)　initialize( ) : Make the queue empty

(d)　enqueueR( ) : Add item at the rear end of the queue.

(e)　enqueueF( ) : Add item at the front end of the queue.

(f)　dequeueR( ) : Delete item from the rear end of the queue.

(g)　dequeueF( ) : Delete item from the front end of the queue.

Timing complexity of various dequeue operations :

enqueue R( ) – 0(1) – constant time.

enqueue F( ) – 0(1) – constant time.

dequeue R( ) – 0(1) – constant time.

dequeue F( ) – 0(1) – constant time.

Advantage of dequeue : The dequeue is a general representation of both stack and queue it can be used both as stack or a queue.

Dequeue as an ADT :

Data type for dequeue in an array

```
#define MAX 30 /* A queue with maximum of 30 elements */
typedef struct DQ
{
    int data [MAX];
    int rear, front;
} DQ;
```

Operations on a dequeue :

i)　　initialize( ) : Make the queue empty.

ii)　　empty( ) : Determine if queue is empty.

iii)　　full( ) : Determine if queue is full.

iv)　　enqueueF( ) : Insert an element at the front end of the queue.

v)　　enqueueR( ) : Insert an element at the rear end of the queue.

vi)　　dequeueR( ) : Delete the rear element.

vii)　　dequeueF( ) : Delete the front element.

viii)　　print( ) : Print elements of the queue.

Prototype of functions used for various operations on queue :

- void intialize (DQ *p);

- int empty (DQ *p);

  function returns 1 or 0, depending on whether the queue pointed by p is empty or not.

- int full (DQ *p);

  Function returns 1 or 0, depending on whether the queue pointed by p is full or not.

- void enqueueF (DQ *p, int x);

- void enqueueR (DQ *p, int x);

- int deleteR (DQ *p);

- int deleteF (DQ *p);

- void print (DQ *p);

  enqueueR( ) and enqueueF( ) will cause an overflow if the queue is full.

  dequeueR( ) and dequeueF( ) will cause an underflow if the queue is empty.

5.4.1　Implementation of Dequeue using a Circular Array :

Expression for clock-wise movement :

rear = (rear +1) % MAX where MAX is the size of the array.

front = (front +1) % MAX

Expression for anti-clockwise movement :

rear = (rear −1 + MAX) % MAX

front = (front −1 + MAX) % MAX

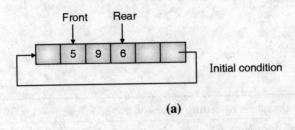

Initial condition

(a)

Insert 2 at Rear end
[rear moves ahead
in clock - wise direction]

(b)

deletion of the front
element
[front moves ahead
in clock - wise direction]

(c)

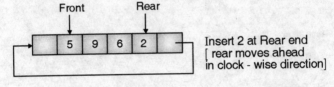

Insert 5 at front
end
[front moves in anti
clock - wise direction]

(d)

Deletion of the rear
element
[from moves in anti
clock - wise direction]

(e)

Fig. 5.4.2 : Various operations on dequeue and movement of front and rear in clock-wise or anti-clockwise direction

> ### 'C' functions for various operations on a dequeue represented using a circular array.

A dequeue can be represented using the following data type.

```c
typedef struct dequeue
{
    int data[MAX];
    int front, rear;
} dequeue;
```

(1) Initialize the queue by setting values of rear and front as -1.

```c
void initialize(dequeue *P)
{
    P → rear = -1;
    P → front = -1;
}
```

(2) Test, whether the dequeue is empty ?

```c
int empty(dequeue *P)
{
    if(P → rear == -1)
        return(1);
    return(0);
}
```

(3) Test, whether the dequeue is full ?

```c
int full(dequeue *P)
{
    if((P → rear + 1) % MAX ==P → front)
        return(1);
    return(0);
}
```

(4) Add item at the rear end of the dequeue.

```c
void enqueueR(dequeue *P, int x)
{
    if(empty(P))
```

```
    {
        P → rear = 0;
        P → front = 0;
        P → data[0] = x;
    }
    else
    {
        P → rear =(P → rear + 1) % MAX;
        P → data[p → rear] = x;
    }
}
```

(5)   Add item at the front end of the dequeue : on addition of item at the
      front end, front will move in anti-clockwise direction.

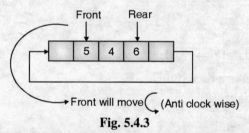

Fig. 5.4.3

```
void enqueueF(dequeue *P, int x)
{
        if(empty(P))
        {
            P → rear = 0;
            P → front = 0;
            P → data[0] = x;
        }
        else
        {
            P → front = (P → front – 1 + MAX) % MAX;
            P → data[P → front] = x;
        }
}
```

6)   Delete an item from the front end of the dequeue :

```
int dequeueF(dequeue *P)
{
   int x;
   x = P → data[P → front];
   if(P → rear == P → front)     /* delete the last element */
         initialize(P);
   else
         P → front =(P → front + 1) % MAX;
   return(x);
}
```

7)   Delete an item from the rear end of the dequeue :

```
int dequeueR(dequeue *P)
{
   int x;
   x = P → data[P → rear];
   if(P → rear == P → front)
         initialize(P)
   else
         P → rear =(P → rear – 1 + MAX) % MAX;
   return(x);
}
```

> **Program 5.4.1 : A program showing various operations
> on a dequeue represented using a
> circular queue.**

```
#include <stdio.h>
#include <conio.h>
#define MAX 30
typedef struct dequeue
   {    int data [MAX];
        int rear, front;
   } dequeue;
```

```
void initialize (dequeue *p);
int empty (dequeue *p);
int full (dequeue *p);
void enqueueR (dequeue *p, int x);
void enqueueF (dequeue *p, int x);
int dequeueF (dequeue *p);
int dequeueR (dequeue *p);
int print (dequeue *p);
void main( )
{
    int x, op, n;
    dequeue q;
    initialize (&q);
    do
    {
    printf("\n1)create\n2)insert(rear)\n3)insert(front)\n4)Delete
            (rear)\n5)Delete(front)");
    printf("\n6)print\n7)Quit");
    printf("\n enter your choice :");
    scanf("%d", &op);
    switch (op)
    {
            case 1 :   printf("\n enter no. of elements :");
                        scanf("%d", &n);
                        initialize(&q);
                        printf("\n enter the data :");
                        for (i = 0; i< n; i++)
                    {
                        scanf("%d", &x);
                        if (full(&q))
                        {
                                printf("\n queue is full ...");
                                exit (0);
                        }
```

```
                    enqueueR(&q, x);
                }
                break;
            case 2 : printf("\n enter element to be
                        inserted:");
                scanf("%d", &x);
                if (full (&q))
                {
                    printf("\n queue is full ...");
                    exit(0);
                }
                enqueR(&q, x);
                break;
            case 3 : printf ("\n enter the elment to be
                        inserted :");
                scanf("%d", &x);
                if (full (&q))
                {
                    printf("\n queue is full ...");
                    exit(0);
                }
                enqueueF(&q, x);
                break;
        case 4 : if (empty(&q))
                {
                    printf("\n queue is empty ...");
                    exit(0);
                }
            x = deleteR(&q);
            printf("\n element = %d", x);
            break;
        case 5 : if (empty (&q))
                {
                    printf("\n queue is empty ...");
                    exit(0);
```

```
                                    }
                                    x = deleteF(&q);
                                    printf("\n element=%d", x);
                                    break;
                        case 6 : printf(&q); break;
                        default : break;
    }while (op! = 7);
}
void initialize(dequeue *P)
{
    P → rear = -1;
    P → front = -1;
}
int empty(dequeue *P)
{
    if(P → rear == -1)
        return(1);
    return(0);
}
int full(dequeue *P)
{
    if((P → rear + 1) % MAX ==P → front)
        return(1);
    return(0);
}
void enqueueR(dequeue *P, int x)
{
    if(empty(P))
    {
        P → rear = 0;
        P → front = 0;
        P → data[0] = x;
    }
    else
```

```
    {
        P → rear =(P → rear + 1) % MAX;
        P → data[p → rear] = x;
    }
}
void enqueueF(dequeue *P, int x)
{
    if(empty(P))
    {
        P → rear = 0;
        P → front = 0;
        P → data[0] = x;
    }
    else
    {
        P → front = (P → front – 1 + MAX) % MAX;
        P → data[P → front] = x;
    }
}
int dequeueF(dequeue *P)
{
    int x;
    x = P → data[P → front];
    if(P → rear == P → front)      /* delete the last element */
        initialize(P);
    else
        P → front =(P → front + 1) % MAX;
    return(x);
}
int dequeueR(dequeue *P)
{
    int x;
    x = P → data[P → rear];
    if(P → rear == P → front)
```

```
            initialize(P);
     else
            P → rear =(P → rear – 1 + MAX) % MAX;
     return(x);
}
void print (dequeue *p)
{  int i;
   i = p → front;
   while (i! = p → rear)
   {      printf("\n%d", p → data[i]);
          i = (i + 1)% MAX;
   }
printf("\n%d", p → data [p → rear]);
}
```

5.5 Priority Queue

Q. Define Priority Queue. Describe the one-way list representation of a Priority Queue with suitable example and diagram. **W - 08**

Priority queue is an ordered list of homogeneous elements. In a normal queue, service is provided on the basis of First-in-first-out. In a priority queue service is not provided on the basis of "first-come-first-served" but rather than each element has a priority based on the urgency of need.

• An element with higher priority is processed before other elements with lower priority.

• Elements with the same priority are processed on "first-come-first served" basis.

An example of priority queue is a hospital waiting room. A patient having a more fatal problem will be admitted before other patients.

Other applications of priority queues is found in long term scheduling of jobs processed in a computer. In practice, short processes are given a priority over long processes as it improves the average response of the system.

5.5.1　Implementation of Priority Queues :

Priority queue can be implemented using a circular array :

As the service must be provided to an element having highest priority, there could be a choice between :

(a)　List is always maintained sorted on priority of elements with the highest priority element at the front. Here, deletion is trivial but insertion is complicated as the element must be inserted at the correct place depending on its priority.

(b)　List is maintained in the "FIFO" form but the service is provided by selecting the element with highest priority. Deletion is difficult as the entire queue must be traversed to locate the element with highest priority. Here, insertion is trivial (at rear end).

Implementation of a Priority Queue using a circular array (Priority queue as an ADT) :

Data type for priority queue in a circular array :

define MAX 30 /* A queue with maximum of 30 elements */

typedef struct pqueue

{ int data [MAX];

　int front, rear;

} pqueue;

Operations on a priority queue :

i)　initialize( ) : Make the queue empty.

ii)　empty( ) : Determine if the queue is empty.

iii)　full( ) : Determine if the queue is full.

iv)　enqueue( ) : Insert an element as per its priority.

v)　dequeue( ) : Delete the front element (front element will have the highest priority.

vi)　print( ) : Print elements of the queue.

Prototype of functions used for various operations on the queue

●　void initialize(pqueue *p);

●　int empty(pqueue *p);

●　int full(pqueue *p);

- void enqueue(pqueue *p, int x);
- int dequeue(pqueue *p);
- void print(pqueue *p);

enqueue( ) operation will cause an overflow if the queue is full.

Dequeue( ) operation will cause an underflow if the queue is empty.

C-implementation of functions :

```
void initialize (pqueue *p)
{  p → rear = - 1;
   p → front = - 1;
}
```
A value of rear or front as -1, indicates that the queue is empty.
```
int empty (pqueue *p)
{ if (P->rear == - 1)
        return (1);        /* queue is empty */
   return (0); /* queue is not empty */
}
int full (pqueue *p)
{ /* if front is next to rear in the circular array then the queue is
full */
    if (p → rear + 1)% MAX == p → front)
        return (1); /* queue is full */
   return (0);
}
void enqueue (pqueue *p, int x)
{ int i;
   if (full(p))
        printf("\n overflow ...");
   else
   {      /* inserting in an empty queue */
        if (empty(p))
            {    p → rear = p → front = 0;
                 p → data [0] = x;
            }
```

```
        else
        {
        /* move all lower priority data right by one place */
i = p → rear ;
while (x > p → data [i])
{      p → data [(i + 1)%MAX] = p → data [i];
        /* position i on the previous element */
        i = (i – 1 + MAX) % MAX; /* anticlockwise movement
                            inside the queue */
        if ((i + 1)% MAX = = p → front)
            break; /* if all elements have been moved */
}
/* insert x */
        i = (i + 1)% MAX;
        p → data [i] = x;
/* re-adjust rear */
    p → rear = (p → rear + 1) % MAX;
}
}
}
int dequeue (pqueue *p)
{  int x;
   if (empty (p))
            printf("\n underflow ...");
        else
        {   x = p → data [p → front];
            if (p → rear = = p → front) /* delete last element */
                initialize (p);
            else
                p → front = (p → front + 1) % MAX;
        }
   return (x);
   }
void print (pqueue *p)
```

```
{  int i, x;
    i = p → front;
   while ( i! = p → rear)
   {      x = p data [i];
          printf ("\n%d", x);
          i = (i + 1) % MAX;
   }
   /* print the last data */
          x = p → data [i];
          printf ("\n%d", x);
   }
```

> **Program 5.5.1 : Program showing various operations on a priority queue.**

```
#include <stdio.h>
#include <conio.h>
#define MAX 30
typedef struct pqueue
{  int data [MAX];
   int rear, front;
} pqueuel
void initialize(pqueue *p);
int empty(pqueue *p);
int full(pqueue *p);
void enqueue(pqueue *p, int x);
int dequeue(pqueue *p);
void print(pqueue *p);
void main( )
{ int x, op, n;
  pqueue q;
  initialize (&q);
do
{
    printf("\n1)create\n2)insert\n3)Delete\n4)print\n5)Quit");
```

```
    printf("\n enter your choice:");
    scanf ("%d", &op);
    switch (op)
    {
    case 1 : printf("\n enter no. of elements :");
             scanf("%d", &n);
             initialize (&q);
             printf("enter the data:");
             for (i = 0; i < n; i++)
             {
                scanf ("%d" &x);
                if (full (&q))
                {       printf("\n queue is full ...");
                        exit(0);
                }
                enqueue (&q, x);
             }
             break;
    case 2 : printf("\n enter the element to be inserted");
             scanf ("%d", &x);
             if (full(&q))
             {
                printf("\n queue is full ...");
                exit(0);
             }
             enqueue (&q, x);
             break;
             case 3 : if (empty (&q))
             {
                     printf("\n queue is empty ...");
                     exit(0);
             }
          x = dequeue (&q);
         printf("\n element = %d", x);
```

```
                break;
            case 4 : print(&q);
                break;
            default : break;
            }
    } while (op! = 5);
}
void initialize (pqueue *p)
{   p → rear = - 1;
    p → front = - 1;
}
/* A value of rear or front as -1, indicate that the queue is empty.
*/
int empty (pqueue *p)
{ if (p->rear == - 1)
            return (1);        /* queue is empty */
    return (0);                /* queue is not empty */
}
int full (pqueue *p)
{ /* if front is next rear in the circular array then the queue is full
*/
    if (p → rear + 1)% MAX == p → front)
            return (1); /* queue is full */
    return (0);
}
void enqueue (pqueue *p, int x)
{ int i;
    if (full (p))
            printf("\n overflow ...");
    else
    {       /* inserting in an empty queue */
            if (empty (p))
                {       p → rear = p → front = 0
                        p → data [0] = x;
```

```
                }
            else
            {
            /* move all lower priority data right by one place */
    i = p → rear ;
    while (x > p → data [i])
    {       p → data [(i + 1)%MAX] = p → data [i];
            /* position i on the previous element */
            i = (i – 1 + MAX) % MAX; /* anticlockwise movement
                                       inside the queue */
            if ((i + 1)% MAX = = p → front)
                break; /* if all elements have been moved */
    }
    /* insert x */
        i = (i + 1)% MAX;
        p → data [i] = x;
    /* re-adjust rear */
      p → rear = (p → rear + 1) % MAX;
    }
  }
}
int dequeue (pqueue *p)
{ int x;
  if (empty (p))
            printf("\n underflow ...");
    else
        {   x = p → data [p → front];
            if (p → rear = = p → front) /* delete last element */
                initialize (p);
            else
                p → front = (p → front + 1) % MAX;
        }
    return (x);
  }
```

```
void print (pqueue *p)
{  int i, x;
   i = p → front;
   while ( i! = p → rear)
   {     x = p data[i];
         printf ("\n%d", x);
         i = (i + 1) % MAX;
   }
   /* print the last data */
         x = p → data[i];
         printf ("\n%d", x);
}
```

5.6 Applications of Queue

Queue is a very useful data structure. Various features of operating system are implemented using a queue.

a)   Scheduling of processes (Round Robin Algorithm)

b)   Spooling (to maintain a queue of jobs to be printed)

c)   A queue of client processes waiting to receive the service from the server process.

d)   Various application software using non-linear data structure tree or graph requires a queue for breadth first traversal.

e)   Simulation of a real life problem with the purpose of understanding its behaviour. The probable waiting time of a person at a railway reservation counter can be found through the technique of computer simulation if the following concerned factors are known :

   1)   Arrival rate

   2)   Service time

   3)   Number of service counters.

   We will discuss some of the applications in detail :

   1)   Josephus problem

   2)   Job scheduling

   3)   Queue simulation.

5.6.1 Josephus Problem :

This is an interesting programming problem known in the literature as Josephus problem. The problem is given as :

- Suppose there are n children standing in a queue.
- Students are numbered from 1 to n in the clockwise direction.
- Students choose a lucky number say m.

They start counting in clock-wise direction from the child designated as 1. The counting proceeds until the mth child is identified. m^{th} child is eliminated from the queue. Counting for the next round begins from the child next to the eliminated one and proceeds until the mth child is identified. This child is then eliminated and the process continues. After few rounds of counting only one child is left and this child is declared as winner.

Implementation :

It is required to write a program to identify a winner of the game. Input to the function are two parameters.

> n : number of children
>
> m : lucky number

Function returns an integer identifying the winner.

```
int winner(int m,int n)
{
   queue q;
   int i;
   init(&q);
        /*create a queue of n integers, numbered from 1 to n.
   Number i stands for i^th child*/
   for(i=1;i<=n;i++)
        enqueue(&q,i);
   for(j=1;j<n;j++) /*n-1 iterations to eliminate n-1 children*/
        {
        for(i=1;i<m;i++) /* skip m-1 children*/
        {
            x=dequeue(&q);
            enqueue(&q,x);
        }
        x=dequeue(&q); /* remove m'th children*/
```

```
}
  x=dequeue(&q); /*last child winner*/
  return(x);
}
```

5.6.2 Job Scheduling :

Programs(jobs) entering a computer for execution are scheduled using some strategies. The purpose is to improve :

i)   CPU utilization

ii) Response time

iii) System utilization

The jobs entering the system are stored in the queue. These jobs can be selected for execution as per some pre-conceived strategy.

We will discuss one of the scheduling methods.

Round Robin technique :

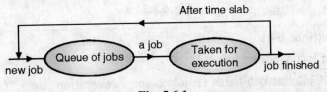

Fig. 5.6.1

Suppose there are n jobs waiting for execution. In Round Robin technique, CPU gives a fixed quantum of time to each job.

- A job is selected from the queue of jobs.

- It is executed for a fixed quantum of time. If the job is not completed by this time then it is removed and pushed back in queue of jobs.

Let us try to understand it with the help of an example.

The table below shows the jobs and the required run time.

Job no.	Run time
1	2 units
2	1 unit
3	2 units

Quantum of time

= 1 unit

Initial status of queue :

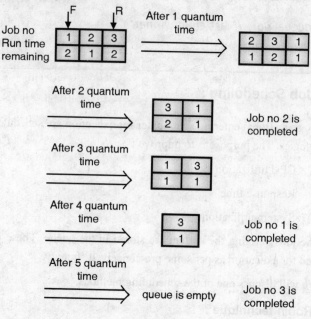

Fig. 5.6.2

```
void RR(Queue q)
{  /* q is a queue of jobs */
/* each job has two fields :1. jobno and 2. execution  time */
job t;
int quantum = 1; int time = 0;
while (! empty (q))
   {      t = dequeue (q);
          time = time + quantum;
          t.execution_time -=quantum;
          if (t.execution_time > 0)
              enqueue (q, t);
          else
              print t.jobno, time;
   }
}
```

5.6.3　Queue Simulation :

Queuing system deals with computing probabilistically, how long users expect to wait on a line, how long the line gets. Waiting time and length of queue depends on :

　　　　1)　Arrival rate of users　　　　2)　Service time.

These parameters are given as probabilistic distribution function. We might be interested in finding how long on average a customer has to wait.

Computer can be used to simulate the behavior of a queue. A bank can utilize this information to determine how many cash counters are needed to ensure reasonable service time.

A typical queue simulation involves processing of events :

　　　　1)　Customer arriving　　　　2)　Customer departing

On arrival, a customer joins the queue and on departure he leaves the queue.

We can use the probabilistic function to generate a stream of ordered pairs. Each pair consists of :

　　　　1)　arrival time　　　2)　service time.

These pairs are enqueued. A simulated clock can be used to give the concept of time. At each tick of the clock, all pending events are processed.

If the event is arrival, we check to see if a cash counter is free. If there is none, we place the arrival on the queue.

The waiting line of customers can be implemented as a queue. A cash counter can be implemented as a shared resource. Whenever the cash counter becomes free, a customer from the queue can be assigned to the shared resource (cash counter).

5.7　MSBTE Questions and Answers

Summer 2008 – Total Marks 14

Q. 1　　Also explain any four terms in Queue. **(Section 5.2)**　　　**(2 Marks)**

Q. 2　　Write a menu driven program in 'C' language for Queue having menus : Store , Retrieve and display Queue.

　　　　(Program 5.2.1)　　　　　　　　　　　　　　　　　**(8 Marks)**

Q. 3   With suitable diagram, explain the principle of circular Queue.

(Section 5.3)   **(4 Marks)**

Winter 2008 – Total Marks 12

Q. 4   Define Priority Queue. Describe the one-way list representation of a
           priority Queue with suitable example and diagram.

(Section 5.5)   **(8 Marks)**

Q. 5   Draw and explain Circular Queue in detail. **(Section 5.3)**   **(4 Marks)**

Summer 2009 – Total Marks 10

Q. 6   Describe priority queues. **(Section 5.5)**   **(2 Marks)**

Q. 7   Write a procedure to insert an element into a queue and to delete an
           element from a queue. Also explain DEQUES.

(Sections 5.2 and 5.4)   **(8 Marks)**

Winter 2009 – Total Marks 10

Q. 8   State any two application of Queue. **(Section 5.1.1)**   **(2 Marks)**

Q. 9   Distinguish between STACK and QUEUE. **(Section 5.1.4)**   **(4 Marks)**

Q. 10   Explain with suitable diagram queue full and queue empty condition
           for circular queue. **(Example 5.3.1)**   **(4 Marks)**

Summer 2010 – Total Marks 16

Q. 11   Explain queue as an abstract data type. **(Section 5.2.1)**   **(4 Marks)**

Q. 12   Write the procedure for inserting and deleting an clement from queue.

(Section 5.2)   **(6 Marks)**

Q. 13   Define circular queue. Also explain advantage of circular queue over
           linear queue with example. **(Section 5.3)**   **(6 Marks)**

□□□

Linked List

Syllabus

Introduction

Terminology : Node, Address, Pointer, Information, Next, Null Pointer, Empty list etc.

Operations on list : searching, Insertion and deletion

Types of Linked lists : Linear list, Circular Linked list, Doubly Linked list,

Array, Stacks, Queues implementation using Linked list

Statistical Analysis

Year	Marks
Summer - 2008	12 Marks
Winter - 2008	12 Marks
Summer - 2009	12 Marks
Winter - 2009	18 Marks
Summer - 2010	14 Marks

6.1 Representation and Implementation of Singly Linked Lists

6.1.1 Comparison between Array and Linked Lists :

Array data structure is simple to use and it is supported by almost all programming languages. It is very simple to understand and time to access any element from an array is constant

- Simple to use

- Simple to define

- Constant access time

- Mapping by compiler

Properties of array data structure

An array element can be accessed by a[i], where a is the name of the array and i is the index.

Compiler maps a[i] to its physical location in memory. Address of a[i] is given by starting address of a + i* size of array element in bytes. This mapping is carried out in constant time, irrespective of which element is accessed. Array data structure suffers from some severe limitations :

- Size of an array is defined at the time of programming.
- Insertion and deletion is time consuming.
- Requires contiguous memory.

First, the size of an array has to be defined when the program is being written and its space is calculated during compilation of the program. This means that the programmer has to take a decision regarding the maximum size of data. If the actual amount of data stored is less than the maximum size, a good amount of memory will be wasted and on the other hand a larger sample of data can not be handled. To avoid the linear cost of insertion and deletion, we need to ensure that the list is not stored contiguously, since otherwise entire parts of list will need to be moved.

Advantages of linked lists :

i) Linked list is an example of dynamic data structure. They can grow and shrink during execution of the program.

ii) Representation of linear data structure. (linear data like polynomial, stack and queue can easily be represented using linked list.

iii)   Efficient memory utilization. Memory is not pre-allocated like static
        data structure. Memory is allocated as per the need. Memory is
        deallocated when it is no longer needed.

iv)   Insertion and deletions are easier and efficient. Insertion and deletion
        of a given data can be carried out in constant time.

6.1.2 Representation :

> **Q.**   What is linked list ? Explain how insertion and deletion can be
>   performed on linked list.   **W - 09**

The linked list consists of a series of structures. They are not required
to be stored in adjacent memory locations. Each structure consists of a data
field and address field. Address field contains the address of its successors.
Fig. 6.1.1 shows the actual representation of the structure.

Data	Address

Fig. 6.1.1 : Representation of the structure

A variable of the above structure type is conventionally known as a
node. Fig. 6.1.2 gives a representation of a linked list of three nodes.

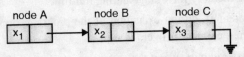

Fig. 6.1.2 : Linked list

A list consisting of three data x_1, x_2, x_3 is represented using a linked
list. Node A stores the data x_1 and the address of the successor (next) node B.
Node B stores the data x_2 and the address of its successor node C. Node C
contains the data x_3 and its address field is grounded (NULL pointer),
indicating it does not have a successor.

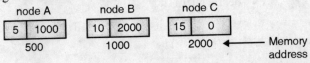

Fig. 6.1.3 : Memory representation of a linked list

Fig. 6.1.3 gives a memory representation of the linked list shown in
Fig. 6.1.2. Nodes A, B and C happen to reside at memory locations 500,
1000 and 2000 respectively. $x_1 = 5$, $x_2 = 10$ and $x_3 = 15$. Node A resides at

the memory location 500, its data field contains a value 5 and its address field contains 1000, which is the address of its successor node. Address field of node C contains 0 as it has no successor.

6.1.3 Implementation :

Structures in "C" can be used to define a node. Address of the successor node can be stored in a pointer type variable.

typedef struct node

{

        int data;

        struct node *next;

}node;

It is a **self referential structure** in "C". It is assumed that the type of data to be stored in each node is predefined to be of integer type. Next field of the structure is a pointer type variable, used for storing address of its successor node. Nodes are manipulated during run-time. A programming language must provide following facilities for run time manipulation of nodes.

- Acquiring memory for storage during run-time.
- Freeing memory during execution of the program, once the need for the acquired memory is over.

In "C" programming language, memory can be acquired through the use of standard library functions malloc( ) and calloc( ). Memory acquired during runtime can be freed through the use of library function free( ).

/* 1 */   node *P;

/* 2 */   P = (node *) malloc(sizeof(node));

/* 3 */   P $\rightarrow$ data = 5;

/* 4 */   P $\rightarrow$ next = NULL

P
↓

| 5 | NULL |

Fig. 6.1.4 : Memory for a node has been allocated during run-time. Its address is stored in the pointer P

In the program segment above, the line 1 declares a variable P with the storage class node *. It can store the address of a node that has been created dynamically. sizeof(node) in line 2 is storage requirement in number of bytes to store a node. malloc(sizeof(node)) returns the address of the allocated memory block and it is assigned to variable P. The address returned by malloc(sizeof(node)) is type casted using type casting operator(node *) before assigning it to the pointer P.

P $\rightarrow$ data = 5, in line 3 stores a value of 5 in the data field of node whose address is stored in pointer P. P $\rightarrow$ next = NULL stores a value of NULL in the next field of the node whose address is stored in the pointer P.

A linked list with the address of the starting node :

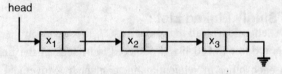

Fig. 6.1.5 : A linked list with the address of the head node

As an array is referenced by its starting address, a linked list is known by the address of its starting node. Address of the starting node is stored in a pointer variable (node * head) head. All manipulations on the linked list can be performed through the address of the starting node. Through the variable "head", first node can be accessed and through the address of the second node stored in the next field of the first node, second node can be accessed and so on.

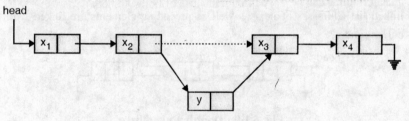

Fig. 6.1.6 : Insertion into a linked list

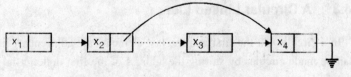

Fig. 6.1.7 : Deletion from a linked list

Insertion into a linked list requires obtaining a new node and then changing values of two pointers. The general idea is shown in Fig. 6.1.6. The dashed line represents the old pointer. It is changed to point to new node. Deletion of a node can be performed in one pointer change. Fig. 6.1.7 shows the result of deleting the node containing x_3. The next field of the node containing x_2 is changed to point to the node containing x_4. Node containing x_3 is freed using the library function free( ) subsequently.

6.1.4 Types of Linked List :

> **Q.** List types of linked list and state the operations performed on linked list.   **S - 08**

6.1.4.1 Singly Linked List :

In this type of linked list two successive nodes of the linked list are linked with each other in sequential linear manner. Movement in forward direction is possible.

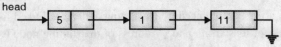

Fig. 6.1.8 : Singly linked list

6.1.4.2 Doubly Linked List :

In this type of linked list each node holds two-pointer fields. In doubly linked list addresses of next as well as preceding elements are linked with current node.

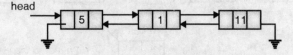

Fig. 6.1.9 : Doubly linked list

6.1.4.3 A Circular Linked List :

In a circular list the first and the last elements are adjacent. A linked list can be made circular by storing the address of the first node in the next field of the last node.

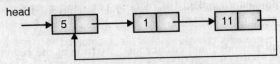

Fig. 6.1.10 : Circular linked list

Example 6.1.1 : With diagram, define Two-way header list.   W - 08

Solution :

The diagram of a two-way header list is shown below.

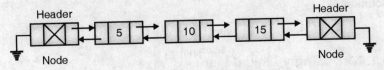

Fig. Ex. 6.1.1

A two-way header list is a doubly linked list with two header nodes, one at the beginning and other at the end. This list can be traversed easily in both forward and backward direction.

Example 6.1.2 : compare grounded header list and circular header list with diagram.   W - 08

Solution :

A grounded header list is shown below.

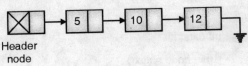

Fig. Ex. 6.1.2(a)

A circular header list is shown below :

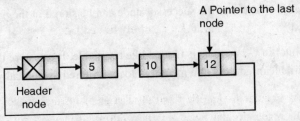

Fig. Ex. 6.1.2(b)

In a circular header list, the last node is converted back to the first node.

- In both grounded and circular list, insertion at the beginning can be carried out in constant time. Timing complexity = O(1).

- In a circular list, insertion at the end can be carried out in constant time. In a grounded list, insertion at the end is time consuming with timing complexity of O(n).

Example 6.1.3 : Define NULL pointer and empty list.　　　　　S - 09

Solution :

A NULL pointer is a pointer containing O address.

$$P = NULL;$$

The above statement will set the pointer to NULL or O address.

An empty list has no elements in it.

$$L = (), \text{represents an empty list}$$

Example 6.1.4 : Define node and pointer.　　　　　W - 09

Solution :

A node is a self reperential structure. Strucutres in "C" can be used to define a node.

```
typedef struct node
    {
        int data;
        struct node * next;
    } node;
```

'data' field stores the data. For each data element, a node is acquird dynamically. Address of the successor node can be stored in the pointer type field "next".

Pointer in C-language is treated like a variable. It can store the address of any variable or address of a memory block, acquired dynamically.

6.2 Basic Linked List Operations

Q. List types of linked list and state the operations performed on linked list.　　　　　S - 08

We can treat a linked list as an abstract data type and perform following basic operations.

1. Creating a linked list.
2. Traversing the linked list.
3. Printing the link list.
4. Counting the nodes in the linked list.
5. Searching an item in the linked list.
6. Inserting an item.
7. Deleting an item.
8. Concatenating two lists.
9. Inversion.
10. Sorting of elements stored in a linked list.
11. Merging of two sorted linked list.
12. Separating a linked list in two linked lists.

6.2.1　Creating a Linked List :

➢　**Program 6.2.1 : Program to create linked list.**

```
#include<conio.h>
#include<stdio.h>
typedef struct node
{
   int data;
   struct node *next;
}node;
void main()
{
   node *HEAD,*P;
   int n,x,i;
   //no. of items to be inserted
   printf("\n no. of items :");
   scanf("%d",&n);
```

```
//get the 1st node with its address in HEAD
HEAD=(node*)malloc(sizeof(node));
//read the data in 1st node
scanf("%d",&(HEAD->data));
HEAD->next=NULL;
//HEAD points to the 1st node,while P points to the last node
P=HEAD; //in case of single node 1st and last node are same
//insert the remaining nodes
for(i=1;i<n;i++)
{
     P->next=(node*)malloc(sizeof(node));
     //new node is inserted as the next node after P
     P=P->next;
     P->next=NULL;
     scanf("%d",&(P->data));
}
}
```

Let us trace the working of the above program manually. Assume n = 3 (3 nodes to be created) with inputs as 5, 1, 9.

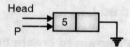

Fig. 6.2.1 : The linked list after insertion of the first item

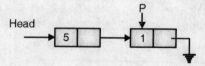

Fig. 6.2.2 : The linked list after first iteration of the "for" loop

The address of the newly acquired node is stored in the next field of the node pointed by P. Subsequently, P is moved to the next node.

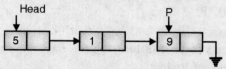

Fig. 6.2.3 : The status of the linked list after insertion of 3 elements

> **Program 6.2.2 : Program to create linked list through 'create' function.**

```
#include<conio.h>
#include<stdio.h>
typedef struct node
{
   int data;
   struct node *next;
}node;
node * create(int);
void main()
{
   node *HEAD;
   int n;
   HEAD = NULL;  //link list is empty
   printf("\n no. of items :");
   scanf("%d",&n);
   HEAD=create(n); //create function returns the address of first
node
}
node * create(int n)
{
   node *head,*P;
   int i;
   head=(node*)malloc(sizeof(node));
   head->next=NULL;
   scanf("%d",&(head->data));
   P=head;
   //insert the remaining nodes
   for(i=1;i<n;i++)
   {
        P->next=(node*)malloc(sizeof(node));
        //new node is inserted as the next node after P
        P=P->next;
```

```
        scanf("%d",&(P->data));
        P->next=NULL;
    }
    return(head);
}
```

6.2.2 Traversing a Linked List :

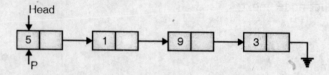

Fig. 6.2.4 : Traversal starts from the first node

Traversal of a linked list always starts from the first node. In order to traverse a linked list in the forward direction, a pointer type variable is assigned the address of the first node.

P = HEAD;

Entire list can be traversed through the following program segment.

P = HEAD;

while(P! = NULL)

    P = P → next; /* next field of the node pointed by P contains the address of the next node */

6.2.3 Counting Number of Nodes in a Linked List through Count Function :

```
int count(node *P)
    {
        int i;
        i = 0;
        while(P ! = NULL)
        {
            i = i + 1;
            P = P → next;
        }
    return(i);
    }
```

> **Program 6.2.3 :** **Program to create linked list interactively and print the list and total number of items in the list.**

```c
#include<conio.h>
#include<stdio.h>
typedef struct node
{
   int data;
   struct node *next;
}node;
node * create(int);
void print(node *);
int count(node *);
void main()
{
   node *HEAD;
   int n,number;
   printf("\n no. of items :");
   scanf("%d",&n);
   HEAD=create(n); //create function returns the address of first
node
   print(HEAD);
   number=count(HEAD);
   printf("\n No of nodes = %d",number);
}
node * create(int n)
{
   node *head,*P;
   int i;
   head=(node*)malloc(sizeof(node));
   head->next=NULL;
   scanf("%d",&(head->data));
   P=head;
   //create subsequent nodes
   for(i=1;i<n;i++)
```

```
    {
            P->next=(node*)malloc(sizeof(node));
            //new node is inserted as the next node after P
            P=P->next;
            scanf("%d",&(P->data));
            P->next=NULL;
    }
    return(head);
}
void print(node *P)
{
    while(P!=NULL)
    {
            printf("<- %d ->",P->data);
            P=P->next;
    }
}
int count(node *P)
{
    int i=0;
    while(P!=NULL)
    {
            P=P->next;
            i++;
    }
    return(i);
}
```

Output

no. of items :4
12
13
14
15

<- 12 -> <- 13 -> <- 14 -> <- 15 ->

No of nodes = 4

6.2.4 Printing a List through Print Function :

```
void print(node *P)
{
    while(P! = NULL)
        {
                printf("\n%d", P → data);
                    P = P → next;
        }
}
```

Above function traverses a linked list and while traversing it prints the integer data stored in the node.

6.2.5 Inserting an Item :

Q.	Write an algorithm to insert new node at the beginning, at middle position and at the end of a single Linked List. **W - 08**
Q.	Write an algorithm to insert new node at the beginning, at middle position and at the end of a single linked list. **S - 09**
Q.	What is linked list ? Explain how insertion and deletion can be performed on linked list. **W - 09**

Inserting a new item, say x, has three situations :

1.   Insertion at the front of the list.
2.   Insertion in the middle of the list.
3.   Insertion at the end of the list.

Algorithm for placing the new item at the beginning of a linked list :

1.   Obtain space for new node.
2.   Assign data to the data field of the new node.
3.   Set the next field of the new node to the beginning of the linked list.
4.   Change the reference pointer of the linked list to point to the new node.

Algorithm for inserting the new data after a node N1 :

1. Obtain space for new node.
2. Assign value to its data field.
3. Search for the node N1.
4. Set the next field of the new node to point to N1 → next.
5. Set the next field of N1 to point to the new node.

➤ **'C' function to insert a data in a linked list after a given data**

```
node *insert(node *head, int x, int key)
{
        /* data x is to be inserted after the key */
/* if key is – 1 then x is to be inserted as a front node */
        node *P, *q;
            /* obtain space for the new node */
        P = (node *) malloc(sizeof(node));
            /* store x in the new node */
        P → data = x;
        if(key = = – 1)
        {
            /* insert the node at the front of the list */
            P → next = head;
            head = P;
        }
        else
        {
            /* search for the key in the linked list */
            q = head;
            while(key! = q → data && q! = NULL)
                    q = q → next;
            if(q ! = NULL)
            {
                    /* if the key is found */
                    P → next = q → next;
```

```
                    q → next = P;
          }
    }
    return(head);
}
```

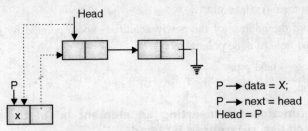

Fig. 6.2.5 : Insertion at the front

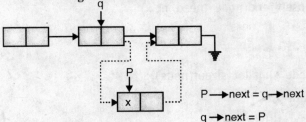

Fig. 6.2.6 : Insertion in between

6.2.5.1   Inserting an Item at the End of a Linked List :

➤   Algorithm :

[Insert an item 'x' in a linked list, referenced by the pointer 'head']

1.   Acquire memory for new node

    i.e   p = (node*) malloc(sizeof (node);

2.   Assign value to the data filed and make its 'next' field 'NULL'

    i.e. $P \rightarrow$ data = x;

        $P \rightarrow$ next = NULL;

3.   If 'head' is 'NULL'

    then

    [head = p ;

goto step 6]

4. Position a pointer q on the last node by traversing the linked list from the first node and until it reaches the last node.

i.e. q = head

while (q $\rightarrow$ next ! = NULL)

q = q $\rightarrow$ next ;

5. Store the address of the newly acquired node, pointed by P, in the next field of node pointed by q.

i.e. q $\rightarrow$ next = p;

6. Stop.

> **'C' function for inserting an element 'x' at the end of linked list, referenced by head.**

```
node *insert_end(node *head,int x)
{
   node *p,*q;
   p=(node *)malloc(sizeof(node));
   p->data=x;
   p->next=NULL;
   if(head==NULL)
        return(p);
   q=head;
   while(q->next!=NULL)
        q=q->next;
   q->next=p;
   return(head);
}
```

6.2.5.2 Inserting a Data 'x' at a Given Location 'LOC' in a Linked List, referenced by 'head' :

> **Algorithm :**

1. Acquire memory for new node with its address in pointer P.

i.e. P = (node *) malloc(sizeof(node));

2. Assign value to data field and make its 'next' field 'NULL'.

i.e. P $\rightarrow$ data =x;

P $\rightarrow$ next = NULL;

3. if (LOC == 1)

then

[insert the node, pointed by P, at the beginning of the linked list. This can be done by following steps.]

(a) Store head in the next field of the node pointed by P

i.e. P $\rightarrow$ next = head;

(b) Move head to the newly connected node.

i.e. head = P;

go to step 7

4. [If Loc > 1]

Position a pointer q on (LOC - 1)th node .

i.e. q = head;

for (i = 1; i < (Loc - 1); i++)

q = q $\rightarrow$ next;

5. if q is NULL

[then report " overflow" and terminate the algorithm.

go to step 7

]

6. Insert the node pointed by P, after the node pointed by q.

i.e. P $\rightarrow$ next = q $\rightarrow$ next;

q $\rightarrow$ next = P;

7. Stop.

➤ **'C' function for inserting an element x at the location 'LOC' in a linked list, referenced by head.**

```
node *insert_LOC(node *head,int x,int LOC)
{
    node *p,*q;
    int i;
```

```
    p=(node *)malloc(sizeof(node));
    p->data = x;
    p->next=NULL;
    if(LOC==1)
    {
        p->next=head;
        return(p);
    }
    q = head;
    for(i=1;i<LOC-1;i++)
        if(q!=NULL)
            q=q->next;
        else
        {
            printf("\nOverflow");
            return(head);
        }
    p->next=q->next;
    q->next=p;
    return(head);
}
```

6.2.5.3   Inserting an Element in a Priority Linked List :

> **Inserting an element 'x' in a sorted list of integers, represented using a linked list. List should remain sorted after insertion.**

                                    Or

> **Insert an element 'x' in a priority linked list. Elements are ordered on increasing priority.**

> **Algorithm :**

   [Existing linked list is referenced by the pointer 'head'. New data to be inserted is 'x'.]

1.   Acquire memory for new node.

     i.e. P = (node *) malloc(sizeof(node));

2. Assign value to its data field and make its next field 'NULL'.

    i.e. P → data = x;

    P → next = NULL;

3. If head is NULL or x is less than the data stored in the first node (i. e. node pointed by 'head')

    then

    [insert the node P at the beginning of the linked list and terminate the algorithm]

    if (head == NULL || x < head → data)

        { P → next = head;

            head = P;

            go to step 5

        }

4. [If head is not NULL and x > head → data]

    Locate the point of insertion, as per the priority of x.

    i.e.

    q = head;

    while (q → next ! = NULL && x > q → next → data)

        q = q → next;

    x should be inserted after the node pointed by q.

    i.e.   P → next = q → next;

        q → next = P;

5. Stop.

> **'C' function to insert an element in priority linked list.**

```
node *insert_priority(node *head,int x)
{
   node *p,*q;
   p=(node *)malloc(sizeof(node));
   p->data=x;
   p->next=NULL;
   if(head==NULL || x<head->data)
   {
        p->next=head;
        head=p;
```

```
        return(head);
    }
    q=head;
    while(q->next!=NULL && x>q->next->data)
        q=q->next;
    p->next=q->next;
    q->next=p;
    return(head);
}
```

6.2.6 Deleting an Item :

Q. What is linked list ? Explain how insertion and deletion can be performed on linked list. **W - 09**

Q. Explain with suitable diagrams-how to delete a node from singly linked list at the beginning, in between and at end of the list. **S - 2010**

Deleting a node from the list is even easier than insertion, as only one pointer value needs to be changed. Here again we have three situations.

1.　Deleting the first item.

2.　Deleting the last item.

3.　Deleting from the middle of the list.

Algorithm for deleting the first item.

1.　Store the address of the first node in a pointer variable, say P.

2.　Move the head to the next node.

3.　Free the node whose address is stored in the pointer variable P.

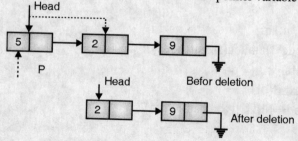

Fig. 6.2.7 : **Deleting the first item**

Algorithm for deleting a node from the middle of the linked list

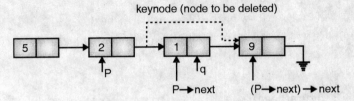

Fig. 6.2.8 : Deletion of middle element

1. Store the address of the preceding node in a pointer variable P. Node to be deleted is marked as key node.

2. Store the address of the key node in a pointer variable q, so that it can be freed subsequently.

3. Make the successor of the key node as the successor of the node pointed by P.

4. Free the node whose address is stored in the pointer variable q.

➤ **'C' function to delete a data from a linked list.**

```
node * delete(node *head, int x)      /* x to be deleted from a
                                         linked list */
{
  node *P, *q;

       if(x == head → data)
       {
            /* deleting the first item */
            P = head;
            head = head → next;
            free (P);
       }
       else
       }
            while(x ! =(P → next) → data && P → next ! = NULL)
                 P = P → next;
            if(P → next ! = NULL)   /* if x exists */
```

```
            {
                q = P → next;
                P → next =(P → next) → next;
                free(q);    /* release space of the key node */
            }
        }
        return(head);
}
```

6.2.6.1　Deletion of the Last Node of a Linked List :

➢　Algorithm :

[Deleting last node of a linked list, referenced by the pointer head]

In order to delete the last node, we must position a pointer q on the last but one node. Address of the node to be deleted is stored in pointer P, So that the memory allocated to it can be freed.

1.　If the first node itself is the last node then

　　[make the linked list empty]

　　　　i.e. if (head → next == NULL)

　　　　　　{　free (head);

　　　　　　　　head = NULL; goto step 4

　　　　　　}

2.　[otherwise]

　　position a pointer q on last but one node

　　i.e. q = head;

　　while (q → next → next ! = NULL)

　　　　q = q → next;

3.　Delete the last node

　　i.e. p = q → next ;

　　　　free (p);

　　　　q → next = NULL;

4.　Stop.

> 'C' function to delete last node of a linked list.

```
node *delete_last(node *head)
{
   node *p,*q;
   if(head->next==NULL)
   {
         free(head);
         head=NULL;
         return(head);
   }
   q=head;
   while(q->next->next!=NULL)
         q=q->next;
   p=q->next;
   free(p);
   q->next=NULL;
   return(head);
}
```

6.2.6.2 Deletion of a Node at Location 'LOC' from a Linked List :

> **Algorithm :**

[Linked list is referenced by the pointer 'head']

1. if (LOC = =1)
    then
    [the node to be deleted is the first node This can be done by following steps]
    (a) Store the address of the first node in the pointer P
         i.e. P = head;
    (b) Move head to the next node
         i.e. head = head → next

(c) Free the memory allocated to the node to be deleted

i.e. free(P); goto step 5

2. [otherwise]

position a pointer q on $(LOC - 1)^{th}$ node.

i.e. q = head;

for (i = 1; i<LOC-1; i++)

q = q →next;

3. if 'q' is 'NULL'

then

[report underflow and terminate the algorithm goto step5]

4. Delete the desired node

i.e. p = q → next;

q → next = p → next;

free (p);

5. Stop.

> **'C' function to delete a node at location 'LOC' from linked list.**

```c
node *delete_LOC(node *head,int LOC)
{
  node *p,*q;
  int i;
  if(LOC==1)
  {
      p=head;
      head=head->next;
      free(p);
      return(head);
  }
  q=head;
  for(i=1;i<LOC-1;i++)
      q=q->next;
  if(q==NULL)
  {
```

```
        printf("\nUnderflow");
        return(head);
    }
    p=q->next;
    q->next=p->next;
    free(p);
    return(head);
}
```

6.2.6.3 Delete a Linked List, Referenced by the Pointer Head :

> **Algorithm :**

1.   if head == NULL

     then

          [go to step 3]

2.   [otherwise] Delete the first node.

     i.e. P = head;

     head = head $\rightarrow$ next;

     free(P);

     goto step 1.

3.   Stop.

> **'C' function to delete a linked list, referenced by the pointer head.**

```
node *delete_list(node *head)
{
    node *p;
    while(head!=NULL)
    {
        p=head;
        head=head->next;
        free(p);
    }
```

```
        return(head);
}
```

6.2.7 Concatenation of Two Linked Lists :

Algorithm for concatenation :

Let us assume that the two linked lists are referenced by head1 and head2 respectively.

(1)   If the first linked list is empty then return head2.

(2)   If the second linked list is empty then return head1.

(3)   Store the address of the starting node of the first linked list in a pointer variable, say P.

(4)   Move the P to the last node of the linked list through simple linked list traversal technique.

(5)   Store the address of the first node of the second linked list in the next field of the node pointed by P. Return head1

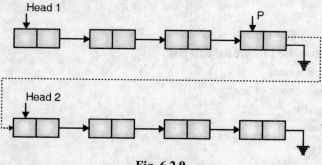

Fig. 6.2.9

➤   **'C' function to concatenate two linked lists.**

```
node * concatenate(node *head1, node *head2)
   {
        node *P;
        if(head1 == NULL)     /* if the first linked list is empty */
            return(head2);
        if(head2 == NULL) /* if the second linked list is empty */
            return(head1);
        P= head1;  /* place P on the first node of the first linked
                    list */
```

```
        while(P → next ! = NULL)  /* Move P to the last node */
            P = P → next;
        P → next = head2;  /* address of the first node of the
                              second linked list stored in the last
                              node of the first linked list */

        return(head1);
}
```

6.2.8 Inversion of Linked List :

A linked list can be reversed by changing the direction of the pointer, iteratively.

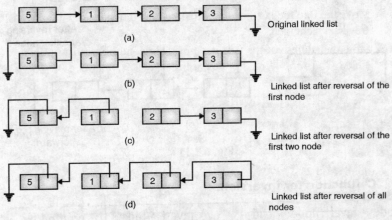

(a)   Original linked list

(b)   Linked list after reversal of the first node

(c)   Linked list after reversal of the first two node

(d)   Linked list after reversal of all nodes

Fig. 6.2.10

Algorithm for reversing the linked list.

Let us take three pointer variables P, q and r.

P references the linked list reversed so far. q points to the linked list to be reversed. r points to the next node of q. Initially,

P = NULL;   q = head;   r = q → next;

```
while(all nodes have not been reversed)
{
        reverse the node pointed by q.
        q → next = P;
        move P, q, r forward by a node.
        P = q;
```

```
        q = r
        r = r → next;
}
```

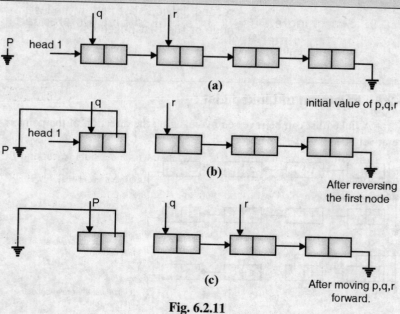

Fig. 6.2.11

➤ **'C' function for inversion.**

```
node * invert(node *head)          /* invert a linked list pointed by
                                       head */
{
   node *P ,*q ,*r;
   P = NULL; q = head; r = q → next;       /* initial values of P, q
                                              and r */
   while(q ! = NULL)    /* until all nodes have been reversed */
   {
        q → next = P;        /* move P, q, r forward by a node */
        P = q;
        q = r;
        if(r ! = NULL)
            r = r → next;
```

```
    }
  return(P);
}
```

6.2.9 Searching a Data 'x' in a Linked List, Referenced by the Pointer Head :

Q. Explain the operation on searching a desired node in the linked list.   W - 09

➢ **Algorithm :**

In order to search an element in a linked list, we start traversing the linked list from the first node. Traversal ends with a success if the element is found . If the element is not found then search ends in a failure.

1.   P = head;
2.   if the data stored in node pointed by P is

        x

            then

                [end the search with success.

                    i.e. return (1)

                ]

3.   Continue searching

        i.e. $P = P \rightarrow$ next.

4.   if end of linked list

        then

                [end with failure

                    i.e. return(0);

                ]

5.   goto step 2

6.   Stop.

➢ **'C' function for searching an element x in a linked list referenced by the pointer head. Function returns 1 if search ends in a success, otherwise, the function returns 0.**

```
int search1(node *head,int x)
{
```

```
        node *p;
        P=head;
        while(P!=NULL)
        {
                if(P->data==x)
                        return(1);
                P=P->next;
        }
        return(0);
}
```

> 'C' function for searching an element x in a linked list referenced by the pointer head. Function returns address of the node if search ends in a success, otherwise, the function returns 'NULL'.

```
node *search2(node *head, int x)
{
    node * P;
    P = head;
    while(P != NULL)
    {
            if (P->data == x)
                return (P);
            P = P -> next;
    }
    return(NULL);
}
```

> 'C' function for searching an element x in a linked list referenced by the pointer head. Function returns location of the node if search ends in a success, otherwise, the function returns '-1'.

```
int search3(node *head,int x)
{
    int i=1;
    node *p;
```

```
    p=head;
    while(p!=NULL)
    {
        if(p->data==x)
            return(i);
        i++;
        p=p->next;
    }
    return(-1);
}
```

6.2.10 Searching an Element x in a Sorted Linked List :

➢ **Algorithm :**

[Linked list is referenced by the pointer head. Elements of the linked list are ordered in ascending order]

In order to search an element in a linked list of sorted elements, we start traversing the linked list from the first node, using a pointer P.

Search ends with success if the element is found in the node pointed by P.

Search ends in a failure under any of the given condition.

(a)   P has become 'NULL'

(b)   P → data is greater than x.

1.   P = head

2.   if P →data is equal to x

    then

            [report success and

                end the traversal

        ]

3.   if P is Null or P → data > x

    then

    [report failure and

        end the traversal

    ]

Continue searching

i.e. $P = P \rightarrow next;$

   goto step 2.

4.   Stop.

➤ **'C' function to search an element in sorted list.**

```c
int search_sorted(node *head,int x)
{
    node *p;
    p=head;
    while(p!=NULL)
    {
        if(p->data==x)
            return(1);
        if(p->data>x)
            return(0);
        p=p->next;
    }
    return(0);
}
```

6.2.11 New Linear Linked List by Selecting Alternate Element :

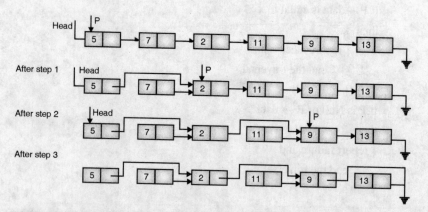

➢ **Algorithm :**

[Linked list is referenced by the pointer head]

1.   P = head
2.   if (P → next is equal to NULL)

       then

            goto step 5
3.   P → next = P → next → next

       P= P → next;
4.   goto step 2

Stop.

```
void create_alternate(node *head)
{
   node *p;
   p=head;
   while(p!=NULL && p->next!=NULL)
   {
        p->next=p->next->next;
        p=p->next;
   }
}
```

6.2.12 Handling of Records through Linked List :

Assume a singly linked list where each node contains student details like name, rollno and percentage of marks. Write a "C" function COUNT() to traverse the linked list and count how many students have obtained more than 60% marks.

Structure used to represent a node

```
typedef struct node
{
   char name [30];
   int rollno;
   float percent;
   struct node *next;
}node;
int COUNT (node *head)
{
```

```
    int n = 0;
    while (head! = NULL)
    {
        if (head -> percent > 60.00)
                n++;
        head = head -> next;
    }
    return (n);
}
```

6.2.13 Merging of sorted Linked List :

Merging of two sorted linked $l1$ and $l2$ with resultant list as l is being explained with help of an example.

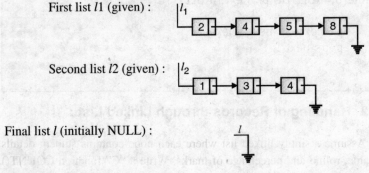

First list $l1$ (given) :

Second list $l2$ (given) :

Final list l (initially NULL) :

Merging

Step 1 : Smaller of the two elements pointed by $l1$ and $l2$ is copied to l. A pointer P is positioned on the last mode of l.

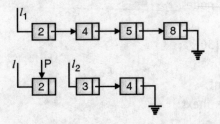

Step 2 : Smaller of the two elements pointed by $l1$ and $l2$ is appended to l. P is positioned on the last node of l.

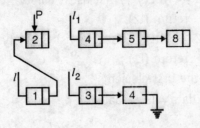

Step 3 : Smaller of the two elements pointed by l1 and l2 is appended to l.
P is positioned on the last node of l.

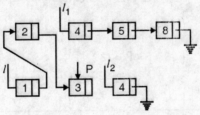

Step 4 : Smaller of the two elements pointed by l1 and l2 is appended to l.
P. is positioned on the last node.

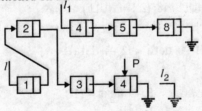

Step 5 : Since, l2 has become NULL, the list l1 is appended at the end
of l.

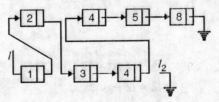

> **'C' function for merging of two sorted lists pointed by l1
and l1**

```
node * merge (node * l1, node * l2)
    { node *l = NULL, *P ;
```

```
            if (l1 == NULL)  //first list is empty
                    return (l2);
            if (l2 == NULL)  //second list is empty
                    return (l1) ;
        // copy the first element
        if (l1 → data < l2 → data)
            {
                        l = P = l1 ;
                        l1 = l1 → next ;
            }
            else
            {       l = P = l2 ;
                    l2 = l2 → next ;
            }
```

// Append remaining data to produce *l*.

```
while (l1 ! = NULL && l2 ! = NULL)
    {
        if (l1 → data < l2 → data)
            {
                    P → next = l1 ;
                    l1 = l1 → next;
                    P = P → next ;
            }
        else
            {
                    P → next = l2 :
                    l2 = l2 → next ;
                    P = P → next ;
            }
    }
// one of the lists l1 or l2 will have some elements
    if (l1 ! = NULL)
```

```
            P → next = l1 ;
        else
            P → next = l2 ;
        return (l) ;
        }
```

6.2.14 Splitting a Linked List at the Middle and Merge with Second Half as First Half :

➤ 'C' program to create a single linked list and split it at the middle and make the second half as the first and vice versa. Display the final list.

```c
#include<stdio.h>
#include<conio.h>
typedef struct node
{
    int data;
    struct node *next;
}node;
void main()
{
    node *head=NULL,*p,*q;
    int n,i,x;
    printf("\n Enter no of nodes :");
    scanf("%d",&n);
    /*  create a linked list of n nodes */
    for(i=0;i<n;i++)

{
        printf("\n Enter the next element :");
        scanf("%d",&x);
```

```
        p=(node*)malloc(sizeof(node));
        p->data=x;
        p->next=NULL;
        if(head==NULL)
            head=q=p;
        else
        {
            q->next=p;
            q=p;
        }
    }
    /* locate the centre of linked list */
    p=q=head;
    while(q->next!=NULL)
    {
        p=p->next;
        q=q->next;
        if(q->next!=NULL)
            q=q->next;
    }
    q->next=head;
    head=p->next;
    p->next=NULL;
    /* Display the final list */
    for(p=head;p!=NULL;p->next)
    {
        printf("\n%d",p->data);
        p=p->next;
    }
}
```

Output

```
Enter no of nodes :3
Enter the next element :12
Enter the next element :23
Enter the next element :34
34
12
23
```

6.2.15 Removing Duplicate Elements from a Linked List :

```
void delete_duplicates (node *head)
{   int x;
    node *p;
    while (head!= NULL)
    { x = head → data;
            \\ delete all subsequent nodes with  x in its data field
            p = head;
            while (p → next != NULL)
            { if (p → next → data == x) //delete
                p →next= p → next→next;
              else
                p = p →next;
            }
            head = head →next; // find the duplicates of the next
element
    }
}
```

6.2.16 Head Node in Linked List :

Sometimes it is useful to keep an extra node at the beginning of a linked list. Such a node is also called sentinel node, a header node, or a dummy node. Fig. 6.2.12 shows a linked list with a header node.

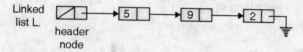

Fig. 6.2.12 : A linked list with a header node

Sentinel nodes are added to simplify algorithms/operations performed on the data structure.

Sentinel node simplifies insert operation : Insert at the front of the list is a special case. An insert operation at the beginning of list causes a change in the referencing pointer with the sentinel node, all cases of insertion become identical.

Sentinel node simplifies delete operation : Deletion from the front of a list is a special case. It changes the start of the list and hence the referencing pointer. With the sentinel node, all cases of deletion become identical.

6.3 Circular Linked List

In a circular linked list, last node is connected back to the first node. In some applications, it is convenient to use circular linked list. A queue data structure can be implemented using a circular linked list, with a single pointer "rear" as the front node can be accessed through the rear node.

Insertion of a node at the start or end of a circular linked list identified by a pointer to the last node of the linked list takes a constant amount of time. It is irrespective of the length of the linked list.

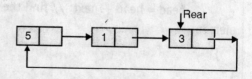

Fig. 6.3.1

Algorithm for traversing a circular list is slightly different than the same algorithm for a singly connected linked list because "NULL" is not encountered.

> ### 'C' function for inserting a number at the rear of a circular linked list.

```
node * insert_rear(node * rear, int x)
{
        node *P;
        P =(node*) malloc(sizeof(node));
            /* acquire memory for the current data */
        P → data = x;
        if(rear = = NULL)
        {
            /* inserting in an empty linked list */
            rear = P;
            /* node is connected back to the same node */
            P → next = P;
            return(rear);
        }
        else
        {
            P → next = rear → next;
            rear → next = P;     /* node P is made a part of
                                    the circle */
            rear =P
            return(rear)
        }
}
```

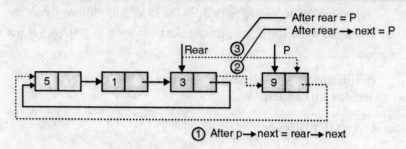

Fig. 6.3.2 : Insertion of a node at rear in circular linked list

➢ **'C' function for inserting a number at the front of the circular linked list.**

```
node * insert_front(node * rear, int x)
{
        node *P;
        P =(node *) malloc(sizeof(node));   /* acquire memory */
        P → data = x;
        if(rear == NULL) //linked list is empty
        {
                rear = P;
                P → next = P;
                return(rear);
        }
        else
        {
                P → next = rear → next;
                rear → next = P;
                return(rear);        /* rear is not moved after
insertion */
        }
}
```

> **'C' function for traversing a circular linked list.**

```
void print(node * rear)
  {
        node *P;
        if(rear ! = NULL)
        {
            P = rear → next;   /* start traversing from the front */
            do
            {
                printf("\n%d", P → data);
                P = P → next;
            } while(P ! = rear → next);
        }
  }
```

In a circular linked list, starting and terminating cases for traversal are same. In such a case, do-while is the most suitable construct for traversing.

> **'C' function for counting of nodes in a circular linked list.**

```
int count (node * rear)
  {     node p;
        int n = 0;
        if (rear == NULL)
            return (0);
        p = rear→ next;
        do
        {
            n = n + 1;
            p = p → next;
        }  while (p! = rear → next);
    return (n);
  }
```

> Write a 'C' function to insert and delete a Nth element in circular linked list ? Give the pictorial representation of the same.

Insertion :

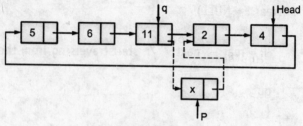

Fig. 6.3.3

q points to $(N-1)^{th}$ element. Element to be inserted is pointed by P.

> **'C' function for insertion.**

```
node * insert_cir_loc(node *head,int x,int loc)
{
    node *p,*q;
    int i;
    p=(node *)malloc(sizeof(node));
    p->data=x;
    p->next=NULL;
    if(loc==1)
        if(head==NULL)
        {
            p->next=p;
            return(p);
        }
        else
        {
            p->next=head->next;
            head->next=p;
            return(head);
        }
```

```
    q=head->next;
    for(i=1;i<loc-1;i++)
         if(q!=head)
             q=q->next;
         else
         {
             printf("\nOverflow");
             return(head);
         }
    p->next=q->next;
    q->next=p;
    return(head);
}
```

Deletion :

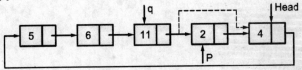

Fig. 6.3.4

q points to $(N-1)^{th}$ element.Element to be deleted is pointed by p

> **'C' function for deletion.**

```
node *delete_cir_loc(node *head,int loc)
{
    node *p,*q;
    int i;
    if(loc==1)
    {
         if(head->next==head)
         {
             free(p);
             return(NULL);
         }
         else
         {
```

```
            p=head->next;
            head->next=p->next;
            free(p);
            return(head);
        }
    }
    q=head->next;
    for(i=1;i<loc-1;i++)
        if(q!=head)
            q=q->next;
        else
        {
            printf("\nUnderflow");
            return(head);
        }
    p=q->next;
    q->next=p->next;
    free(p);
    return(head);
}
```

Example 6.3.1 :　Write an algorithm that will concatenate two circular linked lists, producing a circular linked list.

Solution :

Two linked lists l_1 and l_2 can be Combined by manipulating the following pointers :

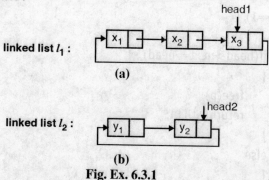

linked list l_1 :

(a)

linked list l_2 :

(b)

Fig. Ex. 6.3.1

Step No.	Operation	Status of l_1 and l_2
1.	P = head2 → next ;	
2.	head2 → next = head1 → next ;	
3.	head1 → next = P	
4.	head1 = head2	

The concatenated list is being referenced through head1.

6.4 Doubly Linked List

Q. What is doubly linked list? Explain with example the method of inserting a node in doubly linked list at beginning and at end.
S - 2010

In a singly linked list, we can easily move in the direction of the link. Finding a node, preceding any node is a time consuming process. The only way to find the node which precedes a node is to start back at the beginning of the list. If we have a problem where moving in either direction is often necessary, then it is useful to have doubly linked lists. Each node has two link fields, one linking in the forward direction and one in the backward direction.

A node in a doubly linked list has at least 3 fields, say "data", "next" and "previous". A doubly linked list is shown in Fig. 6.4.1

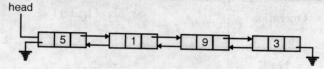

Fig. 6.4.1 : A doubly linked list

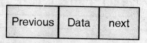

Fig. 6.4.2 : Structure of the node

A node of a doubly linked list can be defined using the following structure.

```
typedef struct dnode
    {
        int data;
        struct dnode *next, *prev;
    } dnode;
```

6.4.1 Creation of a Doubly Linked List :

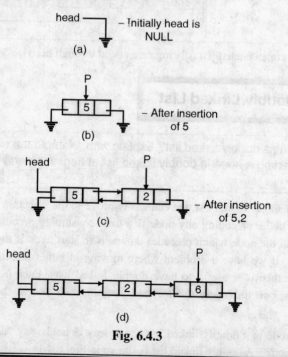

Fig. 6.4.3

Fig. 6.4.3 shows stepwise insertion of 3 elements, namely 5, 2 and 6 Pointer P is used to help insertion at the rear of the linked list.

Algorithm for insertion of x at the rear :

dnode *P, *q;

Step 1 : Acquire memory for the new data

q =(dnode*) malloc(sizeof(dnode));

Step 2 : Store x in the newly acquired node q → data = x;

Step 3 : Make previous and next field as NULL;

q → prev = q → next = NULL;

Fig. 6.4.4 : Status of node after step1 to step3

Case I : Inserting in an empty list(head = NULL)

```
if(head = = NULL)
{
    head = P = q;
}
```

Case II : Inserting in an non-empty list

```
else
{
    P → next = q;
    q → prev = P;
    P = q;
}
```

Note : A linked list can be created through a repeated application of (1) reading a new value of x and then inserting at rear.

> **Program 6.4.1 : A sample program for creation of a doubly linked list and printing its elements in forward and reverse direction**

```
#include<conio.h>
#include<stdlib.h>
#include<stdio.h>
typedef struct dnode
```

```
{
   int data;
   struct dnode *next,*prev;
}dnode;

dnode * create();
void print_forward(dnode *);
void print_reverse(dnode *);
void main()
{
   dnode *head;
   head=NULL;   // initially the list is empty
   head=create();
   printf("\nElements in forward direction :");
   print_forward(head);
   printf("\nElements in reverse direction :");
   print_reverse(head);
}
dnode *create()
{
   dnode *h,*P,*q;
   int i,n,x;
   h=NULL;
   printf("\nEnter no of elements :");
   scanf("%d",&n);
   for(i=0;i<n;i++)
   {
        printf("\nEnter next data: ");
        scanf("%d",&x);
        q=(dnode*)malloc(sizeof(dnode));
        q->data=x;
        q->prev=q->next=NULL;
        if(h==NULL)
            P=h=q;
        else
```

```
            {
                P->next=q;
                q->prev=P;
                P=q;
            }
    }
    return(h);
}
void print_forward(dnode *h)
{
    while(h!=NULL)
    {
        printf("<- %d ->",h->data);
        h=h->next;
    }
}
void print_reverse(dnode *h)
{
    while(h->next!=NULL)   //go to the last node
        h=h->next; // print while moving in the reverse direction
    while(h!=NULL)
    {
        printf("<- %d ->",h->data);
        h=h->prev;
    }
}
```

Output

```
Enter no of elements :4
Enter next data:1
Enter next data:2
Enter next data:3
Enter next data:4
Elements in forward direction :<-1-> <-2-><-3-><-4->
Elements in reverse direction :<-4-> <-3-><-2-><-1->
```

Insertion and deletion are two basic operations on such lists. Consider that a new node pointed to by "p" is to be **inserted** after the node pointed to by q in a doubly linked list as shown in the Fig. 6.4.5.

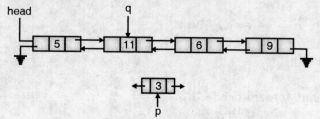

(a) Insertion of a node in a doubly linked list

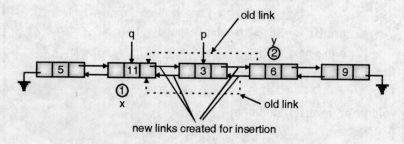

(b) A doubly linked list after the insertion of the node
Fig. 6.4.5

Links of two nodes are altered during insertion. In the Fig. 6.4.5(b), a new node pointed to by p is inserted between the two nodes x and y. Following links must be changed for proper insertion of node pointed by p between x and y.

(1)　Right link of x

(2)　Left link of y

(3)　Left and right links of node pointed to by p

Instructions for making above changes :

p → next = q → next;	//right link of set to y
p → prev = q;	// left link of p set to x
q → next = p;	// right link of x set to p
(p → next) → prev = p;	// left link of y set to p

➤ **'C' function for inserting a node pointed to by p after a node pointed to by q.**

```
void insert(dnode *p, dnode *q)
{
        p → next = q → next;
        p → prev = q;
        q → next = p;
        if(P → next ! = NULL)   /* insertion at the end */
            p → next → prev = p;
}
```

If the right pointer of x is NULL then the insertion is being performed at the end. Hence, there is no question of modifying the left pointer of y.

➤ **'C' function for inserting a node pointed to by p before a node pointed to by q.**

```
dnode * insert (dnode * head, dnode *p, dnode * q)
        {
                if (q → prev == NULL)
                { // insert at the beginning
                        p→ next = q;
                        p→ prev = NULL;
                        q→ prev = p;
                        return (p);
                }
        else
        {   p → prev = q → prev;
            p → next = q;
            p → prev → next = p;
            q → prev = p;
            return (head);
        }
}
```

> **'C' function for inserting a value x, at the beginning of doubly linked list.**

```
dnode * insert2(dnode * head, int x)
{
        dnode *p;
        p =(dnode *) malloc(sizeof(dnode));/* get memory for
the new node */
        p → data = x;
        p → prev = NULL;
        p → next = head;
        if(head ! = NULL)              /* not an empty list */
            head → prev = p;
        return(P);
}
```

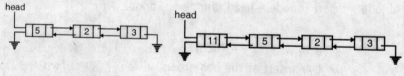

   (a) Original linked list   **(b) Linked list after insertions of 11 at the front**

Fig. 6.4.6

> **'C' function for inserting a value x, at the end of a doubly linked list.**

```
donde * insert3(dnode *head, int x)
{
    dnode *P, *q;
    P =(dnode *) malloc(sizeof(dnode));
    P → data = x;
    P → prev = P → next = NULL;
    if(head == NULL)                   /* empty list */
        return(P);
```

```
    /* go to the last node */
    q = head;
    while(q → next ! = NULL)
        q = q → next;
    P → prev = q
    q → next = P;
}
```

6.4.2 Deletion of a Node :

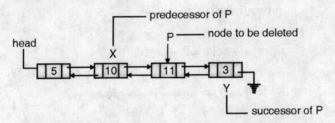

Fig. 6.4.7(a) : Node pointed to by P is to be deleted

When a node, pointed to by P is to be deleted then its predecessor node X and it's successors node Y (as shown in Fig. 6.4.7(a)) will be affected.

- Right link at X should be set to Y.
- Left link at Y should be set to X.
- Release the memory allocated to the node pointed to by P.

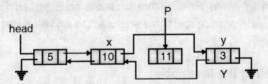

Fig. 6.4.7(b) : Links to be modified as shown above

C-instructions for deletions :

$P \rightarrow$ prev $\rightarrow$ next $= P \rightarrow$ next;   // right at X set to Y

$P \rightarrow$ next $\rightarrow$ prev $= P \rightarrow$ prev;   // left link at Y set to X

free(P);

> ➢ 'C' function for deletion of a node pointed by P in a doubly linked list.

```
dnode * delete_double(dnode *head, dnode *P)
{
        if(P == head)                    /* deleting the head node */
        {
            P → next → prev = NULL;
            head = P → next;
            free(P);
            return(head);
        }
        P → prev → next = P → next;
        if(P → next ! = NULL)            /* not the last node */
            P → next → prev = P → prev;
        free(P);
        return(head);
}
```

- Special care should be taken to delete the first or the last node.

- If the node to be deleted is the first node then head should be advanced to the next node.

- If the node to be deleted is the last node then there is no node to its right.

Example 6.4.1 : Write an algorithm to delete node at beginning at middle position and at the end of a "Doubly" linked list.   `S - 08`

Solution :

1.   Deteting the first node :

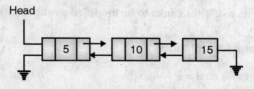

Fig. Ex. 6.4.1

Following steps are needed to delete the first node :

(a) Position a pointer p on the first node.

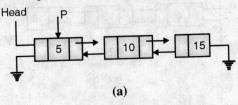

(a)

(b) Head is moved to the next node

$$head = head \rightarrow next$$

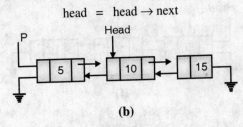

(b)

(c) Left link of head node is grounded

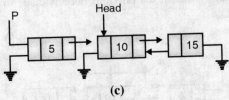

(c)

(d) node, pointed by p is freed

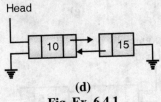

(d)

Fig. Ex. 6.4.1

2. Deleting a node from the middle position :

Following steps are needed to delete a node from the middle position :

(a) Position a pointer p on the required node.

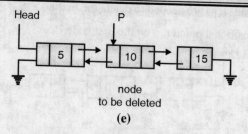

node
to be deleted
(e)

(b) 'Prev' pointer of the next node is made to point to the previous node.

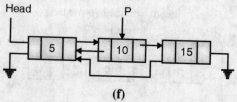

(f)

$$p \rightarrow next \rightarrow prev = p \rightarrow prev$$

(c) 'next' pointer of the previous node is made to point to the next node.

$$P \rightarrow Prev \rightarrow next = p \rightarrow next$$

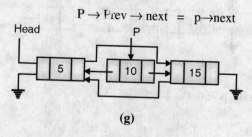

(g)

(d) The node pointed by p is freed.

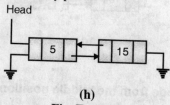

(h)
Fig. Ex. 6.4.1

3.   Deleting the last node :

Following steps are needed to delete the last node :

(a) Position a pointer p on the last node

P = head;

While(p→next!=NULL)

    p = p→next;

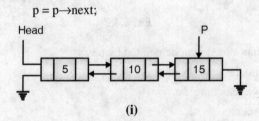

(i)

4.   The 'next' pointer of the last but one node is set to NULL.

p→prev→next = NULL

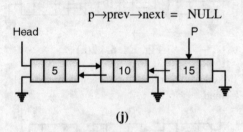

(j)

5.   The node pointed by p is free.

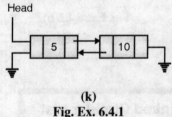

(k)
Fig. Ex. 6.4.1

Example 6.4.2 : With suitable diagram explain 'serching' of a node in Doubly linked list. **S - 08**

Solution :

To search for a data x in a linked list, referenced by the pointer head :

1. We start traversing the linked list from the first node.

2. Traversal ends with success if the element is found. If the element is not found then serarch ends in a failure.

Algorithm :

1.   p = head

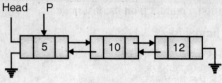

Ex. 6.4.2

2.   If the data stored in node pointed by p is x
      then [end the search with success]

3.   Continue searching i.e.

    $P = p \rightarrow next$

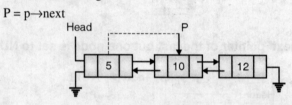

Fig. Ex. 6.4.2(a)

4.   If and of linked list then [end the serach with failure]

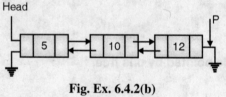

Fig. Ex. 6.4.2(b)

5.   goto step 2
6.   stop.

6.5 Doubly Linked Circular List

- In a doubly linked circular list, the previous pointer of the first node points to the last node.
- Next pointer of the last node points to the first node.
- In a doubly linked circular list, insertion at the front as well as at the rear can be done in constant time order O(1).

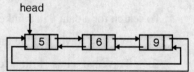

Fig. 6.5.1 : A doubly linked circular list

- If the list is not circular then insertion at the front can be done in constant time order O(1) but the insertion at the rear requires traversing of entire linked list to locate the last node. Time complexity of insertion at the end is of the order of O(n).

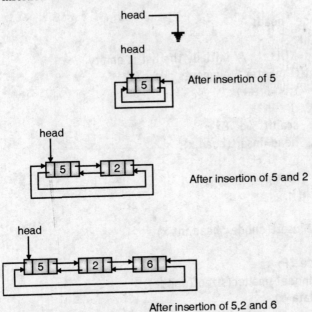

After insertion of 5

After insertion of 5 and 2

After insertion of 5,2 and 6

Fig. 6.5.2

Fig. 6.5.2 showing stepwise insertion of 3 elements namely 5, 2 and 6 in a doubly linked circular list.

> **Program 6.5.1: A sample program for insertion of 5 elements in a doubly circular linked list and subsequently printing of elements stored in the list.**

```
#include<conio.h>
#include<stdlib.h>
#include<stdio.h>
typedef struct dnode
{
   int data;
   struct dnode *next,*prev;
```

```
}dnode;
dnode * insert(dnode *head,int x);
void print(dnode *);
void main()
{
    dnode *head;
    int i,x;
    head=NULL;    // initially the list is empty
    printf("\nEnter 5 elements :");
    for(i=1;i<=5;i++)
    {
        scanf("%d",&x);
        head=insert(head,x);
    }
    print(head);
    getch();
}
dnode *insert(dnode *head,int x)
{
    dnode *P;
    P=(dnode*)malloc(sizeof(dnode));
    P->data=x;
    P->prev=P->next=NULL;
    if(head==NULL)             //inserting in an empty link list
    {            P->prev=P->next=P;
                 return(P);
    }
    P->prev=head->prev;
    P->next=head;
    head->prev->next=P;
    head->prev=P;
    return(head);
}
void print(dnode *head)
{
    dnode *P;
    P=head;
    do
    {
```

```
        printf("<- %d ->",P->data);
        P=P->next;
    }while(P!=head);
}
```

Output

```
Enter 5 elements :  5   4   3   2   1
<- 5 -><- 4 -><- 3 -><- 2 -><- 1 ->
```

6.6 Linked Representation of a Stack

Stack can be representation efficiently through Linked lists. When a stack is represented using a Linked list, it is never full as long as system has memory for dynamic allocation of space for a node. A stack can be represented through a singly connected Linked list.

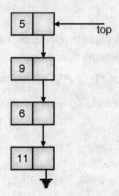

Fig. 6.6.1 : Linked list representation of a stack

Structure of a node :

        typedef struct node

        {

                        int data ;

                        struct node *next ;

        }node ;

• top is a pointer type variable, pointing to the top node

Declaration of top :

        node *top ;

• Memory for a new node can be allocated through malloc( )

(node *) malloc(sizeof(node))

sizeof (node) gives number of bytes required to store a node. Function malloc( ) returns the address of the memory block allocated to store a node. Address returned by malloc( ) is type casted through (node*) so that the address can be treated as an address of a node.

- Initially top is NULL (Empty Stack) ;

- Inserting an element x in an empty stack

  top = (node*) malloc (sizeof (node)) ;

  top $\rightarrow$ data = x ;

  top $\rightarrow$ next = NULL ;

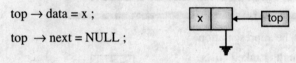

- Subsequent elements can be inserted in the stack through the following operations :

  node *P ;   /* A pointer for acquiring memory for new node */

  P =(node *) malloc (sizeof(node)) ;

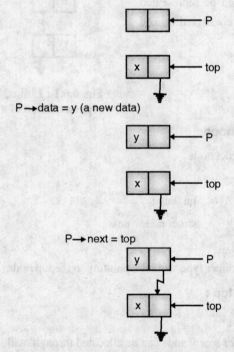

  P $\rightarrow$ data = y (a new data)

  P $\rightarrow$ next = top

- Address of the top node (address is stored in the pointer type variable top) is copied in the next field of node whose address is stored in P

top = P ;

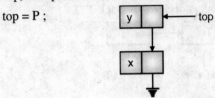

Address of the new node is copied in the pointer top.

- An element from the stack can be deleted through the following operations

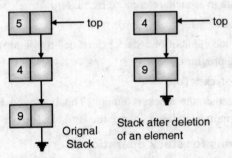

Orignal Stack

Stack after deletion of an element

P = top (save the address of the top node in a pointer P. So that the memory occupied by the node can be freed)

top = top → next ; (top node is deleted)

free(P) ; // memory freed

6.6.1 Functions for Stack Operations :

(a) void init(stack **T) ;

calling the function from the main program

void main(c)

{   stack * top ;

       init(& top) ;

}

Since, the function init( ) modifies the value of top, address of the pointer type variable 'top' must be passed to the function. If the contents of a variable (defined in calling program) is to be modified by the called function then the calling program must pass its address. Pointer variable "top" is passed by address and the corresponding parameter in function init is declared as stack **T.

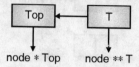

node * Top   node ** T

Contents of the variable top can be accessed through T and it is simply *T.

(b)   void push(stack ** T, int x)

        insert a data in a stack, referenced by *T(top)

(c)   int pop(stack ** T)

        delete the top element of a stack referenced by *T(top) and return it to the calling program.

(d)   int empty(stack * Top)

        check, whether the stack is empty. Top is passed by value as the function empty( ) will not change the variable Top.

➤   **'C' functions for stack operations.**

```c
void init(stack **T)
{
   * T = NULL ; /* make the stack empty)
}
void push(stack ** T, int x)
{
   stack * P ;
   /* set a new node */
   P =(stack *) malloc(sizeof(stack)) ;
   P → data = x ;
   /* attach the node at the front  */
   P → next = *T ;
   * T = P ;
}
int pop(stack **T)
{
```

```
    int x ; stack * P ;
    P = * T ;
    *T = P → next ;
    x = P→ data ;
    free(P) ;
    return(x) ;
}
int empty(stack *Top)
{
    if(Top = = NULL)
    return(1) ;
    return(0) ;
}
```

A program showing usage of stack :

Reverse a string using a stack represented using a linked list

> **Program 6.6.1 : Program to reverse a string represented using a stack.**

```
#include<stdio.h>
#include<conio.h>
typedef struct stack
{
    char data;
    struct stack *next;
} stack;
void init(stack **);
int empty(stack *);
char pop(stack **);
void push(stack **,char);
void main()
{
    stack *TOP;
    char x;
    init(&TOP);
```

```
    printf("\nEnter the string :");
    while((x=getchar())!='\n')
         push(&TOP,x);
    printf("\n");
    while(!empty(TOP))
    {
         x=pop(&TOP);
         printf("%c",x);
    }
}
void init(stack **T)
{
   *T=NULL;
}
int empty(stack *TOP)
{
   if(TOP==NULL)
         return(1);
   return(0);
}
void push(stack **T,char x)
{
   stack *P;
   P=(stack *)malloc(sizeof(stack));
   P->data=x;
   P->next=*T;
   *T=P;
}
char pop(stack **T)
{
   char x;
   stack * P;
   P=*T;
   *T=P->next;
```

```
  x=P->data;
  free(P);
  return(x);
}
```

Output

```
Enter the string :structure
erutcurts
```

6.7 Operations on Queue Implemented using Linked Structure – Linear Queue

Q. With suitable diagram, explain the implementation of linear queue using single linked list.   S - 09

A set of useful operations on a queue includes :

(1) initialize( ) – initializes a queue by setting the value or rear and front pointer to "NULL".

(2) enqueue( ) – inserts an element at the rear end of the queue.

(3) dequeue( ) – deletes the front element and returns the same.

(4) empty( ) – It returns true(1) if the queue is empty and returns false(0) if the queue is not empty.

(5) Print( ) – It prints the queue elements from front to rear.

   (a) Data structure declaration.

```
typedef struct node
{
   int data;
   struct node *next;
}node;
typedef struct Q
{
   node *R;
   node *F;
} Q;
```

(b) Declaring a queue type variable

Q q_1, q_2 ;

Element q_1 of the type Q(queue)

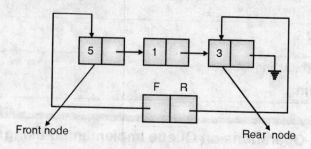

Fig. 6.7.1 : Memory representation of a queue

Data field of the front node is $(q_1.F) \rightarrow$ data

Next field of the front node is $(q_1.F) \rightarrow$ next

Data field of the rear node is $(q_1.R) \rightarrow$ data

Next field of the rear node is $(q_1.R) \rightarrow$ next;

(c) Declaring a queue type pointer

$$Q\ q_1, *P;$$

A queue type variable　　　　　A queue type pointer

P = & q_1;　　　　　　　/* P points to q_1 */

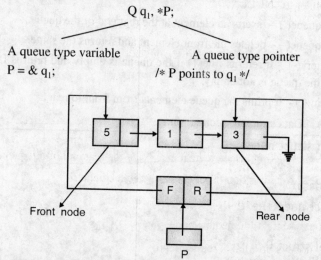

Fig. 6.7.2 : Memory representation of a queue with its address in P

Data field of the front node is $(P \rightarrow F) \rightarrow$ data;

Next field of the front node is $(P \rightarrow F) \rightarrow$ next;

Data field of the rear node is $(P \rightarrow R) \rightarrow$ data;

Next field of the rear node is $(P \rightarrow R) \rightarrow$ next;

> **'C' function to initialize queue.**

```
void initialize(Q *P)
{
  P → R = NULL;
  P → F = NULL;
}
```

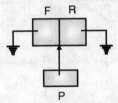

Fig. 6.7.3 : Initial state of a queue. queue is addressed through the pointer P

> **'C' function to check whether queue is empty or not.**

```
int empty(Q *P)
{
  if(P → R == NULL)        /* empty queue */
        return(1);
  return(0);
}
```

enqueue( )

enqueue function inserts a value (say x) at the rear end of the queue.

Steps required for insertion of an element x in a queue :

- Memory is acquired for the new node.
- Value x is stored in the new node.
- New node is inserted at the rear end.
- Special care should be taken for insertion into an empty queue. Both rear and front pointers will point to the only element of the queue.

```
Node *P; Q q;
P =(node *) malloc(sizeof(node));   /* acquire memory */
```

```
P → data = x;                        /* store x in the node */
P → next = NULL;
if(empty(&q))     /* inserting element  in an empty queue */
{
        q.R = q.F = P;
}
else
{
        (q.R) → next = P;
        q.R = P;
}
```

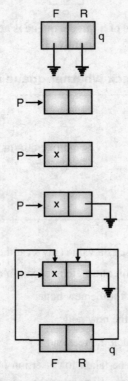

Fig. 6.7.4 : Insertion in an empty queue (stepwise)

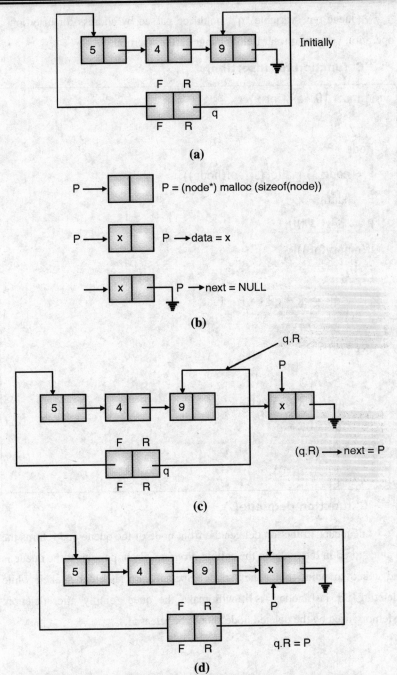

Fig. 6.7.5 : Insertion into a non-empty queue (stepwise)

Queue type variable "q" should be passed by address for insertion( ) operation value of q (rear field) changes after insertion.

> **'C' function for insertion.**

```
void insert(Q *qP, int x)
{
    node *P;
    P =(node *) malloc(sizeof(node));
    P → data = x;
    P → next = NULL;
    if(empty(qP))
    {
        qP → R = qP → F = P;
    }
    else
    {
        qP → R → next = P;
        qP → R = p;
    }
}
```

> **'C' function dequeue( ).**

dequeue( ) function deletes the front node of the queue and returns the value stored in the node, to the calling program. Front pointer of the queue is advanced to point to the next node. Special care should be taken while deleting the last node. As it will make the queue empty after deletion. Memory used by the deleted node should be released.

Steps required for deletion of a node from the queue :

```
Node *P; Q  q;
P = q.F;        /* store the address of the front node in P */
x = P → data
if(q.R == q.F)                 /* deleting the last node */
{
   initialize(&q);             /* make the queue empty */
   free(P);
   return(x);
}
else
{  q.F = P → next;             /* Advance the front pointer */
   free(P);
   return(x);
}
```

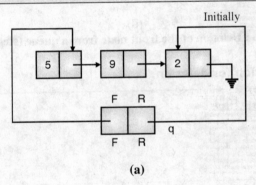

(a)

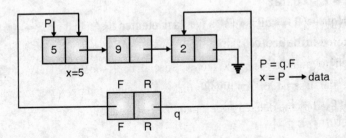

(b)

Fig. 6.7.6 : Deletion of the front node from a queue (stepwise)

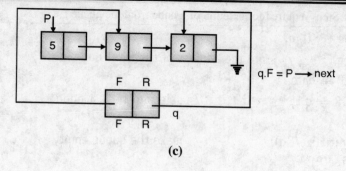

$q.F = P \rightarrow next$

(c)

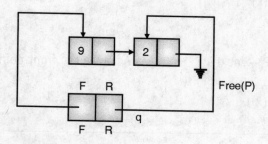

Free(P)

(d)

Fig. 6.7.6 : Deletion of the front node from a queue (stepwise)

➤ **'C' function for deletion.**

```c
int dequeue(Q *qP)
{
    int x;
    node *P;
    P = qP → F;
    x = P → data;
    if(qP → R == qP → F)      /* last element */
            initialize(qP);
    else
            qP → F = P → next;
    free(P);
    return(x);
}
```

➤ 'C' function for printing queue.

Elements of the queue can be printing by traversing the underlying linked list starting from the front node.

void print(Q *qP)

```
{
   node *P;
   P = qP → F; /* start from front */
   while(P! = NULL)
   {
        printf("\n%d", P -> data);
        P = P → next;
   }
}
```

➤ **Program 6.7.1 : A sample program showing various operations on a queue represented using a linked list.**

    (a)   Insert five values in the queue.

    (b)   Print elements of the queue.

    (c)   Delete 2 elements from the queue.

    (d)   Print elements of the queue.

    (e)   Delete the remaining elements of the queue.

```
#include<conio.h>
#include<stdio.h>
#define MAX 10
typedef struct node
{
   int data;
   struct node *next;
}node;

typedef struct Q
{
   node  *R,*F;
```

```
}Q;

void initialise(Q *);
int empty(Q *);
int full(Q *);
void enqueue(Q *,int);
int dequeue(Q *);
void print(Q *);
void main()
{
   Q q;
   int x,i;
   initialise(&q);
   printf("\n Enter 5 elements :");
   for(i=1;i<=5;i++)
   {
        scanf("%d",&x);
        enqueue(&q,x);
   }
            printf("\n displaying queue :");
   print(&q);
   x=dequeue(&q);
   x=dequeue(&q);
            printf("\n after deletion of two elements :");
   print(&q);

   //delete remaining elements
   while(!empty(&q))
        x=dequeue(&q);
   getch();
}
void initialise(Q *qP)
{
   qP->R=NULL;
```

```
   qP->F=NULL;
}
void enqueue(Q *qP,int x)
{
   node *P;
   P=(node*)malloc(sizeof(node));
   P->data=x;
   P->next=NULL;
   if(empty(qP))
   {
        qP->R=P;
        qP->F=P;
   }
   else
   {
        (qP->R)->next=P;
        qP->R=P;
   }
}
int dequeue(Q *qP)
{
   int x;
   node *P;
   P=qP->F;
   x=P->data;
   if(qP->F==qP->R)  //deleting the last element
        initialise(qP);
   else
        qP->F=P->next;
   free(P);
   return(x);
}
void print(Q *qP)
{
```

```
    int i;
    node *P;
    P=qP->F;
    while(P!=NULL)
    {
        printf("\n%d",P->data);
        P=P->next;
    }
}
int empty(Q *qp)
{ if(qp->R==NULL)
    return 1;
    return 0;
}
```

Output

```
Enter 5 elements : 4    5    34 21 90
displaying queue :
4
5
34
21
90
after deletion of two elements :
34
21
90
```

6.7.1 Queue using a Circular Linked List :

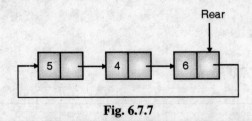

Fig. 6.7.7

In a circular linked list, rear node points back to the front node. Address of the front node can be found through the rear node.

> Address of the front node = rear → next

When a queue is implemented through a singly circular linked list, only one pointer i.e. address of the rear node is required to be maintained. In contrast, when a queue is maintained using a linked list, two pointers must be maintained :

(a)   address of the front node (for deletion)

(b)   address of the rear node (for insertion)

Special care should be taken, while inserting an element in an empty queue. Similarly, after deletion of the last element, the queue should become empty.

Steps for insertion of element x in queue represented using a circular linked list :

(a)   Acquire memory for the node

    P = (node *) malloc(sizeof(node))

(b)   Store the data x in the node

    P → data = x;

If the queue is empty :

(c)   newly acquired node should be connected back to itself.

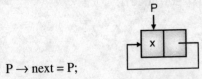

    P → next = P;

(d)   front should point to the only element

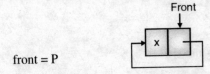

    front = P

If the queue is not empty :

(c)   P → next = rear → next

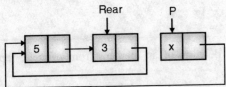

(d)　rear → next = P

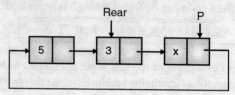

(e)　rear = P

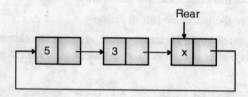

> **'C' function for insertion of an element in a queue represented using a circular linked list.**

```
void enqueue(node **R, int x)  //queue is referenced by address
of rear node.
{
    node *P;
    P =(node *) malloc(sizeof(node));
    P → data = x;
    if(*R == NULL)
    {
        P → next = P;*R = P;
    }
    else
    { P → next = (*R) → next;
      (*R) → next = P;
      *R = P;
    }
}
```

Steps for deletion of an element from a queue represented using a circular linked list.

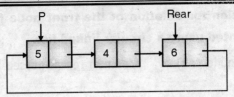

(a)　　P = rear → next;

P Point to the node to be deleted

(b)　　x = P → data;

if (last node is being deleted)

{

(c)　　release the memory of the node being deleted.

free(P);

(d)　　Make the queue empty

rear = NULL;

(e)　　Return the value stored in the front node

return(x);

}

else

{

(c)　　Remove the front node from the queue

rear → next = P → next

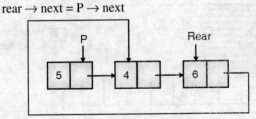

(d)　　release the memory of the node being deleted

free(P)

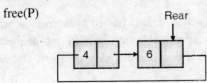

(e)　　return the value stored in the front node

return(x)

}

> ➢ **'C' function for deletion of the front node from a queue represented using a circular linked list.**

```c
int dequeue(node **R)          //pointer rear is passed by address
{
   node *P;
int x;
   P =(*R) → next;          //   '*R' is same as 'rear' as R
contains the address of rear.
   x = P → data;
   if(P → next == P)          /* deleting the last node  */
   {
        *R = NULL;
        free(P);
        return(x);
   }
   (*R) → next = P → next;
   free(P);
   return(x);
}
```

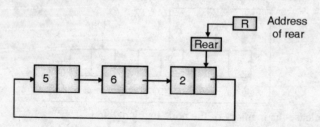

In the above function, rear is passed by address as after deletion, rear may change. Receiving variable in function int dequeue(node **R) is declared as node **R. R contains the address of rear and hence, *R can be used in place of 'rear'.

➤ 'C' function for printing elements of a queue represented using a circular linked list.

```c
void Print(node * rear)
{
    node P;
    P = rear → next;          /* start printing from the front */
    do
    {
        printf("\n%d", P → data);
        P = P → next;
    } while(P! = rear → next);
}
```

In case of a circular linked list, the starting case and the termination case for the loop used for traversal of the linked list are identical.

(1) We start printing from the front node.

(2) We terminate printing on reaching the front node.

Such cases are best handled through do-while loops.

➤ **Program 6.7.2 : Program for showing various operations on a queue represented using circular linked list.**

```c
#include<stdio.h>
#include<conio.h>
typedef struct node
{
 int data;
 struct node *next;
}node;
void init(node **R);
void enqueue(node **R,int x);
int dequeue(node **R);
int empty(node *rear);
void print(node *rear);
void main()
```

```
{
int x,option;
int n = 0,i;
node *rear;
init(&rear);
clrscr();
do
{
 printf("\n 1. Insert\n 2. Delete\n 3. Print\n 4. Quit");
 printf("\n your option:      ");
 scanf("%d",&option);
 switch(option)
 {
  case 1 :
      printf("\n Number of Elements to be inserted");
      scanf("%d",&n);
      for(i=0;i<n;i++)
      {
       scanf("\n %d",&x);
       enqueue(&rear,x);
      }
      break;
  case 2 : if(! empty(rear))
       {
        x = dequeue(&rear);
        printf("\n Element deleted = %d",x);
       }
       else
        printf("\n Uderflow..... Cannot deleted");
       break;
  case 3 : print(rear);
      break;
 }
}while(option != 4);
```

```
 getch();
}
void init(node **R)
{
 *R = NULL;
}
void enqueue(node **R,int x)
{
 node *p;
 p = (node *)malloc(sizeof(node));
 p->data = x;
 if(empty(*R))
 {
   p->next = p;
   *R = p;
 }
 else
 {
   p->next = (*R)->next;
   (*R)->next = p;
   (*R) = p;
 }
}
int dequeue(node **R)
{
 int x;
 node *p;
 p = (*R)->next;
 p->data = x;
 if(p->next == p)
 {
   *R = NULL;
   free(p);
   return(x);
```

```
    }
   (*R)->next = p->next;
   free(p);
   return(x);
}
void print(node *rear)
{
   node *p;
   if(!empty(rear))
   {
     p = rear->next;
   }
   p = p->next;
   do
   {
     printf("\n %d",p->data);
     p = p->next;
   }while(p != rear->next);
}
int empty(node *P)
{
   if(P->next== -1)
          return(1);
   return(0);
}
```

Output

```
1. Insert
2. Delete
3. Print
4. Quit
your option:    1

Element to be inserted  4
            12    23    34   45
```

```
1. Insert
2. Delete
3. Print
4. Quit
your option:    3
            12    23    34    45
1. Insert
2. Delete
3. Print
4. Quit
your option:    2
Element deleted = 4
1. Insert
2. Delete
3. Print
4. Quit
your option:    3
            23    34    45
1. Insert
2. Delete
3. Print
4. Quit
your option:    4
```

6.7.2 Dequeue using Linked Structure :

- Dequeue is already explained in section 5.4.

- Operations on Queue implemented using linked structure is given in section 6.7.

- A dequeue implementation will require two more operations :

    1.   enqueueF() – insert an element at the front end of the queue.

    2.   dequeueR() – delete the rear element of the queue.

These two functions should be added to queue implementation in section 5.4. This will complete the implementation of a dequeue.

C-function for enqueueF() :

```
void enqueueF (Q *qP, int x)
  {
        node *p;
        P = (node *) malloc (sizeof (node));
        P → data = x;
        P → next = NULL ;
        if (empty (qP))
           {
                  qP → R = qP→F = P;
           }
        else
        {
            P→next = qP →F;
            qP →F = P;
        }
  }
```

C-Function for dequeueR() :

```
int dequeueR(Q *qP))
  {
        int x;
        node *p,*2;
  //delete the only element
  if (qP→R ==qP→F)
        {
             P =qP→R;
             X=P→data; free (P);
             qP→R = qP→F = NULL;
             return (x);
        }
  //locate the last but one node
        q=qP→F;
        While (q→next ! =qP→R)
            q=q→next;
        P=q→next;
```

```
        x=P→data;
        q→next=NULL
        qP→R=q;
        free (P);
        return (x)
   }
```

6.8　Priority Queue

Q.　Explain array and linked list representation of priority queue.
W - 09

Priority queue is an ordered list of homogeneous elements. In a normal queue, service is provided on the basis of First-in-first-out. In a priority queue service is not provided on the basis of "first-come-first-served" basis but rather than each element has a priority based on the urgency of need.

- An element with higher priority is processed before other elements with lower priority.

- Elements with the same priority are processed on "first-come-first served" basis.

An example of priority queue is a hospital waiting room. A patient having a more fatal problem will be admitted before other patients.

Other applications of priority queues is found in long term scheduling of jobs processed in a computer. In practice, short processes are given a priority over long processes as it improves the average response of the system.

6.8.1　Implementation of Priority Queues :

Priority queue can be implemented using a circular array :

As the service must be provided to an element having highest priority, there could be a choice between :

(a)　List is always maintained sorted on priority of elements with the highest priority element at the front. Here, deletion is trivial but insertion is complicated as the element must be inserted at the correct place depending on its priority.

(b)   List is maintained in the "FIFO" form but the service is provided by selecting the element with highest priority. Deletion is difficult as the entire queue must be traversed to locate the element with highest priority. Here, insertion is trivial (at rear end).

Implementation of a Priority Queue using a circular array (Priority queue as an ADT) :

Data type for priority queue in a circular array :

```
# define MAX 30 /* A queue with maximum of 30 elements */
typedef struct pqueue
{ int data [MAX];
    int front, rear;
} pqueue;
```

Operations on a priority queue :

i)   initialize( ) : Make the queue empty.

ii)   empty( ) : Determine if the queue is empty.

iii) full( ) : Determine if the queue is full.

iv)   enqueue( ) : Insert an element as per its priority.

v)   dequeue( ) : Delete the front element (front element will have the highest priority.

vi)   print( ) : Print elements of the queue.

Prototype of functions used for various operations on the queue

- void initialize(pqueue *p);

- int empty(pqueue *p);

- int full(pqueue *p);

- void enqueue(pqueue *p, int x);

- int dequeue(pqueue *p);

- void print(pqueue *p);

    enqueue( ) operation will cause an overflow if the queue is full.

    Dequeue( ) operation will cause an underflow if the queue is empty.

C-implementation of functions :

```c
void initialize (pqueue *p)
{  p → rear = - 1;
   p → front = - 1;
}
```
A value of rear or front as -1, indicates that the queue is empty.
```c
int empty (pqueue *p)
{ if (P->rear == - 1)
        return (1);        /* queue is empty */
   return (0); /* queue is not empty */
}
int full (pqueue *p)
{ /* if front is next to rear in the circular array then the queue is
full */
    if (p → rear + 1)% MAX == p → front)
        return (1); /* queue is full */
   return (0);
}
void enqueue (pqueue *p, int x)
{ int i;
   if (full(p))
        printf("\n overflow ...");
   else
   {      /* inserting in an empty queue */
        if (empty(p))
            {   p → rear = p → front = 0;
                p → data [0] = x;
            }
        else
            {
            /* move all lower priority data right by one place */
   i = p → rear ;
   while (x > p → data [i])
```

```
    {       p → data [(i + 1)%MAX] = p → data [i];
            /* position i on the previous element */
            i = (i – 1 + MAX) % MAX; /* anticlock wise movement
 inside the queue */
            if ((i + 1)% MAX = = p → front)
                  break; /* if all elements have been moved */
    }
    /* insert x */
            i = (i + 1)% MAX;
            p → data [i] = x;
    /* re-adjust rear */
        p → rear = (p → rear + 1) % MAX;
    }
  }
}
int dequeue (pqueue *p)
{  int x;
   if (empty (p))
                printf("\n underflow ...");
          else
          {   x = p → data [p → front];
                if (p → rear = = p → front) /* delete last element */
                      initialize (p);
                else
                      p → front = (p → front + 1) % MAX;
          }
   return (x);
   }
void print (pqueue *p)
{  int i, x;
   i = p → front;
   while ( i! = p → rear)
   {      x = p data [i];
          printf ("\n%d", x);
```

```
        i = (i + 1) % MAX;
    }
  /* print the last data */
        x = p → data [i];
        printf ("\n%d", x);
    }
```

> **Program 6.8.1 : Program showing various operations on a priority queue.**

```
#include <stdio.h>
#include <conio.h>
#define MAX 30
typedef struct pqueue
{   int data [MAX];
    int rear, front;
} pqueuel
void initialize(pqueue *p);
int empty(pqueue *p);
int full(pqueue *p);
void enqueue(pqueue *p, int x);
int dequeue(pqueue *p);
void print(pqueue *p);
void main( )
{ int x, op, n;
  pqueue q;
  initialize (&q);
do
{
    printf("\n1)create\n2)insert\n3)Delete\n4)print\n5)Quit");
    printf("\n enter your choice:");
    scanf ("%d", &op);
    switch (op)
    {
    case 1 : printf("\n enter no. of elements :");
```

```
            scanf("%d", &n);
            initialize (&q);
            printf("enter the data:");
            for (i = 0; i < n; i++)
            {
              scanf ("%d" &x);
              if (full (&q))
              {      printf("\n queue is full ...");
                     exit(0);
              }
              enqueue (&q, x);
        }
        break;
   case 2 : printf("\n enter the element to be inserted");
            scanf ("%d", &x);
            if (full(&q))
            {
              printf("\n queue is full ...");
              exit(0);
            }
            enqueue (&q, x);
            break;
            case 3 : if (empty (&q))
            {
                     printf("\n queue is empty ...");
                     exit(0);
            }
        x = dequeue (&q);
       printf("\n element = %d", x);
       break;
       case 4 : print(&q);
       break;
       default : break;
       }
```

```
    } while (op! = 5);
}
void initialize (pqueue *p)
{  p → rear = - 1;
   p → front = - 1;
}
/* A value of rear or front as -1, indicate that the queue is empty.
*/
int empty (pqueue *p)
{ if (P->rear == - 1)
        return (1);        /* queue is empty */
   return (0); /* queue is not empty */
}
int full (pqueue *p)
{ /* if front is next rear in the circular array then the queue is full
*/
    if (p → rear + 1)% MAX == p → front)
        return (1); /* queue is full */
   return (0);
}
void enqueue (pqueue *p, int x)
{ int i;
   if (full (p))
        printf("\n overflow ...");
   else
   {       /* inserting in an empty queue */
        if (empty (p))
            {     p → rear = p → front = 0
                  p → data [0] = x;
            }
        else
            {
            /* move all lower priority data right by one place */
   i = p → rear ;
```

```
    while (x > p → data [i])
    {      p → data [(i + 1)%MAX] = p → data [i];
           /* position i on the previous element */
           i = (i – 1 + MAX) % MAX; /* anticlock wise movement
 inside the queue */
           if ((i + 1)% MAX = = p → front)
                break; /* if all elements have been moved */
    }
    /* insert x */
           i = (i + 1)% MAX;
           p → data [i] = x;
    /* re-adjust rear */
       p → rear = (p → rear + 1) % MAX;
    }
  }
}
int dequeue (pqueue *p)
{  int x;
   if (empty (p))
                printf("\n underflow ...");
           else
           {    x = p → data [p → front];
                if (p → rear = = p → front) /* delete last element */
                    initialize (p);
                else
                    p → front = (p → front + 1) % MAX;
           }
   return (x);
   }
void print (pqueue *p)
{  int i, x;
   i = p → front;
   while ( i! = p → rear)
   {      x = p data[i];
```

```
        printf ("\n%d", x);
        i = (i + 1) % MAX;
    }
    /* print the last data */
        x = p → data[i];
        printf ("\n%d", x);
    }
```

6.9 MSBTE Questions and Answers

Summer 2008 – Total Marks 12

Q. 1   List types of linked list and state the operations performed on linked list. **(Sections 6.1.4, 6.2)**   **(2 Marks)**

Q. 2   Write an algorithm to delete node at beginning, at middle position and at the end of a "Doubly" linked list. **(Example 6.4.1)**   **(6 Marks)**

Q. 3   With suitable diagram, explain 'Searching' of a node in Doubly Linked List. **(Example 6.4.2)**   **(4 Marks)**

Winter 2008 – Total Marks 12

Q. 4   With diagram, define Two-way Header list.
(Example 6.1.1)   **(2 Marks)**

Q. 5   Write an algorithm to insert new node at the beginning, at middle position and at the end of a single Linked List.
(Section 6.2.5)   **(6 Marks)**

Q. 6   Compare a Grounded Header list and Circular Header list with diagram. **(Example 6.1.2)**   **(4 Marks)**

Summer 2009 – Total Marks 12

Q. 7　Define NULL pointer and Empty list. **(Example 6.1.3)**　**(2 Marks)**

Q. 8　Write an algorithm to insert new node at the beginning, at middle position and at the end of a single linked list.

　(Section 6.2.5)　**(6 Marks)**

Q. 9　With suitable diagram, explain the implementation of linear queue using single linked list. **(Section 6.7)**　**(4 Marks)**

Winter 2009 – Total Marks 18

Q. 10　Define node and pointer. **(Example 6.1.4)**　**(2 Marks)**

Q. 11　What is linked list ? Explain how insertion and deletion can be performed on linked list. **(Sections 6.1.2, 6.2.5 and 6.2.6)**　**(4 Marks)**

Q. 12　Explain array and linked list representation of priority queue.

　(Section 6.8)　**(8 Marks)**

Q. 13　Explain the operation on searching a desired node in the linked list.

　(Section 6.2.9)　**(4 Marks)**

Summer 2010 – Total Marks 14

Q. 14　What is doubly linked list? Explain with example the method of inserting a node in doubly linked list at beginning and at end.

　(Sections 6.4 and 6.4.1)　**(6 Marks)**

Q. 15　Explain with suitable diagrams-how to delete a node from singly linked list at the beginning, in between and at end of the list.

　(Section 6.2.6)　**(8 Marks)**

Trees

Statistical Analysis

Year	Marks
Summer - 2008	24 Marks
Winter - 2008	19 Marks
Summer - 2009	26 Marks
Winter - 2009	10 Marks
Summer - 2010	12 Marks

7.1 Introduction to Trees

A tree is a collection of elements called "nodes", one of which is distinguished as a root say r, along with a relation "parenthood" that places a hierarchical structure on the nodes. The root can have zero or more nonempty subtrees T_1, T_2, ... T_k each of whose roots are connected by a directed edge from r.

The root of each subtree is said to be a child of r and r is parent of each subtree root. Fig.7.1.1 is a typical tree using the recursive definition.

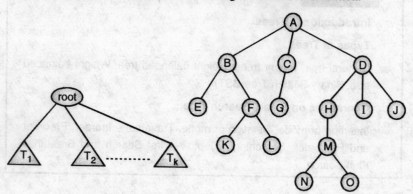

Fig.7.1.1 : Generic tree　　　　**Fig. 7.1.2 : A tree**

7.1.1 Basic Terms :

Q.	Define the terms related to Binary Tree : Level, Depth, Leaf Node, Root Node.	W - 08
Q.	Describe in brief, the terms related to Binary Tree: Level, Depth, Leaf Node, Root Node.	S - 09
Q	Explain the terms with the help of diagram. (i) Siblings (ii) Leaf Node	W - 09

Root : It is a special node in a tree structure and the entire tree is referenced through it. This node does not have a parent. In the tree of Fig. 7.1.2, the root is A.

Parent : It is an immediate predecessor of a node. In the Fig. 7.1.2, A is the parent of B, C, D.

Child : All immediate successors of a node are its children. In the Fig.7.1.2, B, C and D are the children of A.

Siblings : Nodes with the same parent are siblings. H, I and J are siblings as they are children of the   same parent D.

Path : It is number of successive edges from source node to destination node. The path length from node D to node N in Fig.7.1.2 is 3. Node D is connected to N through three edges D-H, H-M, M-N.

Degree of a node :

The degree of a node is a number of children of a node. In Fig. 7.1.2, A and D are nodes of degree 3, B, F and M are nodes of degree 2, C and H are nodes of degree 1 and E, K, L, N, O, I, J are nodes of degree 0. A node of degree 0 is also known as the **leaf node**. A **leaf node** is a terminal node and it has no children.

Leaf node :

A node of degree 0 is also known as a leaf node. A leaf node is a terminal node and it has no children. In the Fig. 7.1.2 E, K, L, G, N, O, I, J are leaf nodes.

Level :

The level of a node in a binary tree is defined as :

1. The root of the tree has level 0
2. The level of any other node in the tree is one more than the level of its father.

The levels of various nodes in the tree of Fig. 7.1.2 is given below.

Nodes	Level
A	0
B, C, D	1
E, F, G, H, I, J	2
K, L, M	3
N, O	4

Depth :

The depth of a binary tree is the maximum level of any node in the tree. This is equal to the node in the tree. This is equal to the longest path from the root to any leaf node. The depth of the tree in Fig. 7.1.2 is 4.

7.2 Binary Tree

Q. Explain the binary tree with suitable example and diagram.

W - 08

A tree is binary if each node of the tree can have maximum of two children. Moreover, children of a node of binary tree are ordered. One child is called the "left" child and the other is called the "right" child. An example of binary tree is shown in Fig.7.2.1.

Node A has two children B and C. Similarly, nodes B and C, each have one child namely G and D respectively.

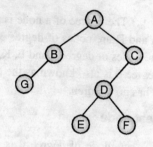

Fig. 7.2.1 : A binary tree

7.2.1 Representation of a Binary Tree Using an Array :

In order to represent a tree in a single one-dimensional array, the nodes are numbered sequentially level by level left to right. Even empty nodes are numbered.

When the data of the tree is stored in an array then the number appearing against the node will work as indices of the node in an array.

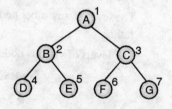

Fig. 7.2.2 : Numbering of nodes

0	1	2	3	4	5	6	7
7	A	B	C	D	E	F	G

Location number zero of the array can be used to store the size of the tree in terms of total number of nodes (existing or not existing).

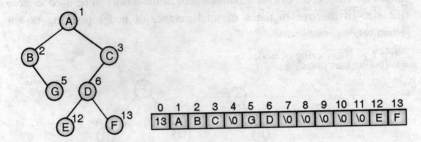

0	1	2	3	4	5	6	7	8	9	10	11	12	13
13	A	B	C	\0	G	D	\0	\0	\0	\0	\0	E	F

Fig. 7.2.3 : Numbering of nodes with some non-existing children

Fig. 7.2.4 : Array representation of the tree shown in Fig. 7.2.3

All non-existing children are shown by "\0" in the array.

Index of the left child of a node $i = 2 \times i$

Index of the right child of a node $i = 2 \times i + 1$

Index of the parent of a node $i = i/2$

Sibling of a node i will be found at the location $i + 1$, if i is a left child of its parent. Similarly, if i is a right child of its parent then its sibling will be found at $i - 1$.

Example 7.2.1 : Explain array representation of binary trees using the following.

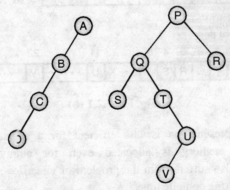

Fig. Ex. 7.2.1 : State and explain limitations of this representation

Solution :

In order to represent a tree in a single one-dimensional array, the nodes are numbered sequentially level by level from left to right. Even empty nodes are numbered. Location number zero of the array can be used to store the size of the tree in terms of total number of nodes (existing or not existing).

Step 1 : Numbering of nodes

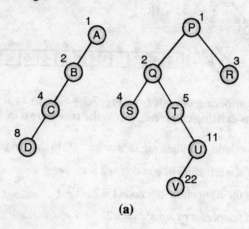

(a)

Step 2 :

Representation :

Left tree

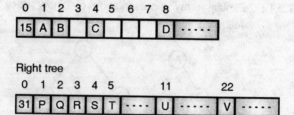

Fig. Ex. 7.2.1 (b)

Array representation is less efficient for a sparse tree. In array representation, memory is allocated even for empty nodes. Array representation also suffers from the problem of underflow. The size of the array is fixed during compile time.

Example 7.2.2 :   Define a binary tree. Show the sequential representation of the binary tree given.

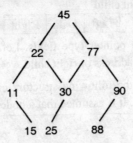

Fig. Ex. 7.2.2

Solution :

A tree is binary if each node of the tree can have maximum of two children. Moreover, children of a node of binary tree are ordered.

One child is called "left" child and the other is called the "right" child.

Array representation of the given tree :

Step 1 : Numbering of nodes :

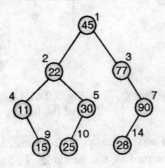

Step 2 : Representation

0	1	2	3	4	5	6	7	8	9	10	11	12	13	14	15
15	45	22	77	11	30		90		15	25				28	

7.2.2 Linked Representation of a Binary Tree :

Linked representation of a binary tree is more efficient than array representation. A node of a binary tree consists of three fields as shown below :

- Data
- Address of the left child

- Address of the right child

| Left | Data | Right |

Left and right are pointer type fields. Left holds the address of left child and right holds the address of right child.

In "C" language, the following structure can be defined to represent one node of a binary tree. It is assumed that a node contains an integer data.

```
typedef struct node
    {    int data;
         struct node *left;
         struct node *right;
    }node;
```

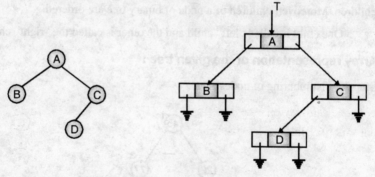

Fig. 7.2.5 : A sample binary   Fig. 7.2.6 : Linked representation
tree   of the binary tree of Fig. 7.2.5

The level of root node is always 0. The immediate children of the root are at level 1 and their immediate children at level 2 and so on.

Height of a node : Height of a node is the distance of the node from its farthest descendant. Height of the node C is 2 as its distance from the descendant H is 2.

Nodes	Height
A	3
C	2
B, F	1
D, E, H, G	0

Height of various nodes of the tree shown in Fig. 7.2.7.

Height of a tree :   Height of a tree is height of the root node. Height of the tree shown in Fig. 7.2.7 is 3 as the height of the root node A is 3.

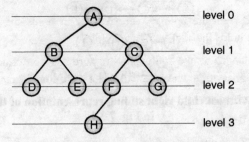

Fig. 7.2.7 : Levels

7.3 A General Tree

In a general tree, number of children per node is not limited to two. Since, the number of children per node can vary greatly, it might not be feasible to make the children direct links in the node. Children of a node can be stored in a linked list with parent node storing the address of its leftmost child.

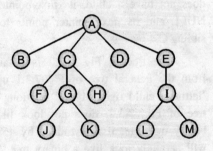

Fig. 7.3.1 : A tree

7.3.1 Node Declaration for a Tree :

```
typedef struct tnode
    { int data;        /* assuming tree stores integer data */
      struct tnode * firstchild;
      struct tnode * nextsibling;
    } tnode;
```

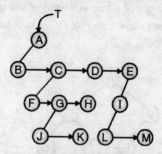

Fig. 7.3.2 : Leftmost child right sibling representation of the tree shown in Fig. 7.3.1

Each node in Fig. 7.3.2 has exactly two links. The first pointer points to its leftmost child and the other pointer points to its next sibling. For example, the first pointer of the node A, points to its leftmost child B. As the root does not have a sibling, its next pointer is NULL. As the node B does not have a child, its first pointer is NULL and its next pointer points to its sibling C.

The tree of Fig. 7.3.2 is obtained from the general tree of Fig. 7.3.1 using 'leftmost child right sibling' relation. The tree of Fig. 7.3.2, does not look like a binary tree, but, if it is rotated by 45°, it will certainly look like a binary tree. The tree of Fig. 7.3.2(a) is obtained by rotating the tree of Fig. 7.3.2 by 45°.

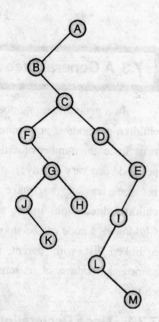

Fig. 7.3.2(a) : Tree of Fig. 7.3.2 is redrawn after it is rotated by 45°

A **forest** is defined as a set of trees. A forest can be represented by a binary tree. It should be clear that the right child of an equivalent binary tree (see Fig. 7.3.2(a)) will always be null. A root does not have a sibling. When a forest is transformed into a binary tree, root will have a right child. Right child of the root will be next tree in a forest. Consider a forest with three trees, as shown in the Fig. 7.3.2(b).

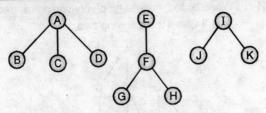

Fig. 7.3.2(b) : A forest containing three trees

Each tree in forest is converted to a binary tree using 'leftmost child right sibling relation'. It is shown in Fig. 7.3.2(c)

Each tree of forest in Fig. 7.3.2(b) is represented by its corresponding binary tree.

Three binary trees of Fig. 7.3.2(c) can be combined by :

(1)　Tree with root node E is the right child of node A.

(2)　Tree with root node I is the right child of node E.

Final tree is shown in Fig. 7.3.2(d).

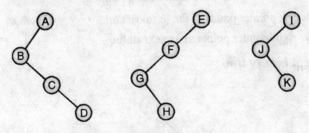

Fig. 7.3.2(c)

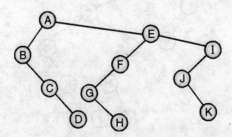

Fig. 7.3.2(d) : Binary tree representation of forest in Fig. 7.3.2(b)

Example 7.3.1 : What is the necessity of converting a tree into binary tree ? Given the following tree :

Fig. Ex. 7.3.1

Covert it into a binary tree and list down the steps for the same.

Solution :

Algorithms for binary tree are simple and widely used. Thus it is easy to give a formal treatment to a binary tree. A tree can be converted into a binary tree using leftmost child right sibling relation.

- The left pointer points to the leftmost child.
- The right pointer points to its next sibling.

Equivalent binary tree :

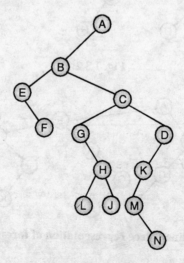

Fig. Ex. 7.3.1(a)

7.4 Types of Binary Tree

Q. Enlist the types of Binary Tree and give their meaning. **S - 09**

7.4.1 Full Binary Tree :

A binary tree is said to be full binary tree if each of its node has either two children or no child at all. Every level is completely filledup. Number of node at any level i in a full binary tree is given by 2^i. A full binary tree is shown in Fig. 7.4.1(a).

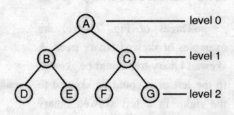

Fig. 7.4.1(a) : Full binary tree of depth 3

Total number of nodes in a full binary tree of height h = $2^0 + 2^1 + 2^2$ ... $+ 2^h = 2^{h+1} - 1$

The height of the tree shown is Fig. 7.4.1(a) is 2 and number of nodes is given by $2^{2+1} - 1 = 8 - 1 = 7$. Hence number of nodes n = $2^{h+1} - 1$

$$\text{Or} \qquad 2^{h+1} = n + 1$$

Taking log on both sides.

$$h + 1 = \log_2 (n + 1)$$

$$\therefore h = (\log_2 (n + 1)) - 1$$

Tournament tree is an example of full binary tree.

7.4.2 Complete Binary Tree :

A complete binary tree is defined as a binary tree where

(i)　　All leaf nodes are on level n or n – 1.

(ii)　　Levels are filled from left to right.

Examples of a complete binary tree are shown in Fig. 7.4.1(b).

Heap is an example of complete binary tree.

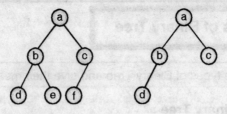

Fig. 7.4.1(b) : Complete binary trees

7.4.3 Skewed Binary Tree :

Threes of Fig. 7.4.1(c) are examples of skewed binary trees. A skewed binary tree could be skewed to the left or it could be skewed to the right. In a left skewed binary tree, most of the nodes have the left child without corresponding right child. Similarly, in a right skewed binary tree, most of the nodes have the right child without a corresponding left child.

Binary search tree could be an example of a skewed binary tree.

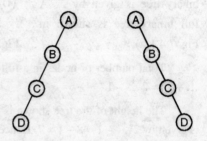

Fig. 7.4.1(c) : Skewed Binary trees

7.4.4 Strictly Binary Tree :

If every non-terminal node in a binary tree consists of non-empty left subtree and right subtree, then such a tree is called strictly binary tree. In other words, a node will have either two children or no child at all. Fig. 7.4.1(d) shows a strictly binary tree.

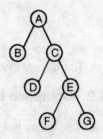

Fig. 7.4.1(d) : Strictly binary tree

7.4.5 Extended Binary Tree (2-Tree) :

In an extended tree, each empty subtree is replaced by a failure node. A failure node is represented by ☐. Nodes with 2 children are called internal nodes, and the nodes with 0 children are called external nodes. Any binary tree can be converted into a extended binary tree by replacing each empty subtree by a failure node.

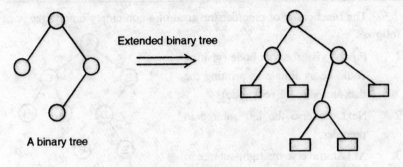

Fig. 7.4.1(e) : Extended binary tree

7.5 Binary Tree Traversal

Most of the tree operations require traversing a tree in a particular order. Traversing a tree is a process of visiting every node of the tree and exactly once. Since, a binary tree is defined in a recursive manner, tree traversal too could b

e defined recursively. For example, to traverse a tree, one may visit the root first, then the left subtree and finally traverse the right subtree. If we impose the restriction that left subtree is visited before the right subtree then three different combination of visiting the root, traversing left subtree, traversing right subtree is possible.

1.   Visit the root, traverse, left subtree, traverse right subtree.

2.   Traverse left subtree, visit the root, traverse right subtree.

3.   Traverse left subtree, traverse right subtree, visit the root.

These three techniques of traversal are known as preorder, inorder and postorder traversal of a binary tree.

7.5.1 Preorder Traversal (Recursive) :

> **Q.** State the principles of Pre-order and In-order traversal of Binary Tree. `S - 08`
>
> **Q.** Write an algorithm to traverse the tree in preorder and post order with example. `S - 2010`

The functioning of preorder traversal of a non-empty binary tree is as follows :

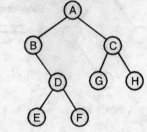

1. Firstly, visit the root node (visiting could be as simple as printing the data stored in the root node).

2. Next, traverse the left subtree in preorder.

3. At last, traverse the right-subtree in preorder.

Fig. 7.5.1 : A sample binary tree

Stepwise preorder traversal of tree is shown in Fig. 7.5.2 is given below :

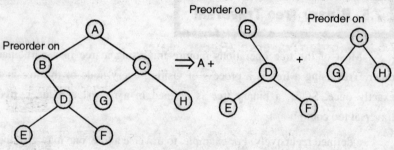

$$\Rightarrow \quad A + (B + \text{Preorder on } \textcircled{D}) + (C + \text{Preorder on } \textcircled{G} + \text{Preorder on } \textcircled{H})$$

$$\Rightarrow \quad A + (B + (D + \text{Preorder on } \textcircled{E} + \text{Preorder on } \textcircled{F})) + (CGH)$$

$$\Rightarrow \quad A + (BDEF) + (CGH)$$

$$\Rightarrow \quad ABDEFCGH$$

Fig. 7.5.2

'C' Function for Preorder Traversal :

```
void preorder (node * T) /* address of the root node is passed in T
*/
{
        if (T! = NULL)
        {
            printf ("\n%d", T → data);   /* visit the root */
            preorder (T → left);          /* preorder traversal on
left subtree */
            preorder (T → right);         /* preorder traversal on
right subtree */
        }
}
```

In words we could say, "visit" a node, traverse left and continue again. When you cannot continue, move right and begin again or move back until you can move right and resume.

7.5.2 Inorder Traversal (Recursive) :

Q. State the principles of Pre-order and In-order traversal of Binary Tree.   S - 08

Q. With the help of example, describe the process of in order traversal of binary tree.   W - 09

The functioning of inorder traversal of a non-empty binary tree is as follows :

1. Firstly, traverse the left subtree in inorder.

2. Next, visit the root node.

3. At last, traverse the right subtree in inorder.

Stepwise inorder traversal of tree shown in Fig. 7.5.3.

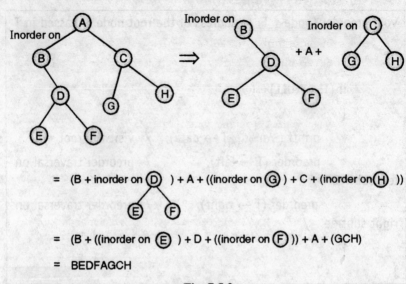

= (B + inorder on (D)) + A + ((inorder on (G)) + C + (inorder on (H)))
          (E) (F)

= (B + ((inorder on (E)) + D + ((inorder on (F))) + A + (GCH)

= BEDFAGCH

Fig. 7.5.3

'C' Function for Inorder Traversal :

```
void inorder (node *T)              /* address of the root node is
passed in T */
{
    if (T! =NULL)
        {
            inorder (T → left);          /* inorder traversal on
left subtree */
            printf ("\n%d", T → data);   /* visit the root */
            inorder (T → right);         /* inorder traversal on
right subtree */
        }
}
```

7.5.3 Postorder Traversal (Recursive) :

> **Q.** Write an algorithm to traverse the tree in preorder and post order with example. **S - 2010**

The functioning of postorder traversal of a non-empty binary tree is as follows :

1. Firstly, traverse the left subtree in postorder.
2. Next, traverse the right subtree in postorder.
3. At last, visit the root node.

Stepwise postorder traversal of tree shown in Fig. 7.5.4 is given below.

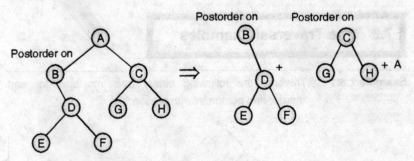

$\Rightarrow$ ((Postorder on D + B)) + ((Postorder on G) + (Postorder or H)+ C) + A
　　　　　　　　E　F

$\Rightarrow$ (((Postorder on E + (Postorder on F)) + D) + B) + GHCA

$\Rightarrow$ EFDBGHCA

Fig. 7.5.4

'C' Function for Postorder Traversal :

> **Q.** Write a 'C/C++' program for postorder traversal of binary tree. **W - 08**

```
void postorder (node * T)        /* address of the root node passed
                                    in T */
```

```
{
    if (T! = NULL)
    {
            postorder (T → left);            /* postorder traversal
on left subtree */
            postorder (T → right);      /* postorder traversal on
right subtree */
            printf ("\n%d", T → data);        /* visit the root */
    }
}
```

7.6 Tree Traversal Examples

Example 7.6.1 :   Traverse the following binary tree into preorder and inorder and postorder with reason.

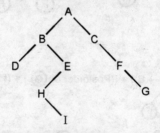

Fig. Ex. 7.6.1

Solution : Preorder traversal : The following of preorder traversal of a non-empty binary tree is as follows :

1.   Firstly, visit the root node.

2.   Next, traverse the left subtree in preorder.

3.   At last, traverse the right subtree in preorder.

     Stepwise preorder traversal on the above tree is given below.

Preorder on

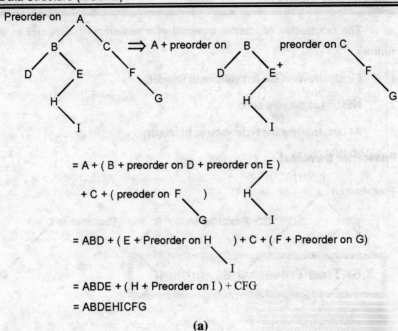

= A + (B + preorder on D + preorder on E)

+ C + (preoder on F   )

= ABD + (E + Preorder on H   ) + C + (F + Preorder on G)

= ABDE + (H + Preorder on I) + CFG

= ABDEHICFG

(a)

Inorder traversal :

Inorder on

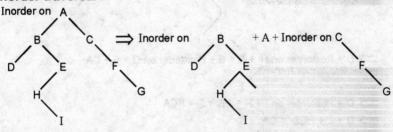

⟹ Inorder on D + B + inorder on E + A + C + inorder on F

⟹ DB + inorder on H + E + AC + F + inorder on G

= DB + H + inorder on I + EACF + G

= DBHIEACFG

(b)

Fig. Ex. 7.6.1

The functioning of inorder traversal of a non-empty binary tree is as follows :

1.　Firstly, traverse the left subtree in inorder.

2.　Next, visit the root node.

3.　At last, traverse the right subtree in inorder.

Postorder traversal :

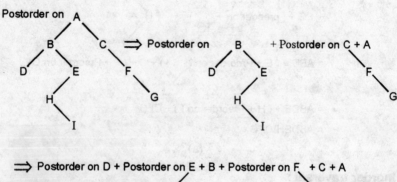

$\Rightarrow$ Postorder on D + Postorder on E + B + Postorder on F + C + A

$\Rightarrow$ D + Postorder on H + E + B + Postorder on G + F + CA

$\Rightarrow$ D + Postorder on I + H + EB + G + FCA

$\Rightarrow$ D + I + HEBGFCA

$\Rightarrow$ DIHEBGFCA

Fig. Ex. 7.6.1 (c)

The functioning of postorder traversal of a non-empty binary tree is as follows :

1.　Firstly, traverse the left subtree in postorder.

2.　Next, traverse the right subtree in postorder.

3.　At last, visit the root node.

Example 7.6.2 : Traverse the following binary tree into preorder and inorder.

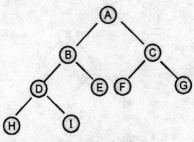

Fig. Ex. 7.6.2

Solution :

Preorder Traversal :

Preorder on

$\Rightarrow$ A + Preorder on B + Preorder on C

$\Rightarrow$ A + B + Preorder on D + Preorder on E + C + Preorder on F + Preorder on G

$\Rightarrow$ AB + D + Preorder on H + Preorder on I + EC + F + G

$\Rightarrow$ ABD + H + I + ECFG　　$\Rightarrow$ ABDHIECFG

Fig. Ex. 7.6.2 (a)

Inorder Traversal :

Inorder on

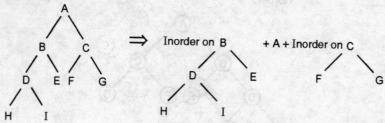

$\Rightarrow$ Inorder on D + B + Inorder on E + A + Inorder on F + C + Inorder on G

$\Rightarrow$ AB + D + Preorder on H+ Preorder on I + EC + F + G

$\Rightarrow$ Inorder on H + D + inorder on I + B + E + A + F + C + G

$\Rightarrow$ H + D + I + BEAFCG

$\Rightarrow$ HDIBEAFCG

Fig. Ex. 7.6.2 (b)

Example 7.6.3 : Perform inorder, preorder and postorder traversal of the following binary tree.

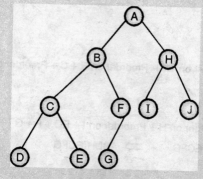

Fig. Ex. 7.6.3

S - 08

Soluation :

Preorder sequence   :   A B C D E F G H I J

Inorder sequence   :   D C E B G F A I H J

Postorder sequence   :   D E C G F B I J H A

Example 7.6.4 : For the given binary tree, perform inorder, preorder and postorder traversal.

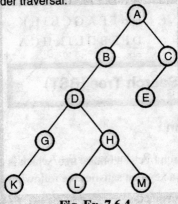

Fig. Ex. 7.6.4

W - 08

Solution :

Preorder sequence	:	A B D G K H L M C E
Inorder sequence	:	K G D L H M A E C
Postorder sequence	:	K G L M H D B E C A

Example 7.6.5 : For the given binary tree, perform inorder, preorder and postorder traversal.

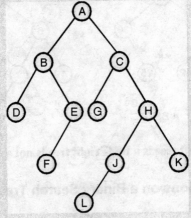

Fig. Ex. 7.6.5

S - 09

Solution :

Preorder sequence　　:　　A B D E F C G H J L K

Inorder sequence　　:　　D B F E A G C L J H K

Postorder sequence　:　　D F E B G L J K H C A

7.7 Binary Search Tree (BST)

7.7.1 Definition :

A binary search tree is a binary tree, which is either empty or in which each node contains a key that satisfies the following conditions :

(1)　All keys are distinct.

(2)　For every node, X, in the tree, the values of all the keys in its left subtree are smaller than the key value in X.

(3)　For every node, X, in the tree, the values of all the keys in its right subtree are larger than the key value in X.

Binary search tree finds its application in searching. In Fig. 7.7.1, the tree on the left is a binary search tree. Tree on the right is not a BST. Left subtree of the node with key 8 has a key with value 9.

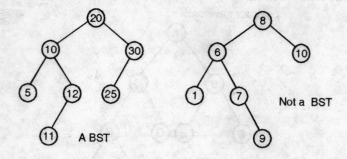

Fig. 7.7.1 : Left tree is a BST, right tree is not a binary search tree

7.7.2 Operations on a Binary Search Tree :

(1)　Initialise　　　　　　　　(2)　Find

(3)　Makeempty　　　　　　　(4)　Insert

(5)　Delete　　　　　　　　　(6)　Create

(7)　Findmin　　　　　　　　(8)　Findmax

Structure of node of a binary search tree :

```
typedef struct BSTnode
{
    int data;
    struct BSTnode *left, *right;
} BSTnode;
```

7.7.2.1   Initialize Operation :

Initially the tree is empty and hence the referencing pointer root should be set to NULL.

➤   'C' function for initialise.

```
BSTnode* initialize()
{
    return(NULL) ;
}
```

7.7.2.2   Find Operation :

> **Q.**   Explain searching a value in Binary search tree with example.
> **S - 08**

It is often required to find whether a key is there in the tree. If the key, X, is found in the node T, the function returns the address of T or NULL if there is no such node.

Recursive algorithm for find :

	return value	condition
Find (root, x)	NULL	if root == NULL
	root	if root → data == x
	return (Find (root → right, x))	if x > root → data
	return (Find (root → left, x))	if x < root → data

If the key, X, is found to be larger than the value stored in node T, we make a recursive call to function with the right subtree. Otherwise, we make a recursive call to function with the left subtree.

'C' Function for find() Recursive :

```
BSTnode *find(BSTnode * root ,int x)
{
    if((root==NULL)
        return(NULL);
    if(root->data==x)
        return(root);
    if(x>root->data)
        return(find(root->right),x));
    return(find(root->left),x));
}
```

'C' Function for find() Non-Recursive :

Q. Write a program for 'Binary Search in 'C' language. **S - 08**

```
BSTnode *find(BSTnode *root,int x)
{
    while(root!=NULL)
    {
        if(x==root->data)
            return(root);
        if(x>root->data)
            root=root->right;
        else
        root=root->left;
    }
    return(NULL);
}
```

7.7.2.3 Makeempty Operation :

This function deletes every node of the tree. It also releases the memory acquired by the node.

'C' Function to Release Memory :

```
BSTnode *makeempty (BSTnode *root)
```

```
{
    if (root ! = NULL)
        {
            makeempty (root → left);
            makeempty (root → right);
            free (root);
        }
        return (NULL);
}
```

7.7.2.4　Insert Operation :

The function insert (T, x), adds element x to an existing binary search tree. T is tested for NULL, if so, a new node is created to hold x. T is made to point to the new node. If the tree is not empty then we search for x as in find() operation.

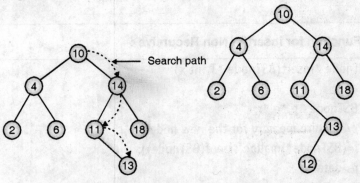

(a) Before insertion of the new key 12　　(b) After inserting 12
Fig. 7.7.2 Insertion operation into a binary search tree

If x is already there in the then insert() operation terminates without insertion as a BST is not allowed to have duplicate keys. If we find a NULL pointer during the find() operation. We replace it by a pointer to a new node holding x. Fig. 7.7.2 shows the insert operation.

'C' Function for insert() – Recursive :

```
BSTnode *insert(BSTnode *T,int x)
{
    if(T==NULL)
```

```
    {
        T=(BST *)malloc(sizeof(BSTnode));
        T->data=x;
        T->left=NULL;
        T->right=NULL;
        return(T);
    }
    if(x > T->data)              // insert in right subtree
    {
        T->right=insert(T->right,x);
        return(T);
    }
    T->left=insert(T->left,x);    //insert in left subtree
    return(T);
}
```

'C' Function for insert() - Non Recursive :

```
BSTnode *insert(BSTnode *T,int x)
{
    BSTnode *p,*q,*r;
    // acquire memory for the new node
    r=(BSTnode*)malloc(sizeof(BSTnode));
    r->data=x;
    r->left=NULL;
    r->right=NULL;
    if(T==NULL)
        return(r);
    // find the leaf node for insertion
    P=T;
    while(p!=NULL)
    {
        q=p;        //save p before advancing
        if(x>p->data)
            p=p->right;
        else
```

```
            p=p->left;
    }
    if(x>q->data)
        q->right=r;  // x as right child of q
    else
        q->left=r;   //x as left child of q
    return(T);
}
```

7.7.2.5 Example on Creation of a BST :

Example 7.7.1 :   Insert the integers 7, 2, 9, 0, 5, 6, 8, 1 into a binary search tree by repeated application of insert operation.

Solution :

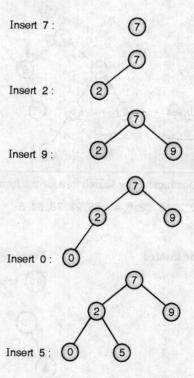

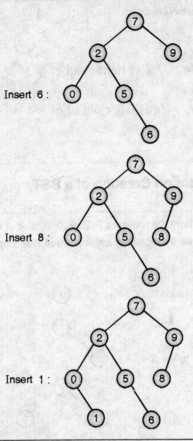

Insert 6 :

Insert 8 :

Insert 1 :

Example 7.7.2 : Construct binary search tree for the following data :

10, 3, 15, 22, 6, 45, 65, 23, 78, 34, 5

Solution :

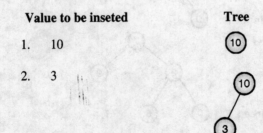

Value to be inseted	Tree
1. 10	10
2. 3	10 / 3

Value to be inseted   **Tree**

3. 15

4. 22

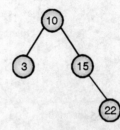

5. 6

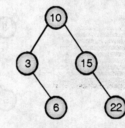

6. 45,65

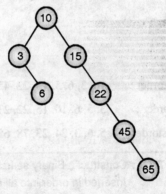

Value to be inseted　　　　　　　　　**Tree**

7.　23,78

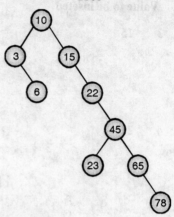

8.　34,5

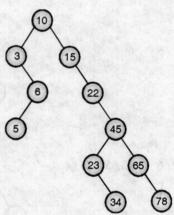

Preorder :　10, 3, 6, 5, 15, 22, 45, 23, 34, 65, 78

Inorder :　3, 5, 6, 10, 15, 22, 23, 34, 45, 65, 78

Postorder :　5, 6, 3, 34, 23, 78, 65, 45, 22, 15, 10

Example 7.7.3 : Construct a Binary search tree from the given list of letters inserted in order into all empty binary search tree
J, R, D, G, T, E, M, H, P, A, F, Q　　S - 09

Solution :

Sr. No.	Letter to be inserted	Tree
1	J	Ⓙ

Sr. No.	Letter to be inserted	Tree
2	R	
3	D	
4	G	
5	T	
6	E	

Sr. No.	Letter to be inserted	Tree
7	M	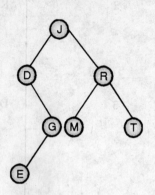
8	H	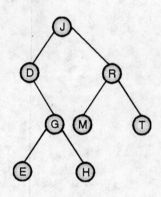
9	P	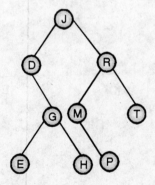

Sr. No.	Letter to be inserted	Tree
10	A	
11	F	
12	Q	

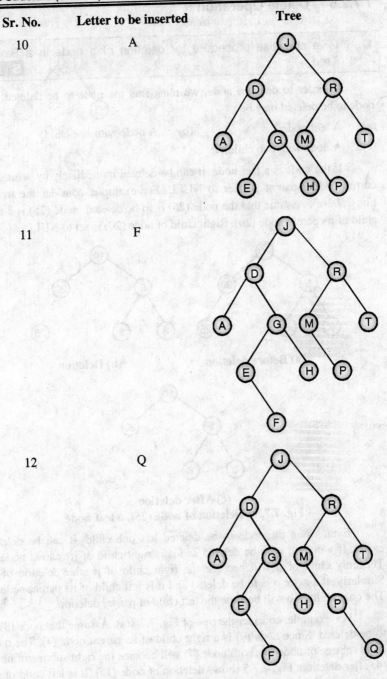

Fig. Ex. 7.7.3

7.7.2.6　Delete Operation :

> **Q.** Give stepwise procedure for deletion of a node in a Binary Tree.　**S - 08**

In order to delete a node, we must find the node to be deleted. The node to be deleted may be :

(a)　A leaf node　　　　(b)　A node with one child

(c)　A node with two children.

If the node is a leaf node, it can be deleted immediately by setting the corresponding parent pointer to NULL. For example, consider the tree of Fig. 7.7.3(a). Assume that the node (25) is to be deleted. node (25) is a right child of its parent node (20). Right child of node (20) is set to NULL.

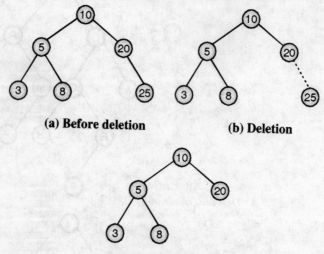

(a) Before deletion　　　　**(b) Deletion**

(c) After deletion
Fig. 7.7.3 : Deletion of node (25), a leaf node

Even when the node to be deleted has one child, it can be deleted easily. If a node q is to be deleted and it is right child of its parent node p. The only child of q will become the right child of p after deletion of q. Similarly, if a node q is to be deleted and it is left child of its parent node p. The only child of q will become the left child of p after deletion.

For example, consider the tree of Fig. 7.7.4(a). Assume that node (9) is to be deleted. Since node (9) is a right child of its parent node (4). The only child subtree of node (9), with node (7) will become the right subtree of node (4) after deletion. Fig. 7.7.5 shows deletion of node (15). It is left child of its parent node (20).

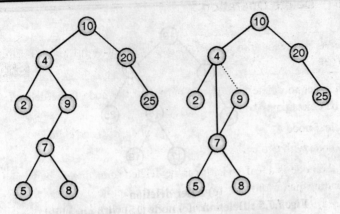

(a) Before deletion   (b) Deletion

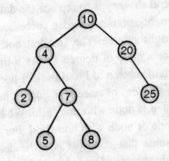

(c) After deletion

Fig. 7.7.4 : Deletion of a node (9) with one child

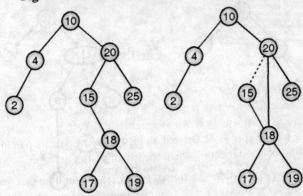

(a) Before deletion   (b) Deletion

Fig. 7.7.5 Contd…

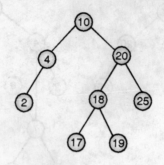

(c) After deletion
Fig. 7.7.5 : Deletion of a node (15) with one child

The case in which the node to be deleted has two children is a bit complicated. The general strategy is to replace the data of this node with the smallest data of the right subtree (inorder successor) and then delete the smallest node in the right subtree. The smallest node in right subtree will either be a leaf node or a node of degree 1. As a first step, the node with smallest value in the right subtree of P (address of node (4)) is found and its address is stored in q. Content of node q is copied in node P. As a second step, the node q is deleted, a node with one child. We have already discussed how to delete a leaf node or node with one child. For example, consider the tree of Fig. 7.7.6. Assume that node (4) is to be deleted. Node (7) is the smallest node in the right subtree of node (4). Value 7 is copied in the node P (earlier node (4)) as shown in the Fig. 7.7.6(b). Now, the node q is deleted.

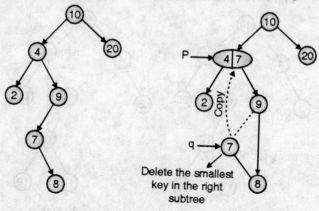

(a) Before deletion   **(b) Deletion**
Fig. 7.7.6 Contd...

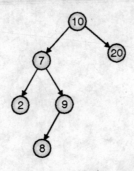

(c) After deletion

Fig. 7.7.6 : Deletion of a node (4) with two children

'C' Function for Deletion :

```c
BSTnode *delete(BSTnode *T,int x)
{
    if(T==NULL)
    {
        printf("\nElement not found :");
        return(T);
    }
    if(x < T->data)           // delete in left subtree
    {
        T->left=delete(T->left,x);
        return(T);
    }
    if(x > T->data)           // delete in right subtree
    {
        T->right=delete(T->right,x);
        return(T);
    }
    // element is found
    if(T->left==NULL && t->right==NULL)   // a leaf node
    {
        temp=T;
        free(temp);
```

```
        return(NULL);
    }
    if(T->left==NULL)
    {
        temp=T;
        T=T->right;
        free(temp);
        return(T);
    }
    if(T->right==NULL)
    {
        temp=T;
        T=T->left;
        free(temp);
        return(T);
    }
    // node with two children
    temp=find_min(T->right);
    T->data=temp->data;
    T->right=delet(T->right, temp ->data);
    return(T);
}
```

7.7.2.7 Create :

A binary search tree can be created by making repeated calls to insert operation.

'C' Function for Tree Creation :

```
BSTnode *create()
{
    int n,x,i;
    BSTnode *root;
    root=NULL;
    printf("\nEnter no. of nodes :");
```

```
    scanf("%d",&n);
    printf("\nEnter tree values :");
    for(i=0;i<n;i++)
    {
        scanf("%d",&x);
        root=insert(root,x);
    }
    return(root);
}
```

7.7.2.8   FindMin :

This function returns to address of the node with smallest value in the tree.

> **'C' function for finding the smallest value is a BST.**

```
BSTnode *findmin (BSTnode *T)
{
        while (T→ left ! = NULL)
            T = T → left ;
        return (T);
}
```

7.7.2.9   FindMax :

This function returns the address of the node with largest value in the tree.

> **'C' function for finding the largest value in a BST.**

```
BSTnode *findmax (BSTnode * T)
{
        while (T → right ! = NULL)
            T = T → right ;
        return (T);
}
```

7.7.3 Program for Various Operations on BST :

> **Program 7.7.1 : Program showing various operations on a binary search tree.**

```c
#include<conio.h>
#include<stdio.h>
#include<stdlib.h>
typedef struct BSTnode
{
    int data;
    struct BSTnode *left,*right;
}BSTnode;

BSTnode *initialise();
BSTnode *find(BSTnode *,int);
BSTnode *insert(BSTnode *,int);
BSTnode *delet(BSTnode *,int);
BSTnode *find_min(BSTnode *);
BSTnode *find_max(BSTnode *);
BSTnode *create();
void inorder(BSTnode *T);
void main()
{
    BSTnode *root,*p;
    int x;
    clrscr();
    initialise();
    root=create();
    printf("\n**** BST created ****");
    printf("\ninorder traversal on the tree ");
    inorder(root);
    p=find_min(root);
    printf("\n smallest key in the tree = %d",p->data);
    p=find_max(root);
```

```
   printf("\nlargest key in the tree = %d",p->data);
   printf("\n **** delete operation ****");
   printf("\nEnter the key to be deleted :");
   scanf("%d",&x);
   root=delet(root,x);
   printf("inorder traversal after deletion :");
   inorder(root);
}
void inorder(BSTnode *T)
{
  if(T!=NULL)
  {
        inorder(T->left);
        printf("%5d",T->data);
        inorder(T->right);
  }
}
BSTnode *initialise()
{
  return(NULL);
}
BSTnode *find(BSTnode *root,int x)
{
  while(root!=NULL)
  {
        if(x==root->data)
            return(root);
        if(x>root->data)
            root=root->right;
        else
        root=root->left;
  }
  return(NULL);
}
BSTnode *insert(BSTnode *T,int x)
```

```
{
    BSTnode *p,*q,*r;
    // acquire memory for the new node
    r=(BSTnode*)malloc(sizeof(BSTnode));
    r->data=x;
    r->left=NULL;
    r->right=NULL;
    if(T==NULL)
        return(r);
    // find the leaf node for insertion
    p=T;
    while(p!=NULL)
    {
        q=p;
        if(x>p->data)
            p=p->right;
        else
            p=p->left;
    }
    if(x>q->data)
        q->right=r;  // x as right child of q
    else
        q->left=r;   //x as left child of q
    return(T);
}
BSTnode *delet(BSTnode *T,int x)
{
    BSTnode *temp;
    if(T==NULL)
    {
        printf("\nElement not found :");
        return(T);
    }
    if(x < T->data)              // delete in left subtree
    {
```

```
        T->left=delet(T->left,x);
        return(T);
}
if(x > T->data)                // delete in right subtree
{
        T->right=delet(T->right,x);
        return(T);
}
// element is found
if(T->left==NULL && T->right==NULL)   // a leaf node
{
        temp=T;
        free(temp);
        return(NULL);
}
if(T->left==NULL)
{
        temp=T;
        T=T->right;
        free(temp);
        return(T);
}
if(T->right==NULL)
{
        temp=T;
        T=T->left;
        free(temp);
        return(T);
}
// node with two children
temp=find_min(T->right);
T->data=temp->data;
T->right=delet(T->right,x);
return(T);
}
```

```
BSTnode *create()
{
    int n,x,i;
    BSTnode *root;
    root=NULL;
    printf("\nEnter no. of nodes :");
    scanf("%d",&n);
    printf("\nEnter tree values :");
    for(i=0;i<n;i++)
    {
        scanf("%d",&x);
        root=insert(root,x);
    }
    return(root);
}
BSTnode *find_min(BSTnode *T)
{
    while(T->left!=NULL)
        T=T->left;
    return(T);
}
BSTnode *find_max(BSTnode *T)
{
    while(T->right!=NULL)
        T=T->right;
    return(T);
}
```

Output

```
Enter no. of nodes : 5
Enter tree values : 34    11 2   99 6
**** BST created ****
inorder traversal on the tree    2   6   11   34   99
 smallest key in the tree = 2
largest key in the tree = 99
 **** delete operation ****
Enter the key to be deleted :11
```

inorder traversal after deletion :   2   6   34   99

7.8 Threaded Binary Trees (TBT)

Q. Explain threaded trees with diagram.   S - 09

In a linked representation of a binary tree, there are more null links than actual pointers. These null links can be replaced by pointers, called threads to other nodes. A left null link of a node is replaced with the address of its inorder predecessor. Similarly, a right null link of a node is replaced with the address of its inorder successor.

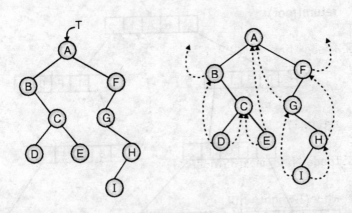

Fig. 7.8.1 : A sample tree before threading   **Fig. 7.8.2 : Tree of Fig. 7.8.1 after threading**

The tree T of Fig. 7.8.2 has 9 nodes and 10 null links, which have been replaced by thread links. If we traverse the tree in inorder the nodes will be visited in the order BDCEAGIHF. Consider a node D. The left null link of D is replaced with a the link pointing to its inorder predecessor. The right null link of D is replaced with a thread link pointing to its inorder successor.

In the memory representation of a tree node we must be able to distinguish between threads and normal pointers. This can be done by adding two extra fields *l*bit and rbit.

*l*bit of a node = 1 left child is normal

*l*bit of a node = 0 left link is replaced with a thread

rbit of a node = 1 right child is normal

rbit of a node = 0 right link is replaced with a thread

In the Fig. 7.8.2, two threads have been left dangling. Node B has no inorder predecessor and the node F has no inorder successor. This problem can be solved by taking a head node.

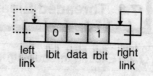

left link | lbit | data | rbit | right link

Fig. 7.8.3 : Initial status of head node

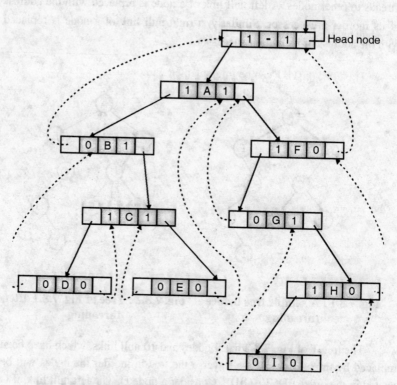

Fig. 7.8.4 : Memory representation of the TBT of Fig. 7.8.2

In "C" language, the following structure can be defined to represent one node of a TBT (threaded binary tree). It is assumed that a node contains a character data.

```c
typedef struct TBTnode
{
    char data;
    struct TBTnode * left;
    struct TBTnode * right;
    int lbit, rbit;
} TBT node;
```

Traversal on TBT can be implemented without using a stack.

7.9 Application of Trees

7.9.1 Expression Trees :

When an expression is represented through a tree, it is known as an expression tree. The leaves of an expression tree are operands, such as constants or variables names and all internal nodes contain operations. Fig. 7.9.1 gives an example of an expression tree.

$$(a + b * c) * e + f$$

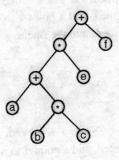

A preorder traversal on the expression tree gives prefix equivalent of the expression. A postorder traversal on the expression tree gives postfix equivalent of the expression.

Fig. 7.9.1

Prefix (expression tree of 7.9.1) = + * + a * b c e f

Postfix (expression tree of 7.9.1) = a b c * + e * f +

Constructing an expression tree :

Here, we will discuss an algorithm for constructing an expression tree from a postfix expression. In case an expression tree is to be converted from infix expression, infix expression should be converted to postfix.

Algorithm :

We read our expression one symbol at a time. If the symbol is an operand, we create a one node tree and push a pointer to it onto a stack. If the symbol is an operator, we pop pointer to two trees T_2 and T_1 from the stack and form a new tree whose root is the operator and whose left and right children point to T_1 and T_2 respectively. A pointer to this new tree is then pushed onto the stack.

As an example, suppose the input is

$$abc * + e * f +$$

The first three symbols are operands, so we create one-node trees push pointers to them onto a stack.

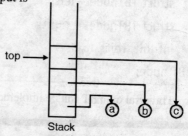

Fig. 7.9.2

Next, 4 * is read, so two pointers to tree are popped, a new tree is formed, and a pointer to it is pushed onto the stack.

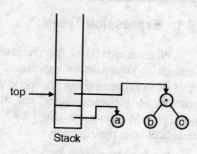

Fig. 7.9.3

Next, a + is read, so two pointers to tree are popped, a new tree is formed, and a pointer to it is pushed onto the stack.

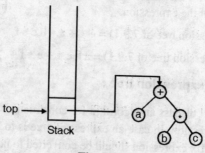

Fig. 7.9.4

Next, e is read, a one node tree is created and a pointer to it is pushed onto the stack.

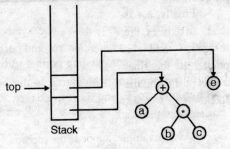

Fig. 7.9.5

Next, a * is read, so two pointers to tree are popped, a new tree is formed, and a pointer to it is pushed onto the stack.

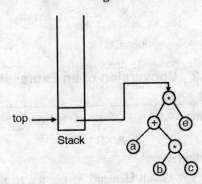

Fig. 7.9.6

Continuing, f is read, a one node tree is created and a pointer to it is pushed onto the stack.

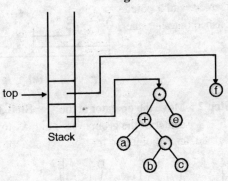

Fig. 7.9.7

Finally, a + is read, two trees are merged, and a pointer to the final tree is pushed on the stack.

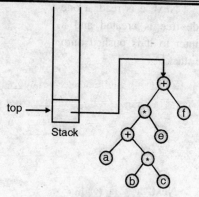

Fig. 7.9.8

7.9.2 Conversion of an Expression into Binary Tree :

Example 7.9.1 :   Construct the binary tree for the following expression.

A + B * C + D * E

Solution :

Step 1 :   Group elements as per the sequence of evaluation. [This step is similar to fully parenthesizing an expression].

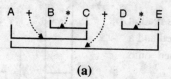

(a)

Step 2 : Move the operator at the center of the group.

Step 3 : Invert the structure.

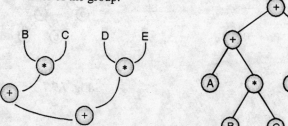

(b)   (c)

Fig. Ex. 7.9.1

Example 7.9.2 : Construct the binary tree for the following expression

$$(A + B) \uparrow (B * C) + D / E$$

Solution :

Step 1 : Group elements as per the sequence of evaluation. [This step is similar to fully parenthesizing an expression].

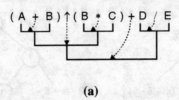

(a)

Step 2 : Move the operator at the center of the group.

Step 3 : Inverting the structure, we get

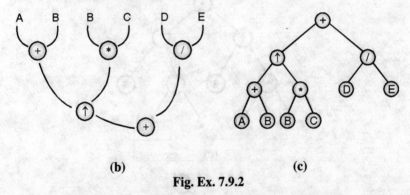

(b)   **(c)**

Fig. Ex. 7.9.2

Example 7.9.3 : Draw the tree structure for the following expressions	
(i) $(2a + 5b)^3 (x - 7y)^4$	W - 08
(ii) $(a - 3b) (2x - y)^3$	W - 08
(iii) $E_1 = (a - 3b) (2x - y)^3$	S - 09
(iv) $E_2 = (2a + 5b)^3 (x - 7y)^4$	S - 09
(v) $(- x + 2y + 3z + 4a + 5b + 6c)^4 * (7d + 4Z)^2$	W - 09
(vi) $(x + 2y + 3z - 4 - 4a + 5b + 6c)^4 * (7b + 4z)^2$	S - 10

Solution :

(i) $(2a + 5b)^3 (x - 7y)^4$

Re- writing the expression after specifying every operator, we get

$((2 * a + 5 * b) \uparrow 3) * ((x - 7 * y) \uparrow 4)$

Stepwise construction of tree :

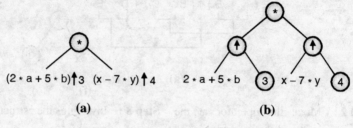

(a)   (b)

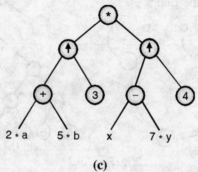

(c)

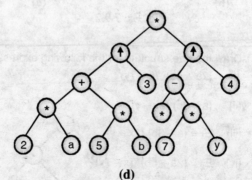

(d)
Fig. Ex. 7.9.3 contd..

(ii) $(a - 3b) (2 x - y)^3$

Fully specifying every operator, we get,

$(a - 3 * b) * (2 * x - y) \uparrow 3$

Stepwise construction of tree :

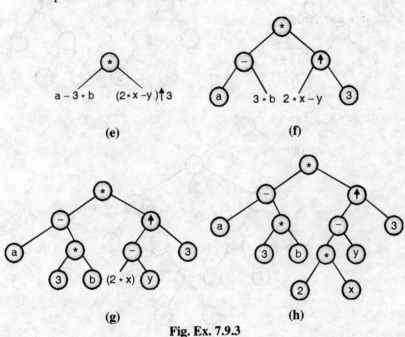

(e)   (f)

(g)   (h)

Fig. Ex. 7.9.3

(iii) $E_1 = (a - 3b) (2x - y)^3$

Fully specifying every operator, we get

$E_1 = (a - 3 * b) * (2 * x - y) \uparrow 3$

Stepwise construction of tree :

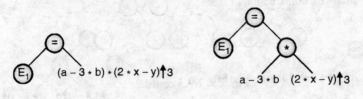

(i)   (j)

Fig. Ex. 7.9.3 contd..

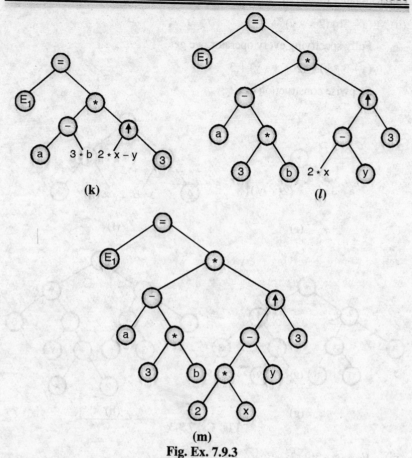

(k)

(l)

(m)

Fig. Ex. 7.9.3

(iv) $E_2 = (2a + 5b)^3 (x - 7y)^4$

Fully specifying every operator, we get

$E_2 = ((2 * a + 5 * b) \uparrow 3) * ((x - 7 * y) \uparrow 4)$

Stepwise construction of tree :

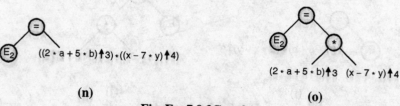

(n)

(o)

Fig. Ex. 7.9.3Contd…

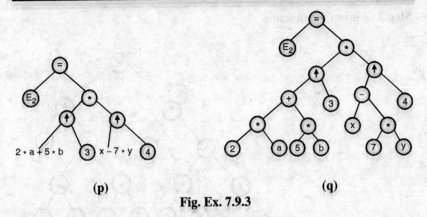

(p)

(q)

Fig. Ex. 7.9.3

(v) $(x + 2y + 3z + 4a + 5b + 6c)^4 * (7d + 4z)^2$

Step 1 : Fully specifying every operater, we get,

$(x + 2 * y + 3 * z + 4 * a + 5 * b + 6 * c) \uparrow 4 * (7 * d + 4 * z) \uparrow 2$

Step 2 : Group elements as per the sequence of evaluation. (This step is similar to fully parenthesizing an expression)

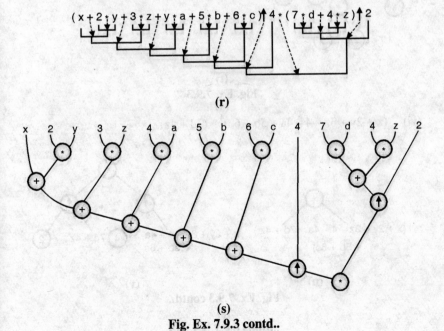

(r)

(s)

Fig. Ex. 7.9.3 contd..

Step 3 : invert the structure.

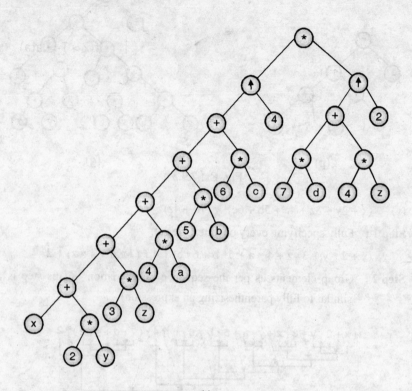

(t)
Fig. Ex. 7.9.3

(vi)　$(x + 2y + 3z - 4 - 4a + 5b + 6c)^4 * (7d + 4z)^2$

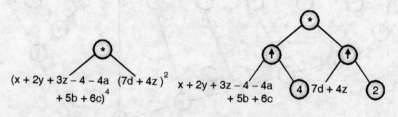

(u)　　　　　　　　　　　　　**(v)**

Fig. Ex. 7.9.3 contd..

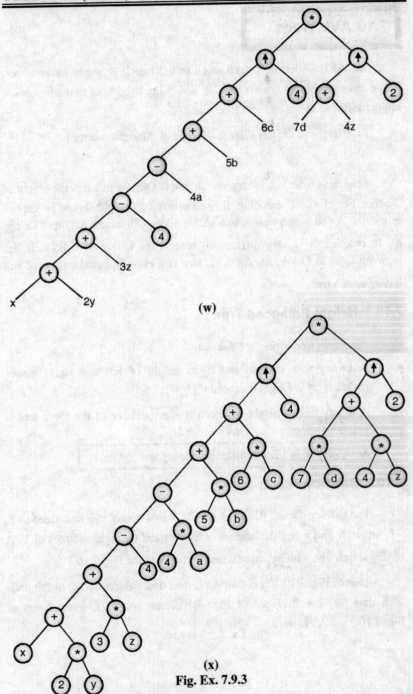

(w)

(x)
Fig. Ex. 7.9.3

7.10 AVL Trees

An AVL (Adelson-Velskii and Landis) tree is a height balance tree. These trees are binary search trees in which the heights of two siblings are not permitted to differ by more than one.

i.e. |Height of the left subtree – height of the right subtree |

$$\leq 1$$

Searching time in a binary search tree is O(h), where h is the height of the tree. For efficient searching, it is necessary that height should be kept to minimum. A full binary search tree with n nodes will have a height of $O(\log_2 n)$. In practice, it is very difficult to control the height of a BST. It lies between O(n) to $O(\log_2 n)$. An AVL tree is a **close approximation** of full binary search tree.

7.10.1 Height Balanced Tree :

- An empty tree is height balanced.

- A binary tree with h_l and h_r as height of left and right subtree respectively is height balanced if $| h_l - h_r | \leq 1$

- A binary tree is height balanced if every subtree of the given tree is height balanced.

> An AVL tree is a height balanced binary search tree.

7.10.2 Balance Factor :

The balance factor, BF(T) of a node T in a binary tree is defined as $h_l - h_r$ where h_l and h_r are the heights of the left and the right subtrees of T. A binary search tree with balance factors is shown in the Fig. 7.10.1.

Tree of Fig. 7.10.1 is not an AVL tree. The balance factor of the node with data 40 is + 2. Trees of Fig. 7.10.2 are non-AVL trees. Trees of Fig. 7.10.3 are AVL-trees.

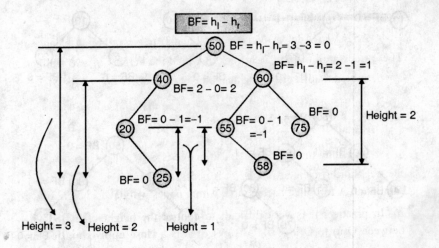

Fig. 7.10.1 : A sample BST with balance factors

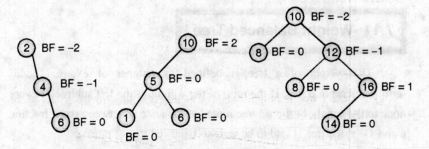

Fig. 7.10.2: Non-AVL trees

The balance factor of a node in an AVL tree could be –1, 0 or 1.

- If the balance factor of a node is 0 then the heights of the left and right subtrees are equal.

- If the balance factor of a node is +1 then the height of the left subtree is one more than the height of the right subtree.

- If the balance factor of a node is –1 then the height of the left subtree is one less than the height of the right subtree.

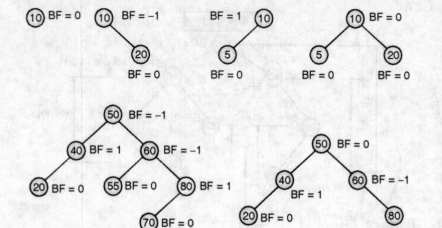

Fig. 7.10.3 : AVL trees

7.11 Weight Balanced Tree

The weight of a tree is defined as number of external nodes (null pointers) in a tree. If the ratio of the weight of the left subtree of every node to the weight of the subtree rooted at the node is between some fraction a and 1 – a, the tree is said to be weight- balanced tree of ratio a.

7.12 MSBTE Questions and Answers

Summer 2008 – Total Marks 24

Q. 1 State the principles of Pre-order and In-order traversal of Binary Tree. **(Sections 7.5.1 and 7.5.2)** **(2 Marks)**

Q. 2 Perform Inorder, Preorder and Postorder traversal of the following Binary Tree. (Refer Fig. No.Q. 2) **(Example 7.6.3)** **(6 Marks)**

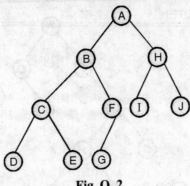

Fig. Q. 2

Q. 3   Explain searching a value in Binary search tree with example.

(Section 7.7.2.2)   **(4 Marks)**

Q. 4   Write a program for 'Binary Search in 'C' language.

(Section 7.7.2.2)   **(4 Marks)**

Q. 5   Give stepwise procedure for deletion of a node in a Binary Tree.

(Section 7.7.2.6)   **(4 Marks)**

Q. 6   Give recursive algorithms for pre-order, in-order and post-order, traversal of Binary Tree. **(Section 7.5)**   **(4 Marks)**

Winter 2008 – Total Marks 19

Q. 7   Define the terms related to Binary Tree : Level, Depth, Leaf Node, Root Node. **(Section 7.7.1)**   **(2 Marks)**

Q. 8   Explain the binary tree with suitable example and diagram.

(Section 7.2)   **(6 Marks)**

Q. 9   For the given binary tree in Fig. No. Q. 9, perform inorder, preorder and postorder traversal. **(Example 7.6.4)**   **(3 Marks)**

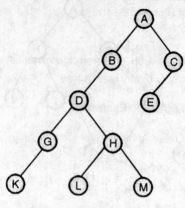

Fig. Q. 9

Q. 10 Write a 'C/C++' program for postorder traversal of binary tree.
(Section 7.5.3)   **(4 Marks)**

Q. 11 Draw the tree structure for the following expressions.

(i) $(2a + 5b)^3 (x - 7y)^4$

(ii) $(a - 3b) (2x - y)^3$ **(Example 7.9.3)**   **(4 Marks)**

> ### Summer 2009 – Total Marks 26

Q. 12 For the given Binary Tree, perform Inorder, Preorder and Post order traversal. **(Example 7.6.5)**   **(6 Marks)**

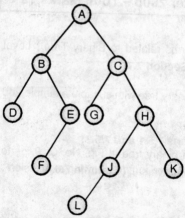

Fig. Q. 12

Q. 13 Enlist the types of Binary Tree and give their meaning.

(Section 7.4) (4 Marks)

Q. 14 Construct a Binary Search Tree from the given list of letters inserted in order into an empty binary search tree :

J,R,D,G,T,E,M,H,P,A,F,Q. (Example 7.7.3) (4 Marks)

Q. 15 Explain threaded trees with diagram. (Section 7.8) (4 Marks)

Q. 16 Draw the 2-tree corresponding to each of the following algebraic expressions :

$E_1 = (a - 3b) (2x - y)^3$

$E_2 = (2a + 5b)^3 (x - 7y)^4$ (Example 7.9.3) (4 Marks)

Q. 17 Describe in brief, the terms related to Binary Tree: Level, Depth, Leaf Node, Root Node. (Section 7.1.1) (4 Marks)

Winter 2009 – Total Marks 10

Q. 18 Explain the terms with the help of diagram.

(i) Siblings (ii) Leaf Node (Section 7.1.1) (2 Marks)

Q. 19 With the help of example, describe the process of in order traversal of binary tree. (4 Marks)

Q. 20 Draw tree structure for the following expression.

$(x + 2y + 3z + 4a + 5b + 6c)^4 * (7d + 4z)^2$ (Example 7.9.3) (4 Marks)

Summer 2010 – Total Marks 12

Q. 21 Write an algorithm to traverse the tree in preorder and post order with example. (Sections 7.5.1 and 7.5.3) (6 Marks)

Q. 22 Draw the tree structure for the following expression :

$(x + 2y + 3z - 4 - 4a + 5b + 6c)^4 * (7d + 4z)^2$

(Example 7.9.3) (6 Marks)

❏❏❏

Note

Graphs

Statistical Analysis

Year	Marks
Summer - 2008	12 Marks
Winter - 2008	12 Marks
Summer - 2009	12 Marks
Winter - 2009	18 Marks
Summer - 2010	18 Marks

8.1 Terminology and Representation

8.1.1 Definition :

Q. Describe in brief, the terms related to graph : nodes , edges , in-degree, out-degree.   **S - 08**

A graph G is a set of vertices (V) and set of edges (E). The set V is a finite, nonempty set of vertices. The set E is a set of pair of vertices representing edges.

$$G = (V, E)$$

$$V(G) = \text{Vertices of graph G}$$

$$E(G) = \text{Edges of graph G}$$

An example of graph is shown in Fig. 8.1.1.

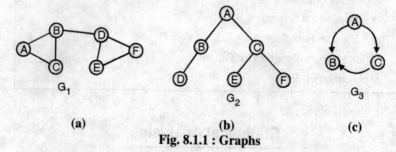

(a)   **(b)**   **(c)**

Fig. 8.1.1 : Graphs

The set representation for each of these graphs is given by

$$V(G_1) = \{A, B, C, D, E, F\}$$

$$V(G_2) = \{A, B, C, D, E, F\}$$

$$V(G_3) = \{A, B, C\}$$

$$E(G_1) = \{(A, B),(A, C),(B, C),(B, D),(D, E),(D, F),(E, F)\}$$

$$E(G_2) = \{(A,B),(A, C),(B, D),(C, E),(C, F)\}$$

$$E(G_3) = \{(A, B),(A, C),(C, B)\}$$

8.1.2 Undirected Graph :

A graph containing unordered pair of vertices is called an undirected graph. In an undirected graph, pair of vertices(A, B) and(B, A) represent the same edge.

The set of vertices V = {1, 2, 3, 4, 5}. The set of edges E = {(1, 2), (1, 3), (1, 5), (2, 3), (2, 4), (3, 4), (4, 5)}.

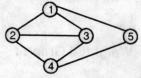

Fig. 8.1.2 : Example of an undirected graph

8.1.3 Directed Graph :

| Q. | Define following terms with respect to graph :
 (ii)   Directed graph   (iv)   Predecessor   **S - 2010** |

A graph containing ordered pair of vertices is called a directed graph. If an edge is represented using a pair of vertices (V_1, V_2) then the edge is said to be directed from V_1 to V_2.

V_1 is called predecessor of V_2 and V_2 is successor of V_1.

The first element of the pair, V_1 is called the start vertex and the second element of the pair, V_2 is called the end vertex. In a directed graph, the pairs (V_1, V_2) and (V_2, V_1) represent two different edges of a graph. Example of a directed graph is shown in Fig. 8.1.3.

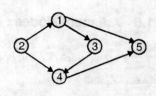

Fig. 8.1.3 : Example of a directed graph

The set of vertices V = {1, 2, 3, 4, 5, 5}.

The set of edges   E = {(1, 3), (1, 5), (2, 1), (2, 4), (3, 4), (4, 5)}.

8.1.4 A Complete Graph :

An undirected graph, in which every vertex has an edge to all other vertices is called a complete graph.

A complete graph with N vertices has $\frac{N(N-1)}{2}$ edges.

Example of a complete graph is shown in Fig. 8.1.4.

Fig. 8.1.4 : A complete graph

8.1.5 Weighted Graph :

A weighted graph is a graph in which edges are assigned some value. Most of the physical situations are shown using weighted graph. An edge may represent a highway link between two cities.

The weight will denote the distance between two connected cities using highway. Weight of an edge is also called its cost. The graph of Fig. 8.1.5 is an example of a weighted graph.

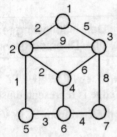

Fig. 8.1.5 : A weighted graph

8.1.6 Adjacent Nodes :

Two vertices V_1 and V_2 are said to be adjacent if there is an edge between V_1 and V_2.

8.1.7 Path :

A path from vertex V_0 to V_n is a sequence of vertices $V_0, V_1, V_2 \dots V_{n-1}, V_n$. Here, V_0 is adjacent to V_1, V_1 is adjacent to V_2 and V_{n-1} is adjacent to V_n. The **length** of a path is the number of edges on the path. A path with n vertices has a length of n – 1. A path is simple if all vertices on the path, except possibly the first and last, are distinct.

8.1.8 Cycle :

A cycle is a simple path that begins and ends at the same vertex. Fig. 8.1.6 is an example of a graph with cycle.

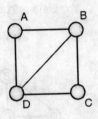

A B D A is a cycle of length 3

B D C B is a cycle of length 3

A B C D A is a cycle of length 4

Fig. 8.1.6 : A graph with cycles

8.1.9 Connected Graph :

A graph is said to be connected if there exists a path between every pair of vertices V_i and V_j.

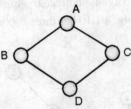

Fig. 8.1.7 : A connected graph

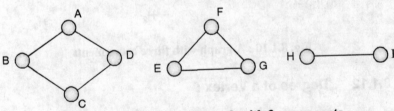

Fig. 8.1.8 : A disconnected graph with 3 components

The graph in Fig. 8.1.7 is a connected graph. But the graph in Fig. 8.1.8 is not connected as there is no path between D and E or between G and H. The graph of Fig. 8.1.8 consists of 3 connected components.

8.1.10 Subgraph :

A subgraph of G is a graph G_1 such that $V(G_1)$ is a subset of $V(G)$ and $E(G_1)$ is a subset of $E(G)$.

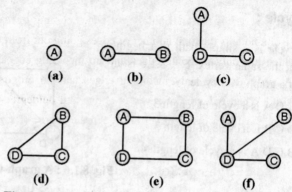

Fig. 8.1.9 : Some sub graphs of the graph of Fig. 8.1.6

8.1.11 Component :

A component H of an undirected graph is a maximal connected subgraph. The graph of Fig. 8.1.10 has three components H_1, H_2 and H_3.

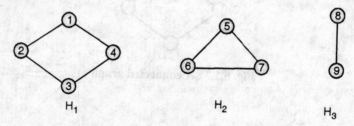

Fig. 8.1.10 : A graph with three components

8.1.12 Degree of a Vertex :

Q.	Describe in brief, the terms related to graph : nodes , edges , in-degree, out- degree.	S - 08
Q.	Explain in-degree and out-degree of a node with example.	W - 09
Q.	Define following terms with respect to graph : (i) In-degree of a node	S - 2010

The total number of edges linked to a vertex is called its degree. The **indegree** of a vertex is the total number of edges coming to that node. The **outdegree** of a node is the total number of edges going out from that node. A vertex, which has only outgoing edges and no incoming edges, is called a **source**. A vertex having only incoming edges and no outgoing edges is called a **sink**. When indegree of a vertex is one and outdegree is zero then such a vertex is called a **pendant** vertex. When the degree of a vertex is 0, it is an **isolated** vertex.

8.1.13　Self Edges or Self Loops :

An edge of the form (V, V) is known as self edge or self loop. An example of self edge is shown in the Fig. 8.1.11.

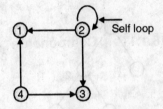

Fig. 8.1.11 : A graph with self loop

8.1.14　Multigraph :

A graph with multiple occurrences of the same edge is known as a multigraph. An example of multigraph is shown in the Fig. 8.1.12.

Fig. 8.1.12 : A multigraph

8.1.15　Tree :

A tree is a connected graph without any cycle. The graphs of Fig. 8.1.13 are not trees as they contain cycles. The graphs of Fig. 8.1.14 are example of trees.

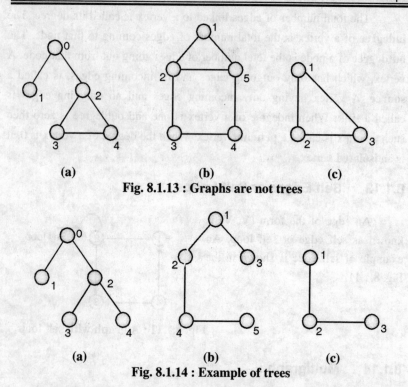

(a) **(b)** **(c)**

Fig. 8.1.13 : Graphs are not trees

(a) **(b)** **(c)**

Fig. 8.1.14 : Example of trees

> **Note :** Tree is a special case of a graph. When a tree is treated as a graph, it need not have a special vertex called the root.

8.1.16 Spanning Trees :

A spanning tree of a graph G = (V, E) is a connected subgraph of G having all vertices of G and no cycles in it. If the graph G is not connected then there is no spanning tree of G. A graph may have multiple spanning trees. Fig. 8.1.16 gives some of the spanning trees of the graph shown in Fig. 8.1.15.

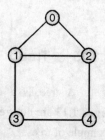

Fig. 8.1.15 : A sample connected graph

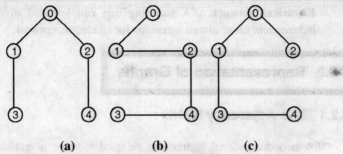

(a) **(b)** **(c)**
Fig. 8.1.16 : Spanning trees of the graph of Fig. 8.1.15

8.1.17 Minimal Spanning Tree :

The cost of a graph is the sum of the costs of the edges in the weighted graph. A spanning tree of a group $G = (V, E)$ is called a minimal cost spanning tree or simply the minimal spanning tree of G if its cost is minimum.

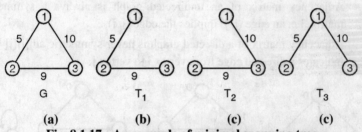

(a) **(b)** **(c)** **(c)**
Fig. 8.1.17 : An example of minimal spanning tree

G $\rightarrow$ A sample weighted graph

T1 $\rightarrow$ A spanning tree of G with cost $5 + 9 = 14$

T2 $\rightarrow$ A spanning tree of G with cost $10 + 9 = 19$

T3 $\rightarrow$ A spanning tree of G with cost $5 + 10 = 15$

Therefore, T_1 with cost 14 is the minimal cost spanning tree of the graph G.

8.1.18 Applications of Spanning Tree :

Spanning trees have many applications. Some of them are :

• **Routing of a packet in a network :** A node can represent a router, located in a city and the link between routers can be represented using an edge. A spanning tree can represent a network with the minimum number of links.

- **Electrical network :** A spanning tree can be used to obtain an independent set of circuit equations for an electric network.

8.2 Representation of Graphs

8.2.1 The Adjacency Matrix :

A two dimensional matrix can be used to store a graph. A graph $G = (V, E)$ where $V = \{0, 1, 2, \ldots n - 1\}$ can be represented using a two dimensional integer array of size $n \times n$.

int adj[20][20]; can be used to store a graph with 20 vertices.

adj[i][j] = 1, indicates presence of edge between two vertices i and j

= 0, indicates absence of edge between two vertices i and j

- A graph is represented using a square matrix.
- Adjacency matrix of an undirected graph is always a symmetric matrix, i.e. an edge (i, j) implies the edge (j, i).
- Adjacency matrix of a directed graph is never symmetric adj[i][j] = 1, indicates a directed edge from vertex i to vertex j.

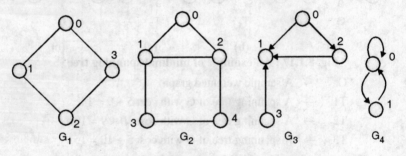

Fig. 8.2.1 : Graphs G_1, G_2, G_3 and G_4

	0	1	2	3
0	0	1	0	1
1	1	0	1	0
2	0	1	0	1
3	1	0	1	0

G_1 (Undirected graph)

	0	1	2	3	4
0	0	1	1	0	0
1	1	0	1	1	0
2	1	1	0	0	1
3	0	1	0	0	1
4	0	0	1	1	0

G_2 (Undirected graph)

	0	1	2	3
0	0	1	1	0
1	0	0	0	0
2	0	1	0	0
3	0	1	0	0

G_3 (Directed graph)

	0	1
0	1	1
1	1	0

G_4 (With self loop)

Fig. 8.2.2 : Adjacency matrix representation of graphs G_1, G_2, G_3 and G_4 of Fig. 8.2.1

Adjacency matrix representation of a weighted graph :

For weighted graph, the matrix adj[ ][ ] is represented as :

If there is an edge between vertices i and j then Adj[i][j] = weight of the edge (i, j) otherwise,

$$Adj[i][j] = 0$$

Fig. 8.2.3 is an example of representation of a weighted graph.

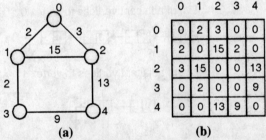

(a)　　　　　　　　(b)

Fig. 8.2.3 : A weighted graph and its adjacency matrix

- Adjacency matrix representation of graphs is very simple to implement.

- Memory requirement : Adjacency matrix representation of a graph wastes lot of memory space. Such matrices are found to be very sparse. Above representation requires space for n^2 elements for a graph with n vertices. If the graph has e number of edges then $n^2 - e$ elements in the matrix will be 0.

- Presence of an edge between two vertices V_i and V_j can be checked in constant time.

    if(adj[i][j] = = 1)

edge is present between vertices i and j

else

edge is absent between vertices i and j.

- Degree of a vertex can easily be calculated by counting all non-zero entries in the corresponding row of the adjacency matrix.

8.2.2 Adjacency List :

> **Q.** Explain the link representation of a Graph with suitable example. **W 08**

A graph can be represented using a linked list. For each vertex, a list of adjacent vertices is maintained using a linked list. It creates a separate linked list for each vertex V_i in the graph $G = (V, E)$

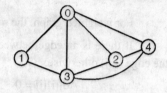

Fig. 8.2.4 : A graph

List of adjacent vertices to vertex 0

Head 0 → 1 → 2 → 3 → 4

List of adjacent vertices to vertex 1

Head 1 → 0 → 3

List of adjacent vertices to vertex 2

Head 2 → 0 → 3 → 4

List of adjacent vertices to vertex 3

Head 3 → 0 → 1 → 2 → 4

List of adjacent vertices to vertex 4

Head 4 → 0 → 2 → 3

Fig. 8.2.5 : Adjacency list for each vertex of graph of Fig. 8.2.4

Adjacency list of a graph with n nodes can be represented by an array of pointers. Each pointer points to a linked list of the corresponding vertex. Fig. 8.2.6 shows the adjacency list representation of graph of Fig. 8.2.4.

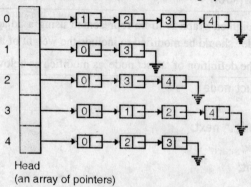

Head
(an array of pointers)

Fig. 8.2.6 : Adjacency list representation of the graph of Fig. 8.2.4

- Adjacency list representation of a graph is very memory efficient when the graph has a large number of vertices but very few edges.

- For an undirected graph with n vertices and e edges, total number of nodes will be n + 2e.

  If e is large then due to overhead of maintaining pointers, adjacency list representation does not remain cost effective over adjacency matrix representation of a graph.

- Degree of a node in an undirected graph is given by the length of the corresponding linked list.

- Finding in-degree of a directed graph represented using adjacency list will require O(e) comparisons. Lists pointed by all vertices must be examined to find the indegree of a node in a directed graph.

- Checking the existence of an edge between two vertices i and j is also time consuming. Linked list of vertex i must be searched for the ertex j.

A graph can be represented using a structure as defined below :

```
# define MAX 30          /* graph has maximum of 30 nodes */

typedef struct node
{
    struct node * next;
```

```
    int vertex;
}node;
node * head[MAX];
```

If a weighted graph is to be represented using a adjacency list, then structure "node" should be modified to include the weight of a edge.

Thus the definition of 'struct node' is modified as below :

```
typedef struct node
{
    struct node * next;
    int vertex;
    int weight;
}node;
```

8.2.3 Examples on Graph representation :

Example 8.2.1 : For the following graph obtain :
        (i)   The in degree and out degree of each vertex,
        (ii)   Its adjacency matrix
        (iii) Its adjacency list representation.   W - 09

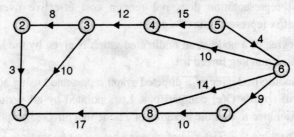

Fig. Ex. 8.2.1

Solution :

(1)

Vertex No.	Indegree	Outdegree
1	3	0
2	1	1
3	1	2
4	2	1
5	1	1·

Vertex No.	Indegree	Outdegree
6	1	3
7	1	1
8	2	1

(2)

	1	2	3	4	5	6	7	8
1	0	0	0	0	0	0	0	0
2	3	0	0	0	0	0	0	0
3	10	8	0	0	0	0	0	0
4	0	0	12	0	0	0	0	0
5	0	0	0	15	0	4	0	0
6	0	0	0	10	0	0	9	14
7	0	0	0	0	0	0	0	10
8	17	0	0	0	0	0	0	0

(a)

(3)   Adjacency list :

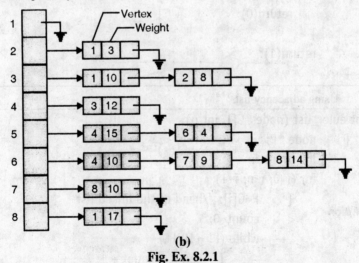

(b)

Fig. Ex. 8.2.1

Example 8.2.2 :   An euler tour of a connected graph G = (V,E) is a cycle that traverses each edge of G exactly once, although it may visit a vertex more than once. For an euler cycle to exist, the degree of each node must be even. Write an algorithm to determine whether the given graph is euler when :

(i) Adjacency matrix is used to represent the graph.

(ii) Adjacency list is used to represent the graph.

Solution :

1. Using adjacency matrix representation.

For the graph to be euler, the degree of each node should be even. The function returns 1 if the graph is euler, 0 otherwise.

```
int euler_matrix (int G[][MAX], int n)
    {    //n is number of vertices
        int i, j, count;
        for (i=0; i <n; i ++)
        {   count = 0;
            for (j=0; j<n; j++)
                    if (G[i][j]==1)
                            count =count + 1;
            if (count%2==1)
            return(0);
        }
        return(1);
    }
```

2. Using adjacency list.

```
int euler_list (node *G[], int n)
    {    node *P;
        int count, i;
        for (i=0; i<n; i++)
            {    P=G[i]; //head of the linked list
                count=0;
                while (P! = NULL)
                    {   count = count + 1;
                        P = P->next;
                    }
                if (count%2==1)
                    return(0);
```

```
          }
       Return(1);
   }
```

Example 8.2.3 : For the adjacency list given below, draw the corresponding graph.

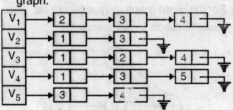

Fig. Ex. 8.2.3

Solution :

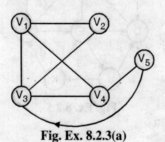

Fig. Ex. 8.2.3(a)

Example 8.2.4 : Find the adjacency matrix for the graph shown below.

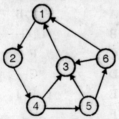

Fig. Ex. 8.2.4

Solution : Adjacency matrix is given below :

	1	2	3	4	5	6
1	0	1	0	0	0	0
2	0	0	0	1	0	0
3	1	0	0	0	0	0

4	0	0	1	0	1	0
5	0	0	1	0	0	1
6	1	0	1	0	0	0

Fig. Ex. 8.2.4(a)

Example 8.2.5 : For the given graph, give adjacent list, edge list and storage representation for adjacency list.　　S - 2010

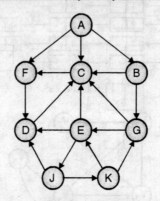

Fig. Ex. 8.2.5

Solution :
Adjacent list :

Vertex	Adjacent vertices
A	F, C, B
B	C, G
C	F
D	C
E	C, D, J
F	D
G	C, E
J	D, K
K	E, G

Edge list :

(A, F), (A, C), (A, B), (B, C), (B, G), (C, F), (D, C)

(E, C), (E, D), (E, J), (F, D), (G, C), (G, E), (J, D), (J, K), (K, E), (K, G)

Adjacency List representation :

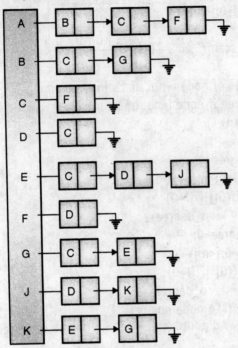

Fig. Ex. 8.2.5(a)

8.2.4 Programs on Graph Representation :

> **Program 8.2.1 : Program to compute the indegree and out degree of every vertex of a directed graph when the graph is represent by an adjacency matrix.**

```
#include<conio.h>
#include<stdio.h>
void main()
{
    int G[10][10],n,i,j,i_degree,o_degree;
    printf("\n Enter no of nodes : ");
    scanf("%d",&n);
    // read the adjacency matrix
    printf("\n Enter adjacency matrix of the graph :");
```

```
    for(i=0;i<n;i++)
        for(j=0;j<n;j++)
        {
            scanf("%d", &G[i][j]);
        }
    // indegree of node i=no. of 1's in i th column
    // outdegree if node i=no. of 1's in i th row
    for(i=0;i<n;i++)
    {
        i_degree=0;
        for(j=0;j<n;j++)
            if(G[j][i]!=0)
                i_degree++;
        o_degree=0;
        for(j=0;j<n;j++)
            if(G[i][j]!=0)
                o_degree++;
        printf("\n node number
%d\tindegree=%d\toutdegree=%d",i,i_degree,o_degree);
    }
}
```

Output

```
Enter no of nodes : 6
Enter adjacency matrix of the graph :0 0 1 0 1 0
0 0 1 1 0 0
0 0 0 0 0 0
0 0 0 0 0 1
0 1 0 1 0 0
1 0 0 0 0 0
node number 0  indegree=1     outdegree=2
node number 1  indegree=1     outdegree=2
node number 2  indegree=2     outdegree=0
node number 3  indegree=2     outdegree=1
node number 4  indegree=1     outdegree=2
node number 5  indegree=1     outdegree=1
```

> **Program 8.2.2 :** **Program to compute the indegree and outdegree of every vertex of a directed graph when the graph is represented by an adjacency list.**

```c
#include<stdio.h>
#include<conio.h>
#include<stdlib.h>
typedef struct node
{
   struct node *next;
   int vertex;
}node;
node * G[20];
/* An array of pointers G[i] is the head of the list of adjacency
   vertices of node i represented using a linked list */
int n;
void read_graph();
int in_degree(int v);
int out_degree(int v);
void insert(int vi,int vj);
void main()
{
   int i_degree,o_degree,i;
   read_graph();
   for(i=0;i<n;i++)
   {
        i_degree=in_degree(i);
        o_degree=out_degree(i);
        printf("\nNode
No=%d\tindegree=%d\toutdegree=%d",i,i_degree,o_degree);
   }
}
void read_graph()
{
   int i,vi,vj,no_of_edges;
```

```
    printf("\nEnter no of vertices : ");
    scanf("%d",&n);
    // initialise G[] with a null
    for(i=0;i<n;i++)
    {
         G[i]=NULL;
         // read edges and insert them in G[]
         printf("\nEnter no of edges : ");
         scanf("%d",&no_of_edges);
         for(i=0;i<no_of_edges;i++)
         {
             printf("\nEnter an edge (u,v) :");
             scanf("%d%d",&vi,&vj);
             insert(vi,vj);
         }
    }
}
void insert(int vi,int vj)
{
    node *p,*q;
    // acquire memory for the new node
    q=(node *)malloc(sizeof(node));
    q->vertex=vj;
    q->next=NULL;
    //insert the node in the linked list number vi
    if(G[vi]==NULL)
         G[vi]=q;
    else
    {
         // go to end of linked list
         p=G[vi];
         while(p->next!=NULL)
             p=p->next;
         p->next=q;
```

```
   }
}
int out_degree(int v)
{
   node *p;
   int o_degree=0;
   p=G[v];
   //count number of nodes in the linked list p
   while(p!=NULL)
   {
        o_degree++;
        p=p->next;
   }
   return(o_degree);
}
int in_degree(int v)
{
   node *p;
   int in_degree,i;
   //all linked list must be searched for the vertex
   in_degree=0;
   for(i=0;i<n;i++)
   {
        p=G[i];
        while(p!=NULL)
        {
             if(p->vertex==v)
                  in_degree++;
             p=p->next;
        }
   }
   return(in_degree);
}
```

Output

Enter no of vertices : 6		
Enter no of edges : 8		
Enter an edge (u,v) :1 2		
Enter an edge (u,v) :1 3		
Enter an edge (u,v) :4 1		
Enter an edge (u,v) :0 2		
Enter an edge (u,v) :5 0		
Enter an edge (u,v) :0 4		
Enter an edge (u,v) :4 3		
Enter an edge (u,v) :3 5		
Node No=0	indegree=1	outdegree=2
Node No=1	indegree=1	outdegree=2
Node No=2	indegree=2	outdegree=0
Node No=3	indegree=2	outdegree=1
Node No=4	indegree=1	outdegree=2
Node No=5	indegree=1	outdegree=1

Function readgraph(), creates an adjacency list for the given graph. Edges are entered as a pair of vertices (V_i, V_j). Edge (V_i, V_j) is entered in the ith linked list and the "vertex" field of the node is set to V_j working of readgraph() is shown below :

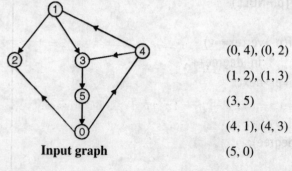

Input graph

(0, 4), (0, 2)

(1, 2), (1, 3)

(3, 5)

(4, 1), (4, 3)

(5, 0)

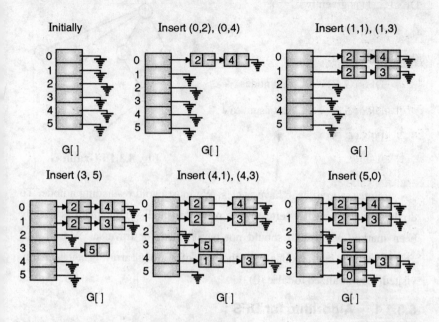

8.3 Traversal of Graphs

Most of graph problems involve traversal of a graph. Traversal of a graph means visited each node and visiting exactly once. Two commonly used techniques are :

(1)   Depth First Search (DFS)

(2)   Breadth First Search (BFS)

8.3.1 Depth First Search (DFS) :

It is like preorder traversal of tree. Traversal can start from any vertex, say V_i · V_i is visited and then all vertices adjacent to V_i are traversed recursively using DFS.

DFS (G, 1) is given by

(a)　Visit (1)

(b)　DFS (G, 2)

　　　DFS (G, 3)　} all nodes

　　　DFS (G, 4)　　adjacent to 1

　　　DFS (G, 5)

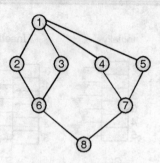

Fig. 8.3.1 : Graph G

Since, a graph can have cycles. We must avoid re-visiting a node. To do this, when we visit a vertex V, we mark it visited. A node that has already been marked as visited, should not be selected for traversal. Marking of visited vertices can be done with the help of a global array visited[]. Array visited[] is initialized to false (0).

8.3.1.1　Algorithm for DFS :

　　n ← number of nodes

(i)　Initialize visited[] to false (0)

　　for (i = 0; i < n; i++)

　　　　visited[i] = 0;

(ii)　void DFS (vertex i)　[DFS starting from i]

　　{

　　　　visited[i] = 1;

　　　　for each w adjacent to i

　　　　　　if(! visited[w])

　　　　　　　　DFS(w);

　　}

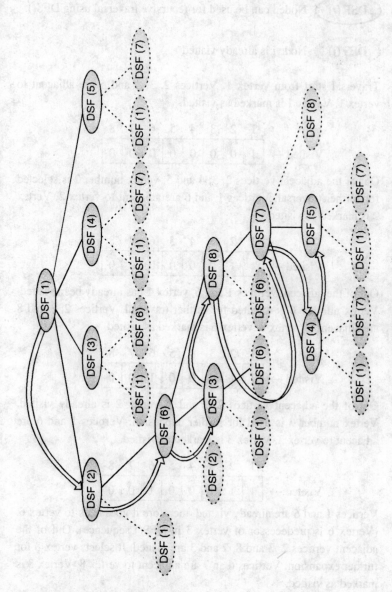

Fig.8.3.2: DFS traversal on graph of Fig. 8.3.1

DFS traversal on graph of Fig. 8.3.1.

> **DSF (i)**   Node i can be used for recursive traversal using DFS().

> **DFS (i)**   Node i is already visited

- Traversal start from vertex 1. Vertices 2, 3, 4 and 5 are adjacent to vertex 1. Vertex **1** is marked as visited.

	1	2	3	4	5	6	7	8
Visited →	1	0	0	0	0	0	0	0

- Out of the adjacent vertices 2, 3, 4 and 5, vertex number 2 is selected for further traversal. Vertices 1 and 6 are adjacent to vertex 2. Vertex 2 is marked as visited.

	1	2	3	4	5	6	7	8
Visited →	1	1	0	0	0	0	0	0

- Out of the adjacent vertices 1 and 6, vertex 1 has already been visited. Vertex number 6 is selected for further traversal. Vertices 2, 3 and 8 are adjacent to vertex 6. vertex 6 is marked as visited.

	1	2	3	4	5	6	7	8
Visited →	1	1	0	0	0	1	0	0

- Out of the adjacent vertices 2, 3 and 8, vertex 2 is already visited. Vertex number **3** is used for further expansion. Vertices 1 and 6 are adjacent to vertex 3. Vertex 3 is marked as visited.

	1	2	3	4	5	6	7	8
Visited →	1	1	1	0	0	1	0	0

- Vertices 1 and 6 are already visited, therefore it goes back to vertex 6. (Vertex 6 is predecessor of vertex 3 in DFS() sequence). Out of the adjacent vertices 2, 3 and 8, 2 and 3 are visited. It selects vertex 8 for further expansion. Vertices 6 an 7 are adjacent to vertex 8. Vertex 8 is marked as visited.

	1	2	3	4	5	6	7	8
Visited →	1	1	1	0	0	1	0	1

- Out of the adjacent vertices 6 and 7, vertex 6 is already visited. Vertex number 7 is used for further expansion. Vertices 4, 5 and 8 are adjacent to vertex number 7. Vertex 7 is marked as visited.

	1	2	3	4	5	6	7	8
Visited →	1	1	1	0	0	1	1	1

- Out of the adjacent vertices 4, 5 and 8, vertex 4 is selected for further expansion. Vertices 1 and 7 are adjacent to vertex 4. Vertex 4 is marked as visited.

	1	2	3	4	5	6	7	8
Visited →	1	1	1	1	0	1	1	1

- Adjacent vertices 1 and 7 are already visited. It goes back to vertex 7 and selects the next unvisited node 5 for further expansion. Vertex 5 is marked as visited.

	1	2	3	4	5	6	7	8
Visited →	1	1	1	1	1	1	1	1

- DFS, traversal sequence → 1, 2, 6, 3, 8, 7, 4, 5

8.3.1.2 Program for DFS using adjacency matrix :

➢ **Program 8.3.1 : Program to implement DFS traversal on a graph represented using an adjacency matrix.**

```
#include<conio.h>
#include<stdio.h>
void DFS(int);
int G[10][10],visited[10],n;
// n->no of vertices
// graph is stored in array G[10][10]
void main()
{
    int i,j;
    printf("\nEnter no of vertices: ");
    scanf("%d",&n);
    // read the adjacency matrix
```

```
    printf("\nEnter adjacency matrix of the graph :");
    for(i=0;i<n;i++)
        for(j=0;j<n;j++)
            scanf("%d",&G[i][j]);

    // visited is initialize to zero
    for(i=0;i<n;i++)
        visited[i]=0;
    DFS(0);
}

void DFS(int i)
{
    int j;
    printf("\n%d",i);
    visited[i]=1;
    for(j=0;j<n;j++)
        if(!visited[j] && G[i][j]==1)
            DFS(j);
}
```

Output

```
Enter no of vertices: 8
Enter adjacency matrix of the graph :0 1 1 1 1 0 0 0
1 0 0 0 0 1 0 0
1 0 0 0 0 1 0 0
1 0 0 0 0 0 1 0
1 0 0 0 0 0 1 0
0 1 1 0 0 0 0 1
0 0 0 1 1 0 0 1
0 0 0 0 0 1 1 0
0
1
5
2
```

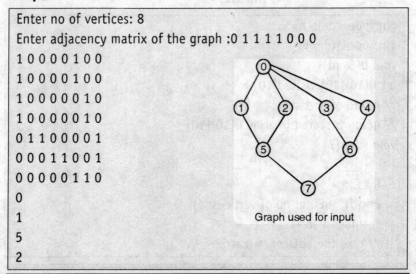

Graph used for input

| 7 |
| 6 |
| 3 |
| 4 |

8.3.1.3　Program for DFS using adjacency list :

> **Program 8.3.2 : Program to implement DFS traversal on a graph represented using an adjacency list.**

```
#include<conio.h>
#include<stdio.h>
typedef struct node
{
   struct node *next;
   int vertex;
}node;
node *G[20];    // heads of linked list
int visited[20];
int n;
void read_graph();    //create adjacency list
void insert(int,int); //insert an edge (vi,vj) in the adjacency list
void DFS(int);
void main()
{
   int i;
   read_graph();
   // initialized visited to 0
   for(i=0;i<n;i++)
        visited[i]=0;
   DFS(0);
}
void DFS(int i)
{
   node *p;
```

```
    printf("\n%d",i);
    p=G[i];
    visited[i]=1;
    while(p!=NULL)
    {
         i=p->vertex;
         if(!visited[i])
              DFS(i);
         p=p->next;
    }
}
void read_graph()
{
    int i,vi,vj,no_of_edges;
    printf("\nEnter no of vertices : ");
    scanf("%d",&n);
    // initialize G[] with a null
    for(i=0;i<n;i++)
    {
         G[i]=NULL;
         // read edges and insert them in G[]
         printf("\nEnter no of edges : ");
         scanf("%d",&no_of_edges);
         for(i=0;i<no_of_edges;i++)
         {
             printf("\nEnter an edge (u,v) :");
             scanf("%d%d",&vi,&vj);
             insert(vi,vj);
         }
    }
}
void insert(int vi,int vj)
{
    node *p,*q;
    // acquire memory for the new node
```

```
    q=(node *)malloc(sizeof(node));
    q->vertex=vj;
    q->next=NULL;
    //insert the node in the linked list number vi
    if(G[vi]==NULL)
        G[vi]=q;
    else
    {
        // go to end of linked list
        p=G[vi];
        while(p->next!=NULL)
            p=p->next;
        p->next=q;
    }
}
```

Output

```
Enter no of vertices : 8
Enter no of edges : 10
Enter an edge (u,v) :0 1
Enter an edge (u,v) :0 2
Enter an edge (u,v) :0 3
Enter an edge (u,v) :0 4
Enter an edge (u,v) :1 5
Enter an edge (u,v) :2 5
Enter an edge (u,v) :3 6
Enter an edge (u,v) :4 6
Enter an edge (u,v) :5 7
Enter an edge (u,v) :6 7
0
1
5
7
2
3
6
4
```

Graph used for input

8.3.1.3.1 Timing Complexity :

Considering the algorithm given in section 8.3.1.3, for each i the for loop will be executed n times.

Hence, the timing complexity = $O(n^2)$

8.3.1.4   Non-recursive DFS traversal :

Non-recursive DFS, uses a stack to remove recursion. All unvisited vertices adjacent to the one being visited are pushed into a stack. Traversal is continued by popping a vertex from the stack.

Algorithm :

```
DFS_Nonrecursive(vertex i)
{
        vertex w;
        stack S;
        initialize the stack S:
        push i in the stack S;
        while(stack is not empty) {
            i = pop(S);
            if(! visited[i])


            {
                    visited[i] = 1;
                    for each w adjacent to i
                            if(! visited[w])
                                    push w in the stack S;

            }
        }
}
```

8.3.1.5　Examples on DFS :

Example 8.3.1 :　Show the working of non-recursive DFS algorithm on the following graph.

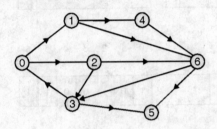

Fig. Ex. 8.3.1

Solution :

Stack contents			Visited[ ]							Vertex visited	Action

			0	1	2	3	4	5	6		
NULL			0	0	0	0	0	0	0	–	initial

↓ top

| 0 | | |

| | | | 0 | 1 | 2 | 3 | 4 | 5 | 6 | | push the |
| | | | 0 | 0 | 0 | 0 | 0 | 0 | 0 | – | initial vertex |

↓
　top

| 1 | 2 | |

| | | | 0 | 1 | 2 | 3 | 4 | 5 | 6 | | pop(), |
| | | | 1 | 0 | 0 | 0 | 0 | 0 | 0 | 0 | visit(), push adjacent vertices |

↓
　top

| 1 | 3 | 6 |

| | | | 0 | 1 | 2 | 3 | 4 | 5 | 6 | | pop(), |
| | | | 1 | 0 | 1 | 0 | 0 | 0 | 0 | 0, 2 | visit(), push adjacent vertices |

↓
　top

| | | | 0 | 1 | 2 | 3 | 4 | 5 | 6 | | pop(), |
| | | | | | | | | | | 0, 2, 6 | visit(), |

Stack contents	Visited[ ]	Vertex visited	Action
1 3 3 5	1 0 1 0 0 0 1		push adjacent vertices
1 3 3 (top)	0 1 2 3 4 5 6 1 0 1 0 0 1 1	0, 2, 6, 5	pop(), visit()
1 3 (top)	0 1 2 3 4 5 6 1 0 1 1 0 1 1	0, 2, 6, 5, 3	pop()
1 (top)	0 1 2 3 4 5 6 1 0 1 1 0 1 1	0, 2, 6, 5, 3	pop(), visit(), push adjacent vertices
4	0 1 2 3 4 5 6 1 1 1 1 0 1 1	0, 2, 6, 5, 3, 1	visit
NULL	0 1 2 3 4 5 6 1 1 1 1 1 1 1	0, 2, 6, 5, 3, 1, 4	complete

Example 8.3.2 : Find DFS for the given graph show each pass separately.

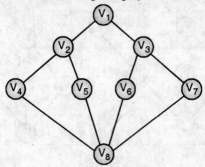

Fig. Ex. 8.3.2

Solution :

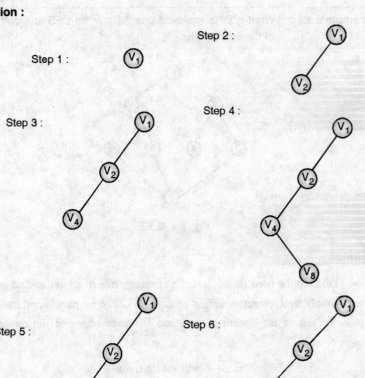

Step 1 :

Step 2 :

Step 3 :

Step 4 :

Step 5 :

Step 6 :

Step 7 :

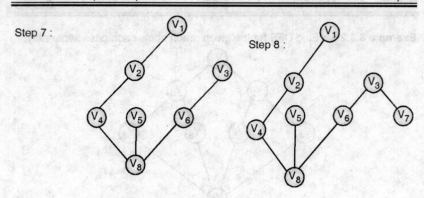

Step 8 :

8.3.1.6 DFS spanning tree :

Example 8.3.3 : What is DFS spanning tree ? Draw the DFS spanning tree of the following graph.

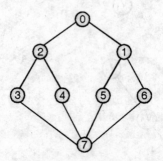

Fig. Ex. 8.3.3

Solution :

DFS can be used for obtaining a spanning tree of an undirected graph. Graph should be connected. Edges of a graph G can be partitioned into two sets E_1 (edges of the spanning tree) and E_2 (back edges or the remaining edges).

$$E_1 \leftarrow \text{Null set (initially)}$$

$$E_2 \leftarrow \text{A set of all edges of the graph G.}$$

In the algorithm for DFS(), whenever a recursive call is made inside the if statement, a new edge will be added to E1.

"for each w adjacent to i
if(! visited[w])
DFS(w);"
Edge(i, w) is added to E1. The same edge is also deleted from E2.

E1 = E1 ∪ {(i, w)}

E2 = E2 − {j, w}

Edges of E_1 will form a spanning tree as DFS will visit each node of the graph and each node will be visited exactly once.

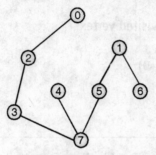

DFS spanning tree of the graph

Fig. Ex. 8.3.3(a)

Example 8.3.4 :   Check whether a given undirected graph is connected. If the graph is not connected then find its components.

Solution :

If G is an undirected graph, then one can determine whether or not it is connected by making a call to DFS. If there is any unvisited node after DFS then the graph G is not connected.

All the connected components of a graph can be obtained by making repeated calls to DFS (V) with V a vertex not yet visited.

8.3.1.7   'C' Function for Checking Whether the Given Graph is Connected :

/* graph is represented using adjacency matrix array visited is initialized to 0

  n = no. of vertices */

```
#define MAX 20
int G[MAX][MAX],visited[MAX],n;
// function connected returns 1 if  graph is connected otherwise 0
int connected()
{
   int i;
   for(i=0;i<n;i++)
         visited[i]=0;
   DFS(0);
   // is there any  unvisited vertex
   for(i=0;i<n;i++)
         if(visited[i]==0)
             return(0);
         return(1);
}
```

8.3.1.8 'C' Function for Finding Components of a Graph :

```
#define MAX 20
int G[MAX][MAX],visited[MAX],n;
// function components() returns no.of components in graph
int components()
{
   int i;
   int count;
   for(i=0;i<n;i++)
         visited[i]=0;
         count=0;
   for(i=0;i<n;i++)
   {
         if(visited[i]==0)
         {
             DFS(i);
             count++;
```

```
        }
    }
    return(count);
}
```

8.3.2 Breadth First Search (BFS) :

Q. Describe Breadth First search technique with suitable example. W - 09

It is another popular approach used for visiting the vertices of a graph. This method starts from a given vertex V_0. V_0 is marked as visited. All vertices adjacent to V_0 are visited next. Let the vertices adjacent to V_0 are V_{10}, V_3, V_{12} ... V_{1n}. V_{11}, V_{12} ... V_{1n} are marked as visited. All unvisited vertices adjacent to V_{11}, V_{12} .....V_{1n} are visited next. The method continues until all vertices are visited. The algorithm for BFS has to maintain a list of vertices which have been visited but not explored for adjacent vertices. The vertices which have been visited but not explored for adjacent vertices can be stored in queue.

- Initially the queue contains the starting vertex.

- In every iteration, a vertex is removed from the queue and its adjacent vertices which are not visited as yet are added to the queue.

- The algorithm terminates when the queue becomes empty.

Fig. 8.3.3 gives the BFS sequence on various graphs.

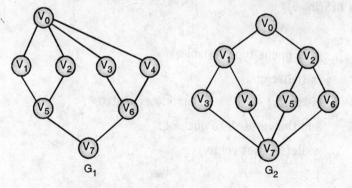

Fig. 8.3.3 Contd...

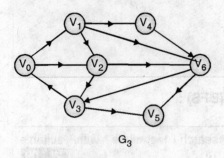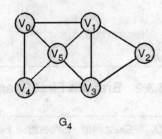

BFS sequence :

$G_1 \to V_0 \mid V_1\, V_2\, V_3\, V_4 \mid V_5\, V_6 \mid V_7$

$G_2 \to V_0 \mid V_1\, V_2 \mid V_3\, V_4\, V_5\, V_6 \mid V_7$

$G_3 \to V_0 \mid V_1\, V_2 \mid V_4\, V_6\, V_3 \mid V_5\, V_6$

$G_4 \to V_0 \mid V_1\, V_4\, V_5 \mid V_2\, V_3$

Fig. 8.3.3 : BFS traversal on G_1, G_2, G_3 and G_4

8.3.2.1 Algorithm for BFS :

Q. Write an algorithm for Breadth-First search on graph. **S - 09**

```
/* Array visited[] is initialize to 0 */
/* BFS traversal on the graph G is carried out beginning at vertex
v */
void BFS(int v)
{
        q : a queue type variable;
        initialize q;
        visited[v] = 1;      /* mark v as visited */
        add the vertex V to queue q;
        while(q is not empty)
        {
            v ← delete an element from the queue;
            for all vertices w adjacent from V
```

```
                {
                    if(!visited[w])
                    {
                        visited[w] = 1;
                        add the vertex w to queue q;
                    }
                }
            }
}
```

8.3.2.2 Examples on BFS :

Example 8.3.5 : Show the working of BFS algorithm on the following graph.

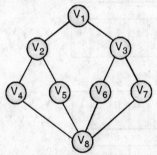

Fig. Ex. 8.3.5

Solution :

Queue	Visited[ ]								Vertex visited	Action
	1	2	3	4	5	6	7	8		
NULL	0	0	0	0	0	0	0	0	–	–
V_1	1	0	0	0	0	0	0	0	V_1	add (q, V_1) visit (V_1)
$V_2\ V_3$	1	1	1	0	0	0	0	0	$V_1\ V_2\ V_3$	delete (q), add and visit adjacent vertices

Queue	Visited[ ]								Vertex visited	Action
$V_3\ V_4\ V_5$	1	2	3	4	5	6	7	8	$V_1\ V_2\ V_3\ V_4$ V_5	delete (q), add and visit adjacent vertices
	1	1	1	1	1	0	0	0		
$V_4\ V_5\ V_6$ V_7	1	2	3	4	5	6	7	8	$V_1\ V_2\ V_3\ V_4$ $V_5\ V_6\ V_7$	delete (q), add and visit adjacent vertices
	1	1	1	1	1	1	1	0		
$V_5\ V_6\ V_7$ V_8	1	1	1	1	1	1	1	1	$V_1\ V_2\ V_3\ V_4$ $V_5\ V_6\ V_7\ V_8$	delete (q), add and visit adjacent vertices
$V_6\ V_7\ V_8$	1	1	1	1	1	1	1	1	$V_1\ V_2\ V_3\ V_4$ $V_5\ V_6\ V_7\ V_8$	delete (q)
$V_7\ V_8$	1	1	1	1	1	1	1	1	$V_1\ V_2\ V_3\ V_4$ $V_5\ V_6\ V_7\ V_8$	delete (q), add and visit adjacent vertices
V_8	1	2	3	4	5	6	7	8	$V_1\ V_2\ V_3\ V_4$ $V_5\ V_6\ V_7\ V_8$	delete (q)
	1	1	1	1	1	1	1			
NULL	1	1	1	1	1	1	1	1	$V_1\ V_2\ V_3\ V_4$ $V_5\ V_6\ V_7\ V_8$	algorithm terminates

Example 8.3.6 : Find the adjacency matrix and adjacency list representation free the following graph. Also list the order of traversal in (i) BFS (ii) DFS.

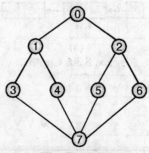

Fig. Ex. 8.3.6

Solution :

Adjacency matrix representation :

	0	1	2	3	4	5	6	7
0	0	1	1	0	0	0	0	0
1	1	0	0	1	1	0	0	0
2	1	0	0	0	0	1	1	0
3	0	1	0	0	0	0	0	1
4	0	1	0	0	0	0	0	1
5	0	0	1	0	0	0	0	1
6	0	0	1	0	0	0	0	1
7	0	0	0	1	1	1	1	0

(a)

Adjacency list representation :

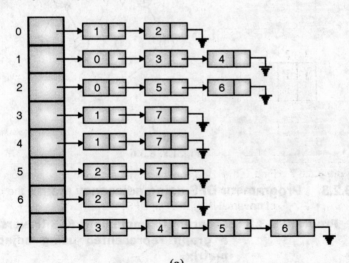

(a)
Fig. Ex. 8.3.6 Contd…

BFS Traversal sequence :

0

1 2

3 4 5 6

7

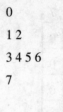
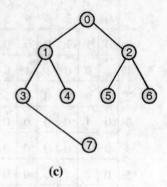

(c)

DFS Traversal sequence :

0 1 3 7 4 5 2 6

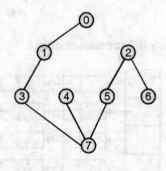

(d)

Fig. Ex. 8.3.6

8.3.2.3 Program for BFS using adjacency matrix :

➤ **Program 8.3.3 : Program to implement BFS traversal on a graph represented using adjacency matrix.**

```
#include<conio.h>
#include<stdio.h>
#define MAX 10
typedef struct Q
{
```

```
   int R,F;
   int data[MAX];
}Q;
int empty(Q *P);
int full(Q *P);
void enqueue(Q *P,int x);
int dequeue(Q *P);
void BFS(int);
int G[MAX][MAX];
int n;
void main()
{
   int i,j,v;
   printf("\nEnter no of vertices : ");
   scanf("%d",&n);
   printf("\nEnter the adjacency matrix of  graph : ");
   for(i=0;i<n;i++)
         for(j=0;j<n;j++)
              scanf("%d",&G[i][j]);
   printf("\nEnter the starting vertex for BFS");
   scanf("%d",&v);
   BFS(v);
   getch();
}
void BFS(int v)
{
   int visited[MAX],i;
   Q q;
   q.R=q.F=-1;
   for(i=0;i<n;i++)
         visited[i]=0;
   enqueue(&q,v);
   printf("\n visit\t%d",v);
   visited[v]=1;
```

```
    while(!empty(&q))
    {
         v=dequeue(&q);
         // visit and add adjacency vertices
         for(i=0;i<n;i++)
             if(visited[i]==0 && G[v][i]!=0)
             {
                     enqueue(&q,i);
                     visited[i]=1;
                     printf("\nvisit\t%d",i);
             }
    }
}
int empty(Q *P)
{
   if(P->R==-1)
         return(1);
   return(0);
}
int full(Q *P)
{
   if(P->R==MAX-1)
         return(1);
   return(0);
}
void enqueue(Q *P, int x)
{
   if(P->R==-1)
   {
         P->R=P->F=0;
         P->data[P->R]=x;
   }
   else
   {
         P->R=P->R+1;
```

```
            P->data[P->R]=x;
   }
}
int dequeue(Q *P)
{
   int x;
   x=P->data[P->F];
   if(P->R==P->F)
   {
        P->R=-1;
        P->F=-1;
   }
   else
        P->F=P->F+1;
   return(x);
}
```

Output

```
Enter no of vertices : 8
Enter the adjacency matrix of  graph :
0 1 1 1 1 0 0 0
1 0 0 0 0 1 0 0
1 0 0 0 0 1 0 0
1 0 0 0 0 0 1 0
1 0 0 0 0 0 1 0
0 1 1 0 0 0 0 1
0 0 0 1 1 0 0 1
0 0 0 0 0 1 1 0
Enter the starting vertex for BFS 0
 visit  0
visit   1
visit   2
visit   3
visit   4
visit   5
visit   6
visit   7
```

8.3.2.4   Program for BFS using adjacency list :

> **Program 8.3.4 :** **Program to implement BFS traversal on a graph implemented through adjacency list.**

```c
#include<conio.h>
#include<stdio.h>
#include<stdlib.h>
#define MAX 20
typedef struct Q
{
   int data[MAX];
   int R,F;
}Q;
typedef struct node
{
   struct node *next;
   int vertex;
}node;
void enqueue(Q *,int);
int dequque(Q *);
int empty(Q *);
int full(Q *);
void BFS(int);
node *G[20];                //heads of the linked list
int n;                      // no of nodes
void readgraph();           //create an adjacency list
void insert(int vi,int vj); //insert an edge (vi,vj)in adj.list
void main()
{
   int i;
   readgraph();
   BFS(0);
}
void BFS(int v)
```

```
{
   int i,visited[MAX],w;
   Q q;
   node *p;
   q.R=q.F=-1;              //initialize
   for(i=0;i<n;i++)
          visited[i]=0;
   enqueue(&q,v);
   printf("\n Visit\t%d",v);
   visited[v]=1;
   while(!empty(&q))
   {
          v=dequeue(&q);
          //insert all unvisited, adjacent vertices of v into queue
          for(p=G[v];p!=NULL;p=p->next)
          {
              w=p->vertex;
              if(visited[w]==0)
              {
                    enqueue(&q,w);
                    visited[w]=1;
                    printf("\nvisit\t%d",w);
              }
          }
   }
}
int empty(Q *P)
{
   if(P->R==-1)
          return(1);
   return(0);
}
int full(Q *P)
{
   if(P->R==MAX-1)
```

```
            return(1);
        return(0);
    }
    void enqueue(Q *P,int x)
    {
        if(P->R==-1)
        {
            P->R=P->F=0;
            P->data[P->R]=x;
        }
        else
        {
            P->R=P->R+1;
            P->data[P->R]=x;
        }
    }
    int dequeue(Q *P)
    {
        int x;
        x=P->data[P->F];
        if(P->R==P->F)
        {
            P->R=-1;
            P->F=-1;
        }
        else
            P->F=P->F+1;
        return(x);
    }
    void readgraph()
    {
        int i,vi,vj,no_of_edges;
        printf("\nEnter no. of vertices :");
        scanf("%d",&n);
        //initialize G[] with NULL
```

```
    for(i=0;i<n;i++)
        G[i]=NULL;
    //read edges and insert them in G[]
    printf("\nEnter no of edges :");
    scanf("%d",&no_of_edges);
    for(i=0;i<no_of_edges;i++)
    {
        printf("\nEnter an edge (u,v)  :");
        scanf("%d%d",&vi,&vj);
        insert(vi,vj);
        insert(vj,vi);
    }
}
void insert(int vi,int vj)
{
    node *p,*q;
    //acquire memory for the new node
    q=(node *)malloc(sizeof(node));
    q->vertex=vj;
    q->next=NULL;
    //insert the node in the linked list for the vertex no. vi
    if(G[vi]==NULL)
        G[vi]=q;
    else
    {
        // go to the end of linked list
        p=G[vi];
        while(p->next!=NULL)
            p=p->next;
        p->next=q;
    }
}
```

Output

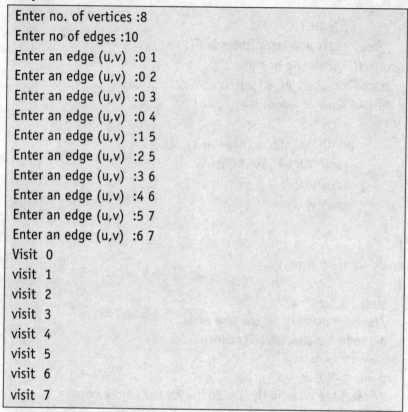

Enter no. of vertices :8
Enter no of edges :10
Enter an edge (u,v) :0 1
Enter an edge (u,v) :0 2
Enter an edge (u,v) :0 3
Enter an edge (u,v) :0 4
Enter an edge (u,v) :1 5
Enter an edge (u,v) :2 5
Enter an edge (u,v) :3 6
Enter an edge (u,v) :4 6
Enter an edge (u,v) :5 7
Enter an edge (u,v) :6 7
Visit 0
visit 1
visit 2
visit 3
visit 4
visit 5
visit 6
visit 7

8.3.2.5   BFS spanning tree :

Example 8.3.7 :   What is BFS spanning tree. Draw the BFS spanning tree of the following graph.

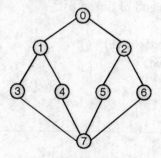

Fig. Ex. 8.3.7

Solution :

BFS can be used for obtaining a spanning tree of an undirected graph. Graph should be connected. A set E of edges of spanning tree can be created during BFS traversal of the graph.

In the algorithm for BFS traversal,

```
loop inside the algorithm for BFS
while(q is not empty)
{
        v ← delete an element from the queue;
        for all vertices w adjacent from V
            if(! visited[w])
            {
                    visited[w] = 1;
                    {
                            add the vertex w to queue q;
                    }
            }
}
```

whenever a new vertex w is added to queue,

an edge (V, w) is added to E.

$$E = E \cup \{(v, w)\}$$

Edges of E will form a spanning tree as BFS will visit each node of the graph and each node will be visited only once.

BFS spanning tree :

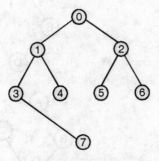

Fig. Ex. 8.3.7(a)

Example 8.3.8 : Consider the graph shown below. Find depth first and breadth first traversals of this graph starting at A.

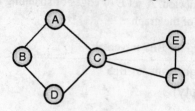

Fig. Ex. 8.3.8

Solution :

(i) Depth first traversal :

	Node No.	Spanning tree
1.	A	A
2.	B	A — B
3.	D	A — B — D
4.	C	A — B — D — C
5.	E	A — B — D — C — E

	Node No.	Spanning tree
6.	F	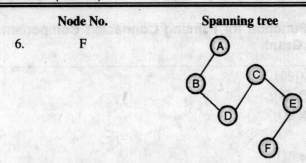

Depth first sequence : ABDCEF

(ii) Breadth first :

Node No.	Spanning tree
A	
BC	
DEF	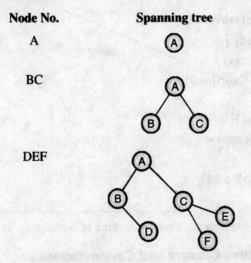

Breadth first sequence : ABCDEF

8.4 Connected Components

Traversal algorithm DFS or BFS can be used for finding out the connected components of a graph. All the connected components of a graph can be obtained by making repeated calls to DFS() or BFS() with V a vertex not yet visited.

8.4.1 'C' Function for Printing Connected Components of a Graph :

```
#define MAX[20]
int G[MAX][MAX];
int visited[MAX];
int n;
int component()
{
   int count,i;
   count=0;
   for(i=0;i<n;i++)
        visited[i]=0;
   for(i=0;i<n;i++)
        if(visited[i]==0)
        {
            BFS(i);
            count++;
        }
        return(count);
}
```

Function components(), returns number of components in a graph.

8.4.2 Transitive Closure and Connectedness :

In many problems, it may be necessary to determine whether there exists a path from the vertex i to vertex j or simply whether the vertex i is connected to vertex j. Transitive closure of a graph G, represented using an adjacency matrix A[][] can defined as follows :

- TC[][], representing transitive closure of G is a matrix of the size n × n where n is number of vertices in G.

- TC[i][j] = 1 if there is a path of length one or more from i to j and 0 otherwise.

- Fig. 8.4.2 shows the transitive closure of the directed graph of Fig. 8.4.1.

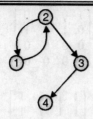

	1	2	3	4
1	1	1	1	1
2	1	1	1	1
3	0	0	0	1
4	0	0	0	0

Fig. 8.4.1 : A digraph   **Fig. 8.4.2 : Transitive closure**

Transitive closure of graph represented using an adjacency matrix A is given by

$A + A^2 + A^3 + \ldots A^n$, where n is number of vertices

8.4.3   Examples on Transitive Closure :

Example 8.4.1 : Compute the transitive closure of the graph of Fig. 8.4.1 using matrix multiplication.

Solution :

$$A = \begin{bmatrix} 0 & 1 & 0 & 0 \\ 1 & 0 & 1 & 0 \\ 0 & 0 & 0 & 1 \\ 0 & 0 & 0 & 0 \end{bmatrix} \text{ adjacency matrix of the graph of Fig. 8.4.1.}$$

$$A^2 = \begin{bmatrix} 0 & 1 & 0 & 0 \\ 1 & 0 & 1 & 0 \\ 0 & 0 & 0 & 1 \\ 0 & 0 & 0 & 0 \end{bmatrix} \times \begin{bmatrix} 0 & 1 & 0 & 0 \\ 1 & 0 & 1 & 0 \\ 0 & 0 & 0 & 1 \\ 0 & 0 & 0 & 0 \end{bmatrix} = \begin{bmatrix} 1 & 0 & 1 & 0 \\ 0 & 1 & 0 & 1 \\ 0 & 0 & 0 & 0 \\ 0 & 0 & 0 & 0 \end{bmatrix}$$

Note : A one in $(i, j)^{th}$ place in A^2 indicates that there is a path of length 2 between the vertices i and j.

$$A^3 = \begin{bmatrix} 1 & 0 & 1 & 0 \\ 0 & 1 & 0 & 1 \\ 0 & 0 & 0 & 0 \\ 0 & 0 & 0 & 0 \end{bmatrix} \times \begin{bmatrix} 0 & 1 & 0 & 0 \\ 1 & 0 & 1 & 0 \\ 0 & 0 & 0 & 1 \\ 0 & 0 & 0 & 0 \end{bmatrix} = \begin{bmatrix} 0 & 1 & 0 & 1 \\ 1 & 0 & 1 & 0 \\ 0 & 0 & 0 & 0 \\ 0 & 0 & 0 & 0 \end{bmatrix}$$

$$A^4 = \begin{bmatrix} 0 & 1 & 0 & 1 \\ 1 & 0 & 1 & 0 \\ 0 & 0 & 0 & 0 \\ 0 & 0 & 0 & 0 \end{bmatrix} \times \begin{bmatrix} 0 & 1 & 0 & 0 \\ 1 & 0 & 1 & 0 \\ 0 & 0 & 0 & 1 \\ 0 & 0 & 0 & 0 \end{bmatrix} = \begin{bmatrix} 1 & 0 & 1 & 0 \\ 0 & 1 & 0 & 1 \\ 0 & 0 & 0 & 0 \\ 0 & 0 & 0 & 0 \end{bmatrix}$$

Transitive closure of A

$$= A + A^2 + A^3 + A^4 = \begin{bmatrix} 0 & 1 & 0 & 0 \\ 1 & 0 & 1 & 0 \\ 0 & 0 & 0 & 1 \\ 0 & 0 & 0 & 0 \end{bmatrix} + \begin{bmatrix} 1 & 0 & 1 & 0 \\ 0 & 1 & 0 & 1 \\ 0 & 0 & 0 & 0 \\ 0 & 0 & 0 & 0 \end{bmatrix}$$

$$+ \begin{bmatrix} 0 & 1 & 0 & 1 \\ 1 & 0 & 1 & 0 \\ 0 & 0 & 0 & 0 \\ 0 & 0 & 0 & 0 \end{bmatrix} + \begin{bmatrix} 1 & 0 & 1 & 0 \\ 0 & 1 & 0 & 1 \\ 0 & 0 & 0 & 0 \\ 0 & 0 & 0 & 0 \end{bmatrix} = \begin{bmatrix} 1 & 1 & 1 & 1 \\ 1 & 1 & 1 & 1 \\ 0 & 0 & 0 & 1 \\ 0 & 0 & 0 & 0 \end{bmatrix}$$

Transitive closure of a graph can be used to check whether a graph is connected. A graph is said to connected (undirected graph) or strongly connected (directed graph) if there is no '0' in the transitive closure matrix of the graph. Graph of Fig. 8.4.1 is not strongly connected as there is no path between vertices

$$(3, 1), (3, 2), (3, 3), (4, 1), (4, 2), (4, 3) \text{ and } (4, 4)$$

Example 8.4.2 : Consider the given graph G.

    (i)   Find all the simple paths from X to Z.

    (ii)   Find all the simple paths from Y to Z.

    (iii)   Find indeg(Y) and outdeg (Y).

    (iv)   Find the adjacency matrix A of the graph G.

    (v)   Find the path P of G using power of the adjacency matrix A.

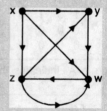

Fig. Ex. 8.4.2

S - 09

Solution :

(i)   Simple paths from X to Z

    (a) $X \to Z$

    (b) $X \to W \to Z$

    (c) $X \to Y \to W \to Z$

(ii) Simple paths from Y to Z

$$Y \to W \to Z$$

(iii) indeg (Y) = 2

outdeg (Y) = 1

(iv) Adjacency matrix representation.

$$A = \quad \begin{array}{c|cccc} & W & X & Y & Z \\ \hline W & 0 & 0 & 0 & 1 \\ X & 1 & 0 & 1 & 1 \\ Y & 1 & 0 & 0 & 0 \\ Z & 1 & 0 & 1 & 0 \end{array}$$

(v) Path matrix using power of matrix A.

Path matrix $P = A + A^2 + A^3 + A^4$

$$A = \begin{bmatrix} 0 & 0 & 0 & 1 \\ 1 & 0 & 1 & 1 \\ 1 & 0 & 0 & 0 \\ 1 & 0 & 1 & 0 \end{bmatrix}$$

$$A^2 = \begin{bmatrix} 0 & 0 & 0 & 1 \\ 1 & 0 & 1 & 1 \\ 1 & 0 & 0 & 0 \\ 1 & 0 & 1 & 0 \end{bmatrix} \times \begin{bmatrix} 0 & 0 & 0 & 1 \\ 1 & 0 & 1 & 1 \\ 1 & 0 & 0 & 0 \\ 1 & 0 & 1 & 0 \end{bmatrix} = \begin{bmatrix} 1 & 0 & 1 & 0 \\ 1 & 0 & 1 & 1 \\ 0 & 0 & 0 & 1 \\ 1 & 0 & 0 & 1 \end{bmatrix}$$

$$A^3 = A^2 \times A = \begin{bmatrix} 1 & 0 & 1 & 0 \\ 1 & 0 & 1 & 1 \\ 0 & 0 & 0 & 1 \\ 1 & 0 & 0 & 1 \end{bmatrix} \times \begin{bmatrix} 0 & 0 & 0 & 1 \\ 1 & 0 & 1 & 1 \\ 1 & 0 & 0 & 0 \\ 1 & 0 & 1 & 0 \end{bmatrix} = \begin{bmatrix} 1 & 0 & 0 & 1 \\ 1 & 0 & 1 & 1 \\ 1 & 0 & 1 & 0 \\ 1 & 0 & 1 & 1 \end{bmatrix}$$

$$A^4 = A^3 \times A = \begin{bmatrix} 1 & 0 & 0 & 1 \\ 1 & 0 & 1 & 1 \\ 1 & 0 & 1 & 0 \\ 1 & 0 & 1 & 1 \end{bmatrix} \times \begin{bmatrix} 0 & 0 & 0 & 1 \\ 1 & 0 & 1 & 1 \\ 1 & 0 & 0 & 0 \\ 1 & 0 & 1 & 0 \end{bmatrix} = \begin{bmatrix} 1 & 0 & 1 & 1 \\ 1 & 0 & 1 & 1 \\ 1 & 0 & 0 & 1 \\ 1 & 0 & 1 & 1 \end{bmatrix}$$

$$P = A + A^2 + A^3 + A^4 = \begin{bmatrix} 1 & 0 & 1 & 1 \\ 1 & 0 & 1 & 1 \\ 1 & 0 & 1 & 1 \\ 1 & 0 & 1 & 1 \end{bmatrix}$$

Note : A non-zero value is written as 1.

8.4.4 Warshall's Algorithm for Computing Transitive Closure of a Graph G :

Q.   Write Warshall's algorithm. For the graph shown in Fig. 2.
   (i)   Prepare adjacency matrix
   (ii) Prepare pathmatrix applying Warshall's algorithm.

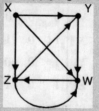

Fig. 2

W - 08

*   It computes the transitive closure of the adjacency matrix using n pass algorithm, where n is the number of vertices.

*   Following formula gives the computation of A[i][j] in the kth pass :

$$A_k[i][j] = A_{k-1}[i][j] \text{ or } A_{k-1}[i][k] \text{ and } A_{k-1}[k][j]$$

8.4.4.1   'C' Function for Computing Transitive Closure of a Graph using Warshall's Algorithm :

```
#define MAX 10
int G[MAX][MAX],TC[MAX][MAX];
int n;
/* Graph is represented using G[MAX][MAX].Its transitive closure
will be computed in TC[MAX][MAX], n is number of vertices  */
void warshall()
{
    int i,j,k;
    // copy G[][] to TC[][]
    for(i=0;i<n;i++)
         for(j=0;j<n;j++)
              TC[i][j]=G[i][j];
```

```
for(k=0;k<n;k++)
      for(i=0;i<n;i++)
          for(j=0;j<n;j++)
                if(TC[i][j]==0)
                        if(TC[i][k]==1 && TC[k][j]==1)
                              TC[i][j]=1;
}
```

Example 8.4.3 : For the graph shown.
        (i)   Prepare adjacency matrix
       (ii)   Prepare Path matrix applying Warshall's algorithm.

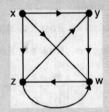

Fig. Ex. 8.4.3

W - 08

Solution :

(i)   **Adjacency matrix :**

	W	X	Y	Z
W	0	0	0	1
X	1	0	1	1
Y	1	0	0	0
Z	1	0	1	0

(ii)   **Finding Path matrix :**

Step 1 : Iterating through W.

Rows of x, y and z contain 1 in the column of W. Therefore, we do the following operations :

$$\text{Row X} = \text{Row X} \cup \text{Row W}$$

$$\text{Row Y} = \text{Row Y} \cup \text{Row W}$$

$$\text{Row Z} = \text{Row Z} \cup \text{Row W}$$

Matrix after the given operations will be

	w	x	y	z
w	0	0	0	1
x	1	0	1	1
y	1	0	0	1
z	1	0	1	1

Step 2 : Iterating through x.

Column of x does not contain 1.

Step 3 : Iterating through y.

Rows of x and z contain 1 in the column of y. Therefore, we do the following operations :

$$\text{Row x} = \text{Row x} \cup \text{Row y}$$

$$\text{Row z} = \text{Row z} \cup \text{Row y}$$

	w	x	y	z
w	0	0	0	1
x	1	0	1	1
y	1	0	0	1
z	1	0	1	1

Step 4 : Iterating through z.

Rows of w, x and y contain 1 in the column of z. Therefore, we do the following operations :

$$\text{Row w} = \text{Row w} \cup \text{Row z}$$

$$\text{Row x} = \text{Row x} \cup \text{Row z}$$

$$\text{Row y} = \text{Row y} \cup \text{Row z}$$

	w	x	y	z	
w	1	0	1	1	
x	1	0	1	1	
y	1	0	1	1	← Final path matrix
z	1	0	1	1	

8.5 Shortest Path Algorithm

Let G = (V,E) be a graph with n vertices. The problem is to find out the shortest distance from a vertex to all other vertices of a graph.

8.5.1 Dijkstra Algorithm :

Q. Explain shortest path algorithm.   W - 09

Q. Explain with suitable example shortest path, algorithm for graph.   S - 2010

Dijkstra's algorithm is also called single source shortest path algorithm. It is based on "greedy" technique. The algorithm maintains a list 'visited[ ]' of vertices, whose shortest distance from the source is already known.

If visited[1], equals 1, then the shortest distance of vertex i is already known. Initially, visited[i] is marked as, for source vertex.

At each step, we mark visited[V] as 1 Vertex V is a vertex at shortest distance from the source vertex. At each step of the algorithm, shortest distance of each vertex is stored in an array 'distance[ ]'.

> **Algorithm :**

(1)   Create cost matrix C[ ][ ] from adjacency matrix adj[ ][ ]. C[i][j] is the cost of going from vertex i to vertex j. If there is no edge between vertices i and j then C[i][j] is infinity.

(2)   Array visited [ ] is initialized to zero.

        for (i = 0; i < n; i++)

            visited[i] = 0;

(3)   If the vertex 0 is the source vertex then visited[0] is marked as 1.

(4)   Create the distance matrix, by storing the cost of vertices from vertex no. 0 to n – 1 from the source vertex 0.

        for (i = 1; i < n; i++)

            distance[i] = cost[0][i];

Initial, distance of source vertex is taken as 0.

i.e. distance[0] = 0;

(5)   for (i = 1; i < n; i++)

- Choose a vertex w, such that distance[w] is minimum and visited[w] is 0.

- Mark visited[w] as 1.

- Recalculate the shortest distance of remaining vertices from the source. Only, the vertices not marked as 1 in array visited[ ] should be considered for recalculation of distance.

  i.e. for each vertex v

  if (visited[v] = = 0)

  distance[v] = min (distance[v],

  distance[w] + cost[w][v])

8.5.1.1 Timing Complexity :

The program contains two nested loops each of which has a complexity of $O(n)$. n is number of vertices. So the complexity of algorithm is $O(n^2)$.

8.5.2 Program on Dijkstra's Algorithm :

> **Program 8.5.1 : Finding minimum distance of vertices from a given source in a graph.**

```
#define INFINITY 9999
#include<stdio.h>
#include<conio.h>
#define MAX 10
void dijkstra(int G[MAX] [MAX],int n,int startnode);

void main( )
{       int G[MAX] [MAX],i,j,n,u;

        printf("\n Enter no. of vertices:");
        scanf("%d",&n);
        printf("\n Enter the adjacency matrix :\n");
        for(i=0;i<n;i++)
            for(j=0;j<n;j++)
                scanf("%d",&G[i] [j]);
```

```
        printf("\n Enter the starting node:");
        scanf("%d",&u);
        dijkstar(G,n,u);
        getch( );
}
void dijkstra(int G[MAX] [MAX],int n,int startnode)
   {    int cost[MAX] [MAX],distance[MAX],pred[MAX];
        int visited[MAX],count,mindistance,nextnode,i,j;
        //pred[] stores the predecessor of each node
        //count gives the number of nodes seen so far
        //create the cost matrix
            for(i=0;i<n;i++)
                    for(j=0;j<n;j++)
                        if(G[i] [j]==0)
                            cost[i] [j]=INFINITY;
                        else
                            cost[i] [j]=G[i] [j];
        //initialize pred[],distance[] and visited[]
        for(i=0;i<n;i++)
        {   distance[i]=cost[startnode] [i];
            pred[i]=startnode;visited[i]=0;
        }
        distance[startnode]=0;visited[startnode]=1;
        count=1;
        while(count<n-1)
        {   mindistance=INFINITY;
            //nextnode gives the node at minimum distance
            for(i=0;i<n;i++)
                    if(distance[i]<mindistance &&!visited[i])
                    {       mindistance=distance[i];
                            nextnode=i;
                    }
            //check if a better path exists through nextnode
                visited[nextnode]=1;
            for(i=0;i<n;i++)
                if(!visited[i])
                        if(mindistance+cost[nextnode] [i]<
```

```
                        distance[i])
                        {
    distance[i]=mindistance+cost[nextnode] [i];
                        pred[i]=nextnode;
                        }
    count++;
}
//Print the path and distance of each node
    for(i=0;i<n;i++)
        if(i!=startnode)
            {       printf("\n Distance of node
%d=%d",i,distance[i]);
                    printf("\n path=%d",i);
                    j=i;
                    do
                    {
                        j=pred[j];
                        printf("<-%d",j);
                    }       while(j!=startnode);
            }
}
```

Output

Enter No. of vertices = 5

Enter the adjacency matrix :

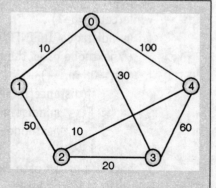

0	10	0	30	100
10	0	50	0	0
0	50	0	20	10
30	0	20	0	60
100	0	10	60	0

Enter the starting node:0

Distance of node number 1=10

  Path=1 ← 0

Distance of node number 2=50

  Path=2← 3← 0

Distance of node number 3=30
    Path=3← 0
Distance of node number 4=60
    Path=4 ←2←3←0

8.5.3 Examples on Dijkstra's Algorithm :

Example 8.5.1 :   Show the working of the Dijkstra Algorithm on the graph
given below.

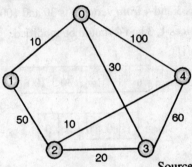

Source vertex is taken as 0

Fig. Ex. 8.5.1

Solution :   **Initial configuration of :**

(a)   Cost matrix

	0	1	2	3	4
0	∞	10	∞	30	100
1	10	∞	50	∞	∞
2	∞	50	∞	20	10
3	30	∞	20	∞	60
4	100	∞	10	60	∞

distance matrix

0	1	2	3	4
0	∞	∞	∞	∞

visited

0	1	2	3	4
0	0	0	0	0

1st Iteration

(a) Select vertex 0 (at minimum distance)

(b) Mark visited[0] as 1

(c) Re-adjust distances of vertices not marked as 1 in visited[ ]. Distance in distance matrix should be altered if there is a better distance path through the selected vertex 0.

- Distance of vertex 1 in distance[ ] matrix is infinity. But the cost of going to vertex 1 from vertex 0 is 10.

- Distances of vertex 3 and 4 in distance[ ] matrix are ∞. But the cost of going to vertices 3 and 4 from vertex 0 is 30 and 100 respectively.

- Distance of vertices 1, 3 and 4 should be modified.

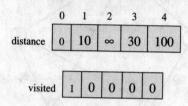

2nd Iteration :

- Select vertex 1 (at minimum distance)

- Mark visited[1] as 1.

- Re-adjust distances.

- Cost of going to vertex 2 form the source vertex 0, via the selected vertex 1 is given by distance[1] + cost[1][2] = 10 + 50 = 60. Distance of 60 is better than the existing distance of ∞.

- Cost of going to vertex 3 from the source vertex 0, via the selected vertex 1 is distance[1] + cost[1][3] = 10 + ∞ = ∞. Which is worse than the existing distance of 30.

- Similarly, the cost of going to vertex 4 from the source, via the selected vertex 1 is ∞. Which is worse than the existing distance of 100.

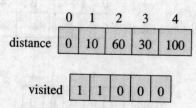

3rd Iteration

Vertex selected = 3

Cost of going to vertex 2 via vertex 3 = distance[3] + cost[3][2] = 30 + 20 = 50

Cost of going to vertex 4 via vertex 3 = distance[3] + cost[3][4] = 30 + 60 = 90

Distances of vertices 2 and 4 should be changed.

	0	1	2	3	4
distance	0	10	50	30	90

visited	1	1	0	1	0

4th Iteration

Vertex selected = 2

Cost of going to vertex 4 via vertex 2 = distance[2] + cost[2][4] = 50 + 10 = 60

Distance of vertex 4 should be changed.

distance	0	10	50	30	60	← final distances

visited	1	1	1	1	0

Example 8.5.2 : Consider the weighted graph in figure with 8 nodes A, B, C, D, E, F, G and H. Find the shortest path from A to all the remaining vertices.

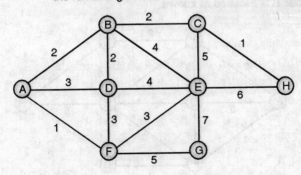

Solution :

Node A is declared as known.

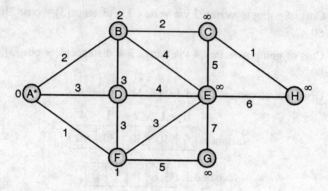

Node F is declared as known.

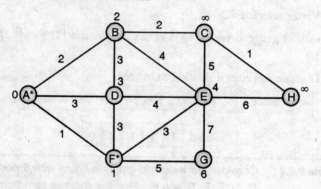

Node B is declared as known.

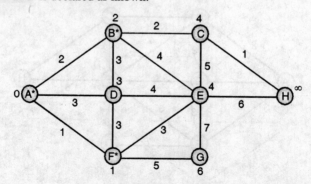

Node D is declared as known

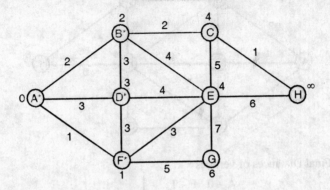

Node C is declared as known

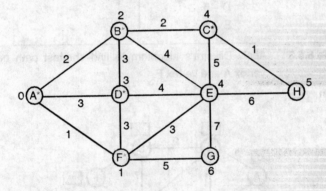

Node E is declared as known

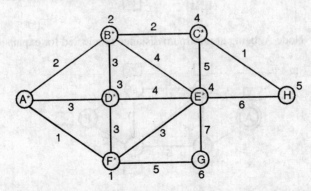

Node H is declared as known

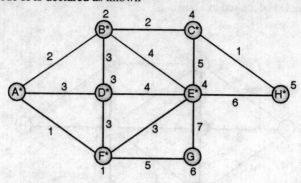

Final Distances of vertices :

A – 0   F – 1
B – 2   G – 6
C – 4   H – 5
D – 3
E – 4

Example 8.5.3 :   Apply Dijkstra's algorithm to find shortest path between vertex A and vertex F.

Solution :

Step 1 :

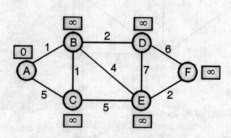

Step 2 :   Node A, being at minimum distance is selected for expansion.

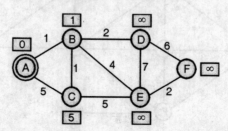

Step 3 : Node B, being at minimum distance is selected for expansion.

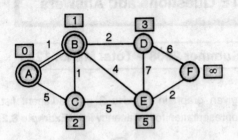

Step 4 : Node C, being at minimum distance is selected for expansion.

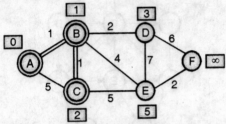

Step 5 : Node D, being at minimum distance is selected for expansion.

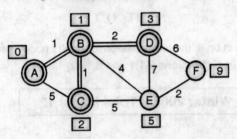

Step 6 : Node E, being at minimum distance is selected for expansion.

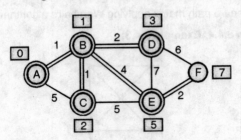

Path from A to F is given by $A \xrightarrow{1} B \xrightarrow{4} E \xrightarrow{2} F$ length of the path = 7.

8.6 MSBTE Questions and Answers

Summer 2008 – Total Marks 12

Q. 1 For the given graph in Fig. No 2 give adjacent list, edge list and storage representation for adjacency list. **(Example 8.2.5)** **(8 Marks)**

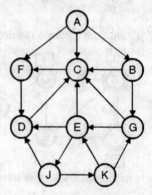

Fig. Q. 1

Q. 2 Describe in brief, the terms related to graph : nodes , edges, in-degree, out – degree. **(Sections 8.1.1 and 8.1.12)** **(4 Marks)**

Winter 2008 – Total Marks 12

Q. 3 Write Warshall's algorithm. For the graph shown in Fig. Q. 3.

(i) Prepare adjacency matrix

(ii) Prepare path matrix applying Warshall's algorithm.

(Section 8.4.4, Example 8.4.3) **(8 Marks)**

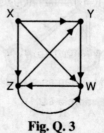

Fig. Q. 3

Q. 4 Explain the link representation of a Graph with suitable example.

(Section 8.2.2) **(4 Marks)**

Summer 2009 – Total Marks 12

Q. 5 Consider the graph G in Fig. No. 2.

i)　　Find all the simple paths from X to Z.

ii)　　Find all the simple paths from Y to Z.

iii)　　Find indeg (Y) and outdeg (Y).

iv)　　Find the adjacency matrix A of the graph G.

v)　　Find the path P of G using powers of the adjacency matrix A.

(Example 8.4.2) **(8 Marks)**

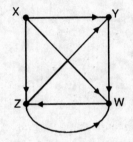

Fig. Q. 5

Q. 6 Write an algorithm for Breadth-First Search on graph.

(Section 8.3.2.1) **(4 Marks)**

Winter 2009 – Total Marks 18

Q. 7 Describe Breadth First search technique with suitable example.

(Section 8.3.2) **(6 Marks)**

Q. 8 Explain shortest path algorithm. **(Section 8.5.1)** **(8 Marks)**

Q. 9 Explain in-degree and out-degree of a node with example.

(Section 8.1.12 and Example 8.2.1) **(4 Marks)**

Summer 2010 – Total Marks 18

Q. 10 Describe depth first search method. **(Section 8.3.1)** **(8 Marks)**

Q. 11 Define following terms with respect to graph :

    (i)   In-degree of a node **(Section 8.1.12)**

    (ii) Directed graph **(Section 8.1.3)**

    (iii) Weighted graph **(Section 8.1.5)**

    (iv) Predecessor **(Section 8.1.3)** **(4 Marks)**

Q. 12 Explain with suitable example shortest path, algorithm for graph.
(Section 8.5.1) **(6 Marks)**

❑❑❑

Hashing

Syllabus

Introduction

Hash functions

Deleting items from hash table.

Statistical Analysis

Year	Marks
Summer - 2008	4 Marks
Winter - 2008	3 Marks
Summer - 2009	4 Marks
Winter - 2009	4 Marks
Summer - 2010	4 Marks

9.1 Introduction to Hashing

Q. What is Hashing ? Give its significance.　**S - 08**

Q. What is hashing? Describe different hash functions (atleast 3). **W - 08**

Q. Explain concept of hashing.　**W - 09**

Q. What is hashing? Explain any one hashing method. **S - 2010**

Sequential search requires, on the average O(n) comparisons to locate an element. So many comparisons are not desirable for a large database of elements. Binary search requires much fewer comparisons on the average O (log n) but there is an additional requirement that the data should be sorted. Even with best sorting algorithm, sorting of elements require O(n log n) comparisons.

There is another widely used technique for storing of data called "hashing". It does away with the requirement of keeping data sorted (as in binary search) and its best case timing complexity is of constant order (O(1)). In its worst case, hashing algorithm starts behaving like linear search.

Best case timing behaviour of searching using hashing = O(1)

Worst case timing Behaviour of searching using hashing = O(n).

Since, there is a large gap between its best case O(1) and worst case O(n) behaviour. It should be implemented properly to get an average case behaviour close to O(1). In hashing , the record for a key value "key" is directly referred by calculating the address from the key value. Address or location of an element or record, x, is obtained by computing some arithmetic function f. f(key) gives the address of x in the table.

(a)　Table used for storing of records is known as hash table.

Function f(key)is known as hash function.

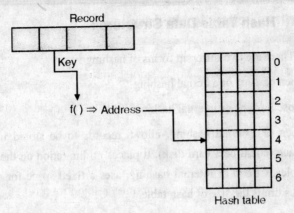

Fig. 9.1.1 : Mapping of record in hash table

Example :

Suppose, we wish to implement a hash table for a set of records where the key is a member of set K of strings as,

K= {"aaa", "bbb", "ccc", "ddd" "eee", "fff", "ggg"}

A function f : key → Index is given by the following table:

N	f(x)
"aaa"	0
"bbb"	1
"ccc"	2
"ddd"	3
"eee"	4
"fff"	5
"ggg"	6

Hash table can be implement using an array of records of length n = 7. To store a record with key x, we simply store it at position f(x) in the array. Similarly, to locate the record having key = x, we simply check to see if it is found at position f(x).

9.1.1   Hash Table Data Structure :

There are two different forms of hashing :

(a)   Open hashing or external hashing

(b)   Close hashing or internal hashing

Open or external hashing, allows records to be stored in unlimited space (could be a hard disk). It places no limitation on the size of the tables. Closed or internal hashing, uses a fixed space for storage and thus limits the size of hash table.

9.1.2   Open Hashing Data Structure :

Q.   What is hashing? Explain any one hashing method.   S - 2010

Fig. 9.1.2 gives the basic data structure for open hashing.

The basic idea is that the records [elements] are partitioned into B classes, numbered 0,1,2.. B–1. Hashing function f(x) mapps a record with key n to an integer value between 0 and B–1. If a record is mapped to location 1 then we say the record is mapped to bucket 1 or the record belongs to class 4. Each bucket in the bucket table is the head of the linked list of records mapped to that bucket.

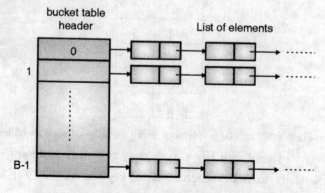

Fig. 9.1.2 : The open hashing data organization

9.1.3 Closed Hashing Data Structure :

A closed hash table keeps the elements in the bucket itself. Only one element can be put in the bucket. If we try to place an element in the bucket f(n) and find it already holds an element, then we say that a collision has occurred. In case of collision, the element should be rehashed to alternate empty location $f_1(x), f_2(x), \ldots$ within the bucket table. In closed hashing, collision handling is a very important issue.

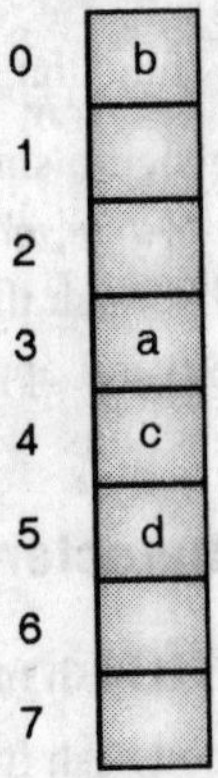

Fig. 9.1.3 : Partially filled hash table

9.2 Hashing Functions

We are designing a container which will be used to hold some number of items of a given set K. In this context, we call the elements of the set K *keys* . The general approach is to store the keys in an array. The position of a key in the array is given by a function h($\cdot$), called a *hash function* , which determines the position of a given key directly from that key.

In the general case, we expect the size of the set of keys, $|K|$, to be relatively large or even unbounded. For example, if the keys are 32-bit integers, then $|K| = 2^{32}$. Similarly, if the keys are arbitrary character strings of arbitrary length, then $|K|$ is unbounded.

On the other hand, we also expect that the actual number of items stored in the container to be significantly less than $|K|$. That is, if n is the number of items actually stored in the container, then $n << |K|$. Therefore, it seems prudent to use an array of size M, where M is at least as great as the maximum number of items to be stored in the container.

Consequently, what we need is a function h : K → {0, 1, ... M – 1}. This function maps the set of values to be stored in the container to subscripts in an array of length *M*.

This function is called a *hash function*.

In general, since, |K| ≥ M the mapping defined by hash function will be a *many-to-one mapping*. That is, there will exist many pairs of distinct keys x and y, such that x ≠ y, for which h(x)=h(y). This situation is called a *collision*. Several approaches for dealing with collisions are explored in the following sections.

9.2.1 Characteristics of a Good Hash Function :

*   A good hash function avoids collisions.
*   A good hash function tends to spread keys evenly in the array.
*   A good hash function is easy to compute.

There are many hashing functions. We will discuss these in the following sections.

9.2.2 Division-Method :

> **Q.** What is hashing? Describe different hash functions (atleast 3).
> **W - 08**
>
> **Q.** Explain different methods used to evaluate Hash Functions.
> **S - 09**

In this method, we use modular arithmetic system to divide the key value by some integer divisor m (may be table size). It gives us the location value, where the element can be placed. We can write,

$$L = (K \bmod m) + 1$$

where $L \Rightarrow$ location in table/file

          $K \Rightarrow$ key value

          $m \Rightarrow$ table size/number of slots in file

suppose, $K = 23, m = 10$ then

          $L = (23 \bmod 10) + 1 = 3 + 1 = 4$

∴ The key whose value is 23 is placed in 4th location.

9.2.3 Midsquare Methods :

> **Q.** What is hashing? Describe different hash functions (atleast 3).
> **W - 08**
>
> **Q.** Explain different methods used to evaluate Hash Functions.
> **S - 09**

In this case, we square the value of a key and take the number of digits required to form an address, from the middle position of squared value. Suppose a key value is 16, then its square is 256. Now if we want address of two digits, then you select the address as 56 (i.e. two digits starting from middle of 256).

9.2.4 Folding Method :

> **Q.** What is hashing? Describe different hash functions (atleast 3).
> **W - 08**
>
> **Q.** Explain different methods used to evaluate Hash Functions.
> **S - 09**

Most machines have a small number of primitive data types for which there are arithmetic instructions. Frequently key to be used will not fit easily in to one of these data types. It is not possible to discard the portion of the key that does not fit into such an arithmetic data type. The solution is to combine the various parts of the key in such a way that all parts of the key affect for final result, such an operation is termed **folding** of the key.

That is the key is actually partitioned into number of parts, each part having the same length as that of the required address. Add the value of each parts, ignoring the final carry to get the required address. This is done in two ways :

(a)   Fold-shifting : Here actual values of each parts of key are added.

(b)   Fold-boundary : Here the reversed values of outer parts of key are added.

Suppose, the key is : 12345678, and the required address is of two digits, then break the key into parts : 12, 34, 56, 78.

Add these, we get 12 + 34 + 56 + 78 = | 1 | 80

                                               Ignore

So we get address as 80. (This is fold-shifting).

For fold boundary, reverse the key parts, we get 21, 34, 56, 87

Add these parts, 21 + 34 + 56 + 87 = | 1 | 98

So we get the address as 98.

                                               Omit

9.2.5 Digit Analysis :

> **Q.** What is hashing? Describe different hash functions (atleast 3).
> W - 08
>
> **Q.** Explain different methods used to evaluate Hash Functions.
> S - 09

This hashing function is a distribution-dependent. Here we make a statistical analysis of digits of the key, and select those digits (of fixed position) which occur quite frequently. Then reverse or shifts the digits to get the address.

For example, if the key is : 9861234. If the statistical analysis has revealed the fact that the third and fifth position digits occur quite frequently, then we choose the digits in these positions from the key. So we get, 62. Reversing it we get 26 as the address.

9.2.6 Length Dependent Method :

> **Q.** What is hashing? Describe different hash functions (atleast 3).
> W - 08
>
> **Q.** Explain different methods used to evaluate Hash Functions.
> S - 09

In this type of hashing function we use the length of the key along with some portion of the key to produce the address, directly. In the indirect method, the length of the key along with some portion of the key is used to obtain intermediate value. Then use any other method to obtain the address values.

9.2.7 Algebraic Coding :

> **Q.** What is hashing? Describe different hash functions (atleast 3).
> W - 08
>
> **Q.** Explain different methods used to evaluate Hash Functions.
> S - 09

Here a n bit key value is represented as a polynomial. The divisor polynomial is then constructed based on the address range required. The modular division of key-polynomial by divisor polynomial, to get the address-polynomial.

$$\text{Let } f(x) = \text{polynomial of n bit key}$$
$$= a_1 + a_2 x + \dots + a_n x^{n-1}$$
$$d(x) = \text{divisor polynomial}$$
$$= x^1 + d_1 + d_2 x + \dots + d_1 x^{1-1}$$

(i.e. if required address is in the range 0 to $k = 2^1 - 1$)

Then the required address-polynomial will be,

$$f(x) \bmod d(x) = ab_1 + b_2 x + \dots + b_1 x^{1-1}$$

where $(b_1, b_2 \dots b_1)_2$ is the address.

9.2.8 Multiplicative Hashing :

This method is based on obtaining an address of a key, based on the multiplication value. If k is the non-negative key, and a constant c, $(0 < c < 1)$, compute kc mod 1, which is a fractional part of kc. Multiply this fractional part by m and take a floor value to get the address

$$h(k) = \lfloor m(kc \bmod 1) \rfloor,$$

$$0 \le h(k) < m.$$

So far we talked about how to map a key to address. But, what happens if the two keys yield the same address values? Well it results in collision. Hence one must resolve these collisions.

9.3 MSBTE Questions and Answers

Summer 2008 – Total Marks 04

Q. 1　What is Hashing ? Give its significance. **(Section 9.1)**　　　**(4 Marks)**

Winter 2008 – Total Marks 03

Q. 2　What is hashing? Describe different hash functions (at least 3).
(Section 9.1, 9.2.2 to 9.2.8)　　　　　　　　　　　**(3 Marks)**

Summer 2009 – Total Marks 04

Q. 3　Explain different methods used to evaluate Hash Functions.
(Section 9.2.2 to 9.2.8)　　　　　　　　　　　　　**(4 Marks)**

Winter 2009 – Total Marks 04

Q. 4　Explain concept of hashing. **(Section 9.1)**　　　　**(4 Marks)**

Summer 10 – Total Marks 04

Q. 5　What is hashing? Explain any one hashing method.
(Section 9.1 and 9.1.2)　　　　　　　　　　　　　**(4 Marks)**

❑❑❑

Lab Experiments

10.1 Program Based on Array

```
/*Program based on array: operation for insertion and deletion */

#include <stdio.h>
#include <conio.h>

void main()
{
  int a[30],n=0,op,i,x,loc;
  clrscr();
  do
    {
    printf("\n\n1)Read initial Data in the array");
    printf("\n2)Insert\n3)Delete\n4)Quit");
    printf("\nEnter your choice : ");
    scanf("%d",&op);
    switch(op)
     {
         case 1: printf("\nEnter no. of data : ");
             scanf("%d",&n);
             printf("\nEnter %d elements : ",n);
             for(i=0;i<n;i++)
                  scanf("%d",&a[i]);
             break;
```

```
        case 2: printf("\nEnter a location from %d to %d :
",1,n+1);
              scanf("%d",&loc);
              if(loc>=1 & loc<= n+1)
                {
                    printf("\nEnter the data to be inserted : ");
                    scanf("%d",&x);
                    for(i=n-1;i>=loc-1;i--)
                            a[i+1]=a[i];
                            a[loc-1]=x;
                    n++;
                    printf("\nData after insertion :");
                    for(i=0;i<n;i++)
                            printf("%d ",a[i]);
                }
              else
                printf("\n Invalid location ");
              break;
        case 3: printf("\nEnter a location from %d to %d : ",1,n);
              scanf("%d",&loc);
              if(loc>=1 & loc<= n)
                {
                    for(i=loc;i<n;i++)
                            a[i-1]=a[i];
                    n--;
                    printf("\nData after deletion :");
                    for(i=0;i<n;i++)
                            printf("%d ",a[i]);
                }
              else
                printf("\n Invalid location ");
              break;
    }
  }while(op!=4);
}
```

Output

1)Read initial Data in the array
2)Insert
3)Delete
4)Quit
Enter Your Choice : 2

Enter a location from 1 to 1 : 1

Enter the data to be inserted : 12

Data after insertion :12

1)Read initial Data in the array
2)Insert
3)Delete
4)Quit
Enter Your Choice : 2

Enter a location from 1 to 2 : 2

Enter the data to be inserted : 34

Data after insertion :12 34

1)Read initial Data in the array
2)Insert
3)Delete
4)Quit
Enter Your Choice :2

Enter a location from 1 to 3 : 3

Enter the data to be inserted :6

```
Data after insertion :12  34  6

1)Read initial Data in the array
2)Insert
3)Delete
4)Quit
Enter Your Choice : 3

Enter a location from 1 to 3 : 2

Data after deletion :12   6

1)Read initial Data in the array
2)Insert
3)Delete
4)Quit
Enter Your Choice :4
```

10.2 Sorting Methods

10.2.1 Bubble Sort, Selection Sort and Insertion Sort :

```
/*Implement sorting methods - bubble sort, selection sort
insertion sort.*/

void insertion_sort(int [],int);
void selection_sort(int a[],int n);
void bubble_sort(int a[],int n);

void main()
{
   int a[50],n,i,op;
   clrscr();
   do
```

```
   {
     printf("\n1)insertion \n2)Selection \n3)Bubble \n4)Quit");
     printf("\nEnter your choice : ");
     scanf("%d",&op);
     switch(op)
      {
        case 1: printf("\nEnter no. of elements :");
            scanf("%d",&n);
            printf("\nEnter array elements :");
            for(i=0;i<n;i++)
               scanf("%d",&a[i]);
            insertion_sort(a,n);
            break;
        case 2: printf("\nEnter no. of elements :");
            scanf("%d",&n);
            printf("\nEnter array elements :");
            for(i=0;i<n;i++)
               scanf("%d",&a[i]);
            selection_sort(a,n);
            break;
        case 3: printf("\nEnter no of elements :");
            scanf("%d",&n);
            printf("\nEnter array elements :");
            for(i=0;i<n;i++)
               scanf("%d",&a[i]);
            bubble_sort(a,n);
            break;
      }
   } while(op!=4);

}

void insertion_sort(int a[],int n)
{
```

```c
   int i,j,temp,k;
   printf("\n Unsorted Data:");
   for(k=0;k<n;k++)
    printf("%5d",a[k]);

   for(i=1;i<n;i++)
   {
        temp=a[i];
        for(j=i-1;j>=0 && a[j]>temp; j--)
            a[j+1]=a[j];
            a[j+1]=temp;
    printf("\n After pass  %d", i);
       for(k=0;k<n;k++)
        printf("%5d",a[k]);

   }
}
void selection_sort(int a[],int n)
{
   int i,j,temp,k;
   printf("\n Unsorted Data:");
   for(k=0;k<n;k++)
    printf("%5d",a[k]);

   for(i=0;i<n-1;i++)
   {     k=i;
         for(j=i+1;j<n;j++)
           if(a[j]<a[k])
             k=j;
          temp=a[i];
          a[i]=a[k];
          a[k]=temp;
    printf("\n After pass  %d",i+1);
       for(k=0;k<n;k++)
```

```
        printf("%5d",a[k]);

    }
}
void bubble_sort(int a[],int n)
{
    int i,j,k,temp;
    printf("\n Unsorted Data:");
    for(k=0;k<n;k++)
     printf("%5d",a[k]);
    for(i=1;i<n;i++)
     {
       for(j=0;j<n-1;j++)
          if(a[j]>a[j+1])
            {
                temp=a[j];
                a[j]=a[j+1];
                a[j+1]=temp;
            }
       printf("\nAfter pass   %d",i);
       for(k=0;k<n;k++)
        printf("%5d",a[k]);
     }
}
```

Output

```
1)insertion
2)Selection
3)Bubble
4)Quit
Enter your choice : 1

Enter no of elements :4
```

```
Enter array elements :5
7
33
2

Unsorted Data:  5   7   33   2
After pass 1=   5   7   33   2
After pass 2=   5   7   33   2
After pass 3=   2   5   7   33
1)insertion
2)Selection
3)Bubble
4)Quit
Enter your choice : 2

Enter no of elements :4

Enter array elements :55   2  1
88

Unsorted Data:  55   2   1   88
After pass  1   1   2   55   88
After pass  2   1   2   55   88
After pass  3   1   2   55   88
1)insertion
2)Selection
3)Bubble
4)Quit
Enter your choice : 3
Enter no of elements :4

Enter array elements :2
6
33
11
```

```
Unsorted Data:    2    6    33    11
After pass  1    2    6    11    33
After pass  2    2    6    11    33
After pass  3    2    6    11    33
1)insertion
2)Selection
3)Bubble
4)Quit
Enter your choice : 4
```

10.2.2 Quick Sort and Merge Sort :

```c
/*Implement Quick sort and Merge sort using recursion */

#include<conio.h>
#include<stdio.h>

void quick_sort(int [],int,int);
int partition(int [],int,int);
void mergesort(int a[] ,int i , int j);
void merge(int a[],int i1, int j1, int i2, int j2);
void main()
{
   int a[30],n,i,op;
   clrscr();
   do
     {
       printf("\n1)Quick Sort \n2)Merge Sort \n3)Quit");
       printf("\nEnter your choice : ");
       scanf("%d",&op);
       switch(op)
        {
          case 1: printf("\nEnter no of elements :");
                scanf("%d",&n);
```

```
                printf("\nEnter array elements :");
                for(i=0;i<n;i++)
                        scanf("%d",&a[i]);
                quick_sort(a,0,n-1);
                printf("\nSorted array is :");
                for(i=0;i<n;i++)
                        printf("%d  ",a[i]);
                break;

        case 2: printf("\nEnter no. of elements :");
                scanf("%d",&n);
                printf("\nEnter array elements :");
                for(i=0;i<n;i++)
                        scanf("%d",&a[i]);
                mergesort(a,0,n-1);
                printf("\nSorted array is :");
                for(i=0;i<n;i++)
                        printf("%d    ",a[i]);
                break;

    }
   }while(op!=3);
}
void quick_sort(int a[],int l,int u){
   int j;
   if(l<u)
   {
        j=partition(a,l,u);
        quick_sort(a,l,j-1);
        quick_sort(a,j+1,u);
   }
}
int partition(int a[],int l,int u)
{
```

```
    int v,i,j,temp;
    v=a[l];
    i=l;
    j=u+1;
    do
    {
    do
    {    i++;
    }while(a[i]<v && i<=u);

    do
    {    j--;
    }while(a[j]>v);

    if(i<j)
    {
         temp=a[i];
         a[i]=a[j];
         a[j]=temp;
    }
    }while(i<j);
    a[l]=a[j];
    a[j]=v;
    return(j);
}
void mergesort(int a[] ,int i , int j)
  {
   int mid;
   if(i<j)
    { mid=(i+j)/2;
      mergesort(a,i,mid);   //left recursion
      mergesort(a,mid+1,j); //right recursion
      merge(a,i,mid,mid+1,j); //merging of two sorted sub-arrays
    }
    }
```

```
void merge(int a[],int i1, int j1, int i2, int j2)
 {
   int temp[50];//array used for merging
   int i,j,k;
   i=i1;//beginning of the first list
   j=i2;//beginning of the second list
   k=0;
   while(i<=j1 && j <=j2) //while elements in both lists
    {
  if(a[i]<a[j])
    temp[k++]=a[i++];
  else
    temp[k++]=a[j++];
    }
   while(i<=j1)//copy remaining elements of the first list
    temp[k++]=a[i++];
   while(j<=j2)//copy remaining elements of the second list
    temp[k++]=a[j++];
 //Transfer elements from temp[] back to a[]
  for(i=i1,j=0;i<=j2;i++,j++)
    a[i]=temp[j];
}
```

Output

```
1)Quick Sort
2)Merge Sort
3)Quit
Enter your choice : 1

Enter no of elements :3

Enter array elements :55
4
```

```
1

Sorted array is :1  4  55
1)Quick Sort
2)Merge Sort
3)Quit
Enter your choice : 2

Enter no of elements :5

Enter array elements :8
6
3
44
1

Sorted array is :1   3   6   8   44
1)Quick Sort
2)Merge Sort
3)Quit
Enter your choice : 3
```

10.3 Various Searching Methods

```c
/*Program for various searching methods */

#include <stdio.h>
#include <conio.h>

int binsearch(int a[],int i ,int j,int key);/*Recursive binary
search*/
int linsearch(int a[],int n , int key);

void main()
```

```
{
 int a[30],key,n,i,result,op;
 clrscr();
 do
   {
   printf("\n1)Linear Search\n2)Binary Search\n3)Quit");
   printf("\nEnter Your Choice : ");
   scanf("%d",&op);
   switch(op)
     {
         case 1: printf("\n Enter No. of elements : ");
             scanf("%d" ,&n);
             printf("\n Enter a  list of %d elements : ",n);
             for(i=0;i<n;i++)
                 scanf("%d",&a[i]);
             printf("\n Enter the the element to be searched : ");
             scanf("%d",&key);
             result=linsearch(a,n,key);
             if(result==-1)
                 printf("\n Not found : ");
             else
                 printf("\n Found at location= %d",result+1);
             break;

         case 2: printf("\n Enter No. of elements : ");
             scanf("%d" ,&n);
             printf("\n Enter a sorted list of %d elements : ",n);
             for(i=0;i<n;i++)
                 scanf("%d",&a[i]);
             printf("\n Enter the the element to be searched : ");
             scanf("%d",&key);
             result=binsearch(a,0,n-1,key);
             if(result==-1)
                 printf("\n Not found : ");
```

```
            else
                printf("\n Found at location= %d",result+1);
            break;

    }
    }while(op!=3);
}

int binsearch(int a[],int i, int j,int key)
{
  int c;
  if(i>j)
   return(-1);
  c=(i+j)/2;
  if(key==a[c])
     return(c);
  if(key>a[c])
     return(binsearch(a,c+1,j,key));
  return(binsearch(a,i,c-1,key));
}

int linsearch(int a[],int n , int key)
{
  int i;
  for(i=0;i<n;i++)
    {
  if(a[i]==key)
      return(i);
    }

  return(-1);
}
```

Output

```
1)Linear Search
2)Binary Search
3)Quit
Enter Your Choice : 1

 Enter No. of elements : 3

 Enter a  list of 3 elements : 6
55
2

 Enter the element to be searched : 55

 Found at location= 2
1)Linear Search
2)Binary Search
3)Quit
Enter Your Choice : 2

 Enter No. of elements : 3

 Enter a sorted list of 3 elements : 47
8
6

 Enter the element to be searched : 8

 Found at location= 2
1)Linear Search
2)Binary Search
3)Quit
Enter Your Choice : 3
```

10.4 Use of Stack for Expression

```
/* program for conversion of:
          1. infix into its postfix form
          2. Evaluation of postfix expression
  operators supported '+,-,*,/,%,^,(,)
  operands supported -- all single character operands
*/

#include<stdio.h>
#include<conio.h>
#include<ctype.h>
#define MAX 50

typedef struct stack
{
   int data[MAX];
   int top;
}stack;

int  precedence(char);
void init(stack *);
int  empty(stack *);
int  full(stack *);
int  pop(stack *);
void push(stack *,int );
int  top(stack *); //value of the top element
void infix_to_postfix(char infix[],char postfix[]);
void eval_postfix(char postfix[]);
int  evaluate(char x,int op1,int op2);

void main()
 { char infix[30],postfix[30];
```

```
   clrscr();
   printf("\nEnter an infix expression : ");
   gets(infix);
   infix_to_postfix(infix,postfix);
   printf("\nPostfix : %s ",postfix);
   printf("\nPostfix evaluation : ");
   eval_postfix(postfix);
   getch();
 }
void infix_to_postfix(char infix[],char postfix[])
{  stack s;
   char x;
   int i,j;//i-index for infix[],j-index for postfix
   char token;
   init(&s);
   j=0;
   for(i=0;infix[i]!='\0';i++)
     {    token=infix[i];
          if(isalnum(token))
               postfix[j++]=token;
          else
              if(token == '(')
                   push(&s,'(');
              else
                   if(token == ')')
                     while((x=pop(&s))!='(')
                          postfix[j++]=x;
                   else
                   {

   while(precedence(token)<=precedence(top(&s)) &&
!empty(&s))
                          {
                               x=pop(&s);
                               postfix[j++]=x;
```

```
                              }
                              push(&s,token);
                    }
        }
    while(!empty(&s))
    {
        x=pop(&s);
        postfix[j++]=x;
    }
postfix[j]='\0';
}
void eval_postfix(char postfix[])
{
    stack s;
    char x;
    int op1,op2,val,i;
    init(&s);
    for(i=0;postfix[i]!='\0';i++)
    {   x=postfix[i];
        if(isalpha(x))
            { printf("\nEnter the value of %c : ",x);
            scanf("%d",&val);
            push(&s,val);
            }
        else
        {    //pop two operands and evaluate
            op2=pop(&s);
            op1=pop(&s);
            val=evaluate(x,op1,op2);
            push(&s,val);
        }
    }
    val=pop(&s);
    printf("\nvalue of expression = %d",val);
```

```
}

int evaluate(char x,int op1,int op2)
{
   if(x=='+')  return(op1+op2);
   if(x=='-')  return(op1-op2);
   if(x=='*')  return(op1*op2);
   if(x=='/')  return(op1/op2);
   if(x=='%')  return(op1%op2);

}




int precedence(char x)
{
   if(x == '(')                    return(0);
   if(x == '+' || x == '-')         return(1);
   if(x == '*' || x == '/' || x == '%') return(2);
   return(3);
}

void init(stack *s)
{
   s->top=-1;
}

int empty(stack *s)
{
   if(s->top==-1)  return(1);
   return(0);
}
```

```
int full(stack *s)
{
   if(s->top==MAX-1)    return(1);
   return(0);
}

void push(stack *s,int x)
{
   s->top=s->top+1;
   s->data[s->top]=x;
}

int pop(stack *s)
{
   int x;
   x=s->data[s->top];
   s->top=s->top-1;
   return(x);
}

int top(stack * p)
{
   return(p->data[p->top]);
}
```

Output

```
Enter an infix expression : a+(d-c)*e/f

Postfix : adc-e*f/+
Postfix evaluation :
Enter the value of a : 2
```

Enter the value of d : 3

Enter the value of c : 4

Enter the value of e : 5

Enter the value of f : 6

value of expression = 2

10.5 Recursive Programs

```c
/*Recursive Program:Factorial,Fibonacci,Ackerman function,Tower
of Hanoi*/

#include <stdio.h>
#include <conio.h>
int factorial(int n);
int fibonacci(int n);
int ackerman(int m,int n);
void TOH(int n, char x, char y,char z);

void main()
  {
    int op,m,n,value;
    clrscr();
    do
      {
      printf("\n\n1)Factorial\n2)Fibonacci\n3)Ackerman\n4)Tower
of Hanoi\n5)Quit");
      printf("\nEnter Your Choice : ");
      scanf("%d",&op);
      switch(op)
        {
```

```
        case 1: printf("\nEnter a Number : ");
            scanf("%d",&n);
            value=factorial(n);
            printf("\n\nFactoral of %d = %d",n,value);
            break;
        case 2: printf("\nEnter Term No. : ");
            scanf("%d",&n);
            value=fibonacci(n);
            printf("\n\nTerm No. %d = %d",n,value);
            break;
        case 3: printf("\nEnter 2 Numbers : ");
            scanf("%d%d",&m,&n);
            value=ackerman(m,n);
            printf("\n\nAckerman function of(%d,%d) =
%d",m,n,value);
            break;
        case 4: printf("\Enter No. of plates : ");
            scanf("%d",&n);
            TOH(n,'A','B','C');
            break;
    }
    }while(op!=5);
}

int factorial(int n)
{
   if(n==0)
   return(1);
   return(n*factorial(n-1));
}
int fibonacci(int n)
{
   if(n==0)
   return(0);
```

```
    if(n==1)
    return(1);
    return(fibonacci(n-1)+fibonacci(n-2));
  }
 int ackerman(int m,int n)
  {
   if(m==0)
    return(n+1);
   if(n==0)
    return(ackerman(m-1,1));
    return(ackerman(m-1,ackerman(m,n-1)));
  }

 void TOH(int n, char x, char y,char z)
  {
    if(n>0)
     {
   TOH(n-1,x,z,y);
   printf("\n%c -> %c",z,y);
   TOH(n-1,z,y,x);
     }
  }
```

Output

```
1)Factorial
2)Fibonacci
3)Ackerman
4)Tower of Hanoi
5)Quit
Enter Your Choice : 1

Enter a Number : 5

Factorial of 5 = 120
```

```
1)Factorial
2)Fibonacci
3)Ackerman
4)Tower of Hanoi
5)Quit
Enter Your Choice : 2

Enter Term No. : 5


Term No. 5 = 5

1)Factorial
2)Fibonacci
3)Ackerman
4)Tower of Hanoi
5)Quit
Enter Your Choice : 3

Enter 2 Numbers : 1
2


Ackerman function of(1,2) = 4

1)Factorial
2)Fibonacci
3)Ackerman
4)Tower of Hanoi
5)Quit
Enter Your Choice : 4
Enter No. of plates :3


C -> B
```

```
B -> C
A -> C
C -> B
B -> A
A -> B
C -> B

1)Factorial
2)Fibonacci
3)Ackerman
4)Tower of Hanoi
5)Quit
Enter Your Choice : 5
```

10.6 Implementation of Queue

10.6.1 Queue using an Array :

```c
/* Simulation of  queue using an array */
#include<conio.h>
#include<stdio.h>
#define MAX 5

typedef struct Q
{
   int R,F;
   int data[MAX];
}Q;

void initialise(Q *P);
int empty(Q *P);
int full(Q *P);
void enqueue(Q *P,int x);
int dequeue(Q *P);
```

```
void print(Q *P);
void main()
{
   Q q;
   int op,x;
   initialise(&q);
   clrscr();
   do
     {
         printf("\n\n1)Insert\n2)Delete\n3)Print\n4)Quit");
         printf("\nEnter Your Choice:");
         scanf("%d",&op);
         switch(op)
           {
              case 1: printf("\n Enter a value:");
                    scanf("%d",&x);
                    if(!full(&q))
                         enqueue(&q,x);
                    else
                         printf("\nQueue is full !!!!");
                    break;
              case 2: if(!empty(&q))
                       {
                           x=dequeue(&q);
                           printf("\Deleted Data=%d",x);
                       }
                    else
                    printf("\nQueue is empty !!!!");
                    break;
              case 3: print(&q);break;
            }
     }while(op!=4);
}

void initialise(Q *P)
```

```
{
    P->R=-1;
    P->F=-1;
}

int empty(Q *P)
{
    if(P->R==-1)
          return(1);
    return(0);
}

int full(Q *P)
{
    if(P->R==MAX-1)
          return(1);
    return(0);
}

void enqueue(Q *P,int x)
{
    if(P->R==-1)
    {
          P->R=P->F=0;
          P->data[P->R]=x;
    }
    else
    {
          P->R=P->R+1%MAX;
          P->data[P->R]=x;
    }
}

int dequeue(Q *P)
{
```

```
    int x;
    x=P->data[P->F];
    if(P->R==P->F)
    {
        P->R=-1;
        P->F=-1;
    }
    else
        P->F=P->F+1;
    return(x);
}

void print(Q *P)
{
    int i;
    if(!empty(P))
    {
        printf("\n");
        for(i=P->F;i<=P->R;i++)
            printf("%d\t",P->data[i]);
    }
}
```

Output

```
1)Insert
2)Delete
3)Print
4)Quit
Enter Your Choice:1

 Enter a value:3

1)Insert
2)Delete
3)Print
```

```
4)Quit
Enter Your Choice:1

 Enter a value:6

1)Insert
2)Delete
3)Print
4)Quit
Enter Your Choice:1

 Enter a value:8

1)Insert
2)Delete
3)Print
4)Quit
Enter Your Choice:3

3      6      8

1)Insert
2)Delete
3)Print
4)Quit
Enter Your Choice:2
Deleted Data=3


1)Insert
2)Delete
3)Print
4)Quit
Enter Your Choice:4
```

10.6.2 Circular Queue using an Array :

```c
/* A program for circular queue using an array */
#include<conio.h>
#include<stdio.h>
#define MAX 10

typedef struct Q
{
   int R,F;
   int data[MAX];
}Q;

void initialise(Q *P);
int empty(Q *P);
int full(Q *P);
void enqueue(Q *P,int x);
int dequeue(Q *P);
void print(Q *P);
void main()
{
   Q q;
   int op,x;
   initialise(&q);
   clrscr();
   do
     {
         printf("\n\n1)Insert\n2)Delete\n3)Print\n4)Quit");
         printf("\nEnter Your Choice:");
         scanf("%d",&op);
         switch(op)
           {
              case 1: printf("\n Enter a value:");
```

```
                        scanf("%d",&x);
                        if(!full(&q))
                                enqueue(&q,x);
                        else
                                printf("\nQueue is full !!!!");
                        break;
                case 2: if(!empty(&q))
                        {
                                x=dequeue(&q);
                                printf("\Deleted Data=%d",x);
                        }
                        else
                        printf("\nQueue is empty !!!!");
                        break;
                case 3: print(&q);break;
            }
    }while(op!=4);
}

void initialise(Q *P)
{
   P->R=-1;
   P->F=-1;
}

int empty(Q *P)
{
   if(P->R==-1)
        return(1);
   return(0);
}
```

```c
int full(Q *P)
{
    if((P->R+1)%MAX==P->F)
        return(1);
    return(0);
}

void enqueue(Q *P,int x)
{
    if(P->R==-1)
    {
        P->R=P->F=0;
        P->data[P->R]=x;
    }
    else
    {
        P->R=(P->R+1)%MAX;
        P->data[P->R]=x;
    }
}

int dequeue(Q *P)
{
    int x;
    x=P->data[P->F];
    if(P->R==P->F)
    {
        P->R=-1;
        P->F=-1;
    }
    else
        P->F=(P->F+1)%MAX;
```

```
    return(x);
}

void print(Q *P)
{
    int i;
    if(!empty(P))
    {
         printf("\n");
         for(i=P->F;i!=P->R;i=(i+1)%MAX)
             printf("%d\t",P->data[i]);
         printf("%d\t",P->data[i]);
    }
}
```

Output

```
1)Insert
2)Delete
3)Print
4)Quit
Enter Your Choice:1


 Enter a value:6


1)Insert
2)Delete
3)Print
4)Quit
Enter Your Choice:1


 Enter a value:8
```

1)Insert
2)Delete
3)Print
4)Quit
Enter Your Choice:1

 Enter a value:9

1)Insert
2)Delete
3)Print
4)Quit
Enter Your Choice:3

6   8   9

1)Insert
2)Delete
3)Print
4)Quit
Enter Your Choice:2
Deleted Data=6

1)Insert
2)Delete
3)Print
4)Quit
Enter Your Choice:4

10.6.3 Queue using a Linked List :

```c
/* Queue represented using a linked list.*/

#include<conio.h>
#include<stdio.h>

typedef struct node
{
   int data;
   struct node *next;
}node;

typedef struct Q
{
   node  *R,*F;
}Q;

void initialise(Q *);
int empty(Q *);
int full(Q *);
void enqueue(Q *,int);
int dequeue(Q *);
void print(Q *);
void main()
{
   Q q;
   int x,i,op;
   initialise(&q);
   clrscr();
   do
     {
         printf("\n\n1)Insert\n2)Delete\n3)Print\n4)Quit");
         printf("\n Enter Your Choice:");
```

```
        scanf("%d",&op);
        switch(op)
          {
            case 1: printf("\n Enter a value:");
                    scanf("%d",&x);
                    enqueue(&q,x);
                    break;
            case 2: if(!empty(&q))
                      {
                          x=dequeue(&q);
                          printf("\Deleted Data=%d",x);
                      }
                    else
                        printf("\nQueue is empty !!!!");
                    break;
            case 3: print(&q);break;
          }
    }while(op!=4);
}

void initialise(Q *qP)
{
  qP->R=NULL;
  qP->F=NULL;
}
void enqueue(Q *qP,int x)
{
  node *P;
  P=(node*)malloc(sizeof(node));
  P->data=x;
  P->next=NULL;
  if(empty(qP))
  {
        qP->R=P;
```

```
            qP->F=P;
   }
   else
   {
         (qP->R)->next=P;
         qP->R=P;
   }
}
int dequeue(Q *qP)
{
   int x;
   node *P;
   P=qP->F;
   x=P->data;
   if(qP->F==qP->R)  //deleting the last element
         initialise(qP);
   else
         qP->F=P->next;
   free(P);
   return(x);
}
void print(Q *qP)
{
   int i;
   node *P;
   P=qP->F;
   printf("\n");
   while(P!=NULL)
   {
         printf("%d ",P->data);
         P=P->next;
   }
}
int empty(Q *qp)
```

```
{
   if(qp->R==NULL)
        return 1;
   return 0;
}
```

Output

```
1)Insert
2)Delete
3)Print
4)Quit
Enter Your Choice:1

 Enter a value:5


1)Insert
2)Delete
3)Print
4)Quit
Enter Your Choice:1

 Enter a value:9

1)Insert
2)Delete
3)Print
4)Quit
Enter Your Choice:1

 Enter a value:7

1)Insert
2)Delete
```

```
3)Print
4)Quit
Enter Your Choice:3

5 9 7

1)Insert
2)Delete
3)Print
4)Quit
Enter Your Choice:2
Deleted Data=5

1)Insert
2)Delete
3)Print
4)Quit
Enter Your Choice:4
```

10.7 Operations on Singly Linked List

```c
/*Operations on SLL(singly linked list) */

#include<stdio.h>
#include<conio.h>
#include<stdlib.h>
typedef struct node
  { int data;
    struct node *next;
  }node;


node *create();
```

```c
node *insert_b(node *head,int x);
node *insert_e(node *head,int x);
node *insert_in(node *head,int x);
node *delete_b(node *head);
node *delete_e(node *head);
node *delete_in(node *head);
node *reverse(node *head);
void search(node *head);
void print(node *head);

void main()
{ int op,op1,x;
  node *head=NULL;
  clrscr();
  do
   {
     printf("\n\n1)create\n2)Insert\n3)Delete\n4)Search");
     printf("\n5)Reverse\n6)Print\n7)Quit");
     printf("\nEnter your Choice:");
     scanf("%d",&op);
     switch(op)
      { case 1:head=create();break;
      case 2:printf("\n\t1)Beginning\n\t2)End\n\t3)In between");
          printf("\nEnter your choice : ");
          scanf("%d",&op1);
          printf("\nEnter the data to be inserted : ");
          scanf("%d",&x);
          switch(op1)
```

```
            { case 1: head=insert_b(head,x);
                 break;
              case 2: head=insert_e(head,x);
                 break;
              case 3: head=insert_in(head, x);
                 break;
            }
          break;
     case 3:printf("\n\t1)Beginning\n\t2)End\n\t3)In between");
          printf("\nEnter your choice : ");
          scanf("%d",&op1);
          switch(op1)
            { case 1:head=delete_b(head);
                 break;
              case 2:head=delete_e(head);
                 break;
              case 3:head=delete_in(head);
                 break;
            }
          break;
     case 4:search(head);break;
     case 5:head=reverse(head);
          print(head);
          break;
     case 6:print(head);break;
     }
   }while(op!=7);
}
```

```
node *create()
{ node *head,*p;
 int i,n;
 head=NULL;
 printf("\n Enter no of data:");
 scanf("%d",&n);
 printf("\nEnter the data:");
 for(i=0;i<n;i++)
  {
   if(head==NULL)
   p=head=(node*)malloc(sizeof(node));
   else
    {
   p->next=(node*)malloc(sizeof(node));
   p=p->next;
    }
    p->next=NULL;
    scanf("%d",&(p->data));
  }
 return(head);
}

node *insert_b(node *head,int x)
{   node *p;
  p=(node*)malloc(sizeof(node));
  p->data=x;
  p->next=head;
```

```
    head=p;
    return(head);
}

node *insert_e(node *head,int x)
{   node *p,*q;
    p=(node*)malloc(sizeof(node));
    p->data=x;
    p->next=NULL;
    if(head==NULL)
      return(p);
    //locate the last node
    for(q=head;q->next!=NULL;q=q->next)
    ;
    q->next=p;
    return(head);
}

node *insert_in(node *head,int x)
{   node *p,*q;
    int y;
    p=(node*)malloc(sizeof(node));
    p->data=x;
    p->next=NULL;
    printf("\Insert after which number ? : ");
    scanf("%d",&y);
    //locate the lthe data 'y'
    for(q=head ; q != NULL && q->data != y ; q=q->next)
```

```
    ;
    if(q!=NULL)
     {
    p->next=q->next;
    q->next=p;
     }
    else
      printf("\nData not found ");
    return(head);
}
node *delete_b(node *head)
{
  node *p,*q;
  if(head==NULL)
    {
    printf("\n Underflow....Empty Linked List");
     return(head);
     }
  p=head;
  head=head->next;
  free(p);
  return(head);

}
node *delete_e(node *head)
{
  node *p,*q;
  if(head==NULL)
```

```
    {
   printf("\nUnderflow....Empty Linked List");
   return(head);
    }
  p=head;
  if(head->next==NULL)
    { // Delete the only element
     head=NULL;
     free(p);
     return(head);
    }
//Locate the last but one node
  for(q=head;q->next->next !=NULL;q=q->next)
  ;
  p=q->next;
  q->next=NULL;
  free(p);
  return(head);
}
node *delete_in(node *head)
{
 node *p,*q;
 int x,i;
 if(head==NULL)
   {
   printf("\nUnderflow....Empty Linked List");
   return(head);
   }
```

```c
  printf("\nEnter the data to be deleted : ");
  scanf("%d",&x);
  if(head->data==x)
    { // Delete the first element
      p=head;
      head=head->next;
      free(p);
      return(head);
    }
//Locate the node previous to one to be deleted
  for(q=head;q->next->data!=x && q->next !=NULL;q=q->next )
  ;
  if(q->next==NULL)
    {
      printf("\nUnderflow.....data not found");
      return(head);
    }
  p=q->next;
  q->next=q->next->next;
  free(p);
  return(head);
}
void search(node *head)
{ node *p;
  int data,loc=1;
  printf("\nEnter the data to be searched: ");
  scanf("%d",&data);
  p=head;
  while(p!=NULL && p->data != data)
```

```
  { loc++;
    p=p->next;
  }
 if(p==NULL)
  printf("\nNot found:");
 else
  printf("\nFound at location=%d",loc);
}
void print(node *head)
{ node *p;
 printf("\n\n");
 for(p=head;p!=NULL;p=p->next)
  printf("%d  ",p->data);
}
node *reverse(node *head)
 { node *p,*q,*r;
  p=NULL;
  q=head;
  r=q->next;
  while(q!=NULL)
   {
  q->next=p;
  p=q;
  q=r;
  if(q!=NULL)
    r=q->next;
   }
  return(p);
}
```

Output

```
1)create
2)Insert
3)Delete
4)Search
5)Reverse
6)Print
7)Quit
Enter your Choice:1

 Enter no of data:3

Enter the data:5
6
9

1)create
2)Insert
3)Delete
4)Search
5)Reverse
6)Print
7)Quit
Enter your Choice:2

     1)Beginning
     2)End
     3)In between
```

Enter your choice : 1

Enter the data to be inserted : 3

1)create
2)Insert
3)Delete
4)Search
5)Reverse
6)Print
7)Quit
Enter your Choice:4

Enter the data to be searched: 6

Found at location=3

1)create
2)Insert
3)Delete
4)Search
5)Reverse
6)Print
7)Quit
Enter your Choice:3

　　1)Beginning
　　2)End

      3)In between
Enter your choice : 3

Enter the data to be deleted : 6

1)create
2)Insert
3)Delete
4)Search
5)Reverse
6)Print
7)Quit
Enter your Choice:5

9 5 3

1)create
2)Insert
3)Delete
4)Search
5)Reverse
6)Print
7)Quit
Enter your Choice:7

10.8 Operations on a Tree

```c
// program showing various operations on binary search tree
#include<conio.h>
#include<stdio.h>
#include<stdlib.h>

typedef struct BSTnode
{
    int data;
    struct BSTnode *left,*right;
}BSTnode;

BSTnode *find(BSTnode *,int);
BSTnode *insert(BSTnode *,int);
BSTnode *delet(BSTnode *,int);
BSTnode *create();
void inorder(BSTnode *T);
void preorder(BSTnode *T);
void postorder(BSTnode *T);

void main()
{
    BSTnode *root=NULL,*p;
    int x,op;
    clrscr();
    do
      { printf("\n\n1)Create\n2)Delete\n3)Search \n4)Preorder");
```

```c
      printf("\n5)Inorder\n6)Postorder\n7)Insert\n8)Quit");
      printf("\nEnter Your Choice :");
      scanf("%d",&op);
       switch(op)
        {
          case 1: root=create();break;
          case 2:    printf("\nEnter the key to be deleted :");
              scanf("%d",&x);
              root=delet(root,x);
              break;
          case 3:    printf("\nEnter the key to be searched :");
              scanf("%d",&x);
              p=find(root,x);
              if(p==NULL)
                printf("\n ***** Not Found****");
              else
                printf("\n ***** Found*****");
              break;
          case 4: preorder(root);break;
          case 5: inorder(root);break;
          case 6: postorder(root);break;
          case 7: printf("\nEnter a data to be inserted : ");
              scanf("%d",&x);
              root=insert(root,x);
        }
    }while(op!=8);
}

void inorder(BSTnode *T)
```

```
{
  if(T!=NULL)
  {
        inorder(T->left);
        printf("%d\t",T->data);
        inorder(T->right);
  }
}

void preorder(BSTnode *T)
{       if(T!=NULL)
    { printf("%d\t",T->data);
     preorder(T->left);
     preorder(T->right);
    }
}
void postorder(BSTnode *T)
{       if(T!=NULL)
    {
     postorder(T->left);
     postorder(T->right);
     printf("%d\t",T->data);
    }
}

BSTnode *find(BSTnode *root,int x)
{
  while(root!=NULL)
  {
```

```
        if(x==root->data)
            return(root);
        if(x>root->data)
            root=root->right;
        else
        root=root->left;
    }
    return(NULL);
}

BSTnode *insert(BSTnode *T,int x)
{
    BSTnode *p,*q,*r;
    // acquire memory for the new node
    r=(BSTnode*)malloc(sizeof(BSTnode));
    r->data=x;
    r->left=NULL;
    r->right=NULL;
    if(T==NULL)
        return(r);
    // find the leaf node for insertion
    p=T;
    while(p!=NULL)
    {
        q=p;
        if(x>p->data)
            p=p->right;
        else
            if(x<p->data)
```

```
                          p=p->left;
                else
                  {
                        printf("\n Duplicate data : ");
                        return(T);
                  }
    }
    if(x>q->data)
        q->right=r;  // x as right child of q
    else
        q->left=r;   //x as left child of q
    return(T);
}

BSTnode *delet(BSTnode *T,int x)
{
    BSTnode *temp;
    if(T==NULL)
    {
        printf("\n Element not found :");
        return(T);
    }
    if(x < T->data)              // delete in left subtree
    {
        T->left=delet(T->left,x);
        return(T);
    }
    if(x > T->data)              // delete in right subtree
    {
```

```
        T->right=delet(T->right,x);
        return(T);
}

// element is found
if(T->left==NULL && T->right==NULL)    // a leaf node
{
        temp=T;
        free(temp);
        return(NULL);
}
if(T->left==NULL)
{
        temp=T;
        T=T->right;
        free(temp);
        return(T);
}
if(T->right==NULL)
{
        temp=T;
        T=T->left;
        free(temp);
        return(T);
}
// node with two children
//go to the inorder successor of the node
temp=T->right;
```

```
    while(temp->left !=NULL)
     temp=temp->left;
    T->data=temp->data;
    T->right=delet(T->right,temp->data);
    return(T);
}


BSTnode *create()
{
    int n,x,i;
    BSTnode *root;
    root=NULL;
    printf("\nEnter no. of nodes :");
    scanf("%d",&n);
    printf("\nEnter tree values :");
    for(i=0;i<n;i++)
    {
        scanf("%d",&x);
        root=insert(root,x);
    }
    return(root);
}
```

Output

```
1)Create
2)Delete
3)Search
4)Preorder
5)Inorder
6)Postorder
```

7)Insert

8)Quit

Enter Your Choice :1

Enter no. of nodes :3

Enter tree values :6

8

4

1)Create

2)Delete

3)Search

4)Preorder

5)Inorder

6)Postorder

7)Insert

8)Quit

Enter Your Choice :3

Enter the key to be searched :8

***** Found*****

1)Create

2)Delete

3)Search

4)Preorder

5)Inorder

6)Postorder

7)Insert

8)Quit

Enter Your Choice :4

6   4   8

1)Create

2)Delete

3)Search

4)Preorder

5)Inorder

6)Postorder

7)Insert

8)Quit

Enter Your Choice :5

4   6   8

1)Create

2)Delete

3)Search

4)Preorder

5)Inorder

6)Postorder

7)Insert

8)Quit

Enter Your Choice :6

4   8   6

1)Create

2)Delete

3)Search

4)Preorder

5)Inorder

6)Postorder

7)Insert

8)Quit

Enter Your Choice :2

Enter the key to be deleted :6

1)Create

2)Delete

3)Search

4)Preorder

5)Inorder

6)Postorder

7)Insert

8)Quit

Enter Your Choice :3

Enter the key to be searched :6

***** Not Found****

1)Create

```
2)Delete
3)Search
4)Preorder
5)Inorder
6)Postorder
7)Insert
8)Quit
Enter Your Choice :8
```

10.9 BFS and DFS on a Graph

```c
/*BSF and DSF on a graph represented using adjacency matrix*/
#include<conio.h>
#include<stdio.h>
#define MAX 10

typedef struct Q
{
    int R,F;
    int data[MAX];
}Q;

int empty(Q *P);
int full(Q *P);
void enqueue(Q *P,int x);
int dequeue(Q *P);
void BFS(int);
void DFS(int);
```

```
int G[MAX][MAX];
int n=0;
int visited[MAX];
void main()
{
   int i,j,v,op;
   printf("\nEnter no of vertices : ");
   scanf("%d",&n);
   printf("\nEnter the adjacency matrix of  graph : ");
   for(i=0;i<n;i++)
        for(j=0;j<n;j++)
            scanf("%d",&G[i][j]);

   do{
     printf("\n\n1)DFS\n2)BFS\n3)QUIT");
     printf("\nEnter Your choice : ");
     scanf("%d",&op);
     switch(op)
      { case 1:printf("\nEnter the starting vertex for DFS : ");
              scanf("%d",&v);
              for(i=0;i<n;i++)
                visited[i]=0;
              DFS(v);break;
        case 2:printf("\nEnter the starting vertex for BFS : ");
              scanf("%d",&v);
              BFS(v);break;
      }
    }while(op!=3);
```

```
}

void BFS(int v)
{
   int visited[MAX],i;
   Q q;
   q.R=q.F=-1;
   for(i=0;i<n;i++)
     visited[i]=0;
   enqueue(&q,v);
   printf("\n visit\n",v);
   visited[v]=1;
   while(!empty(&q))
   {
        v=dequeue(&q);
        // visit and add adjacency vertices
        for(i=0;i<n;i++)
           if(visited[i]==0 && G[v][i]!=0)
           {
                   enqueue(&q,i);
                   visited[i]=1;
                   printf("\n%d",i);
           }
   }
}
int empty(Q *P)
{
   if(P->R==-1)
```

```
        return(1);
    return(0);
}

int full(Q *P)
{
    if(P->R==MAX-1)
        return(1);
    return(0);
}

void enqueue(Q *P,int x)
{
    if(P->R==-1)
    {
        P->R=P->F=0;
        P->data[P->R]=x;
    }
    else
    {
        P->R=P->R+1;
        P->data[P->R]=x;
    }
}

int dequeue(Q *P)
{
    int x;
    x=P->data[P->F];
```

```
    if(P->R==P->F)
    {
            P->R=-1;
            P->F=-1;
    }
    else
            P->F=P->F+1;
    return(x);
}

void DFS(int i)
{
    int j;
    printf("\n%d",i);
    visited[i]=1;
    for(j=0;j<n;j++)
            if(!visited[j] && G[i][j]==1)
                DFS(j);
}
```

Output

```
Enter no of vertices : 3

Enter the adjacency matrix of  graph : 0

1

1

1

0

1
```

```
1
1
0

1)DFS
2)BFS
3)QUIT
Enter Your choice : 1


Enter the starting vertex for DFS : 0


0
1
2


1)DFS
2)BFS
3)QUIT
Enter Your choice : 2


Enter the starting vertex for BFS : 1


 visit


0
2


1)DFS
2)BFS
```

3)QUIT

Enter Your choice : 3

10.10　Hashing with Linear Probing

```
/* Hashing *  /
/* Program Details - Hashing , handle collision  using linear
probing*/
#include <stdio.h>
#include <conio.h>
#define SIZE 10              /* size of the hash table*/
#define FALSE 0
#define TRUE 1
#define h(x) x%SIZE          /*hashing function */
void insert( int data[],int flag[],int x);
int search(int data[],int flag[],int x);
void print(int data[],int flag[]);

void main()
 { int data[SIZE],flag[SIZE],i,j,x,op,loc;
  /* array data[]  - is a hash table
     array flag[]  - if flag[i] is 1 then the i th place of the hash
             table is filled */
   for(i=0;i<SIZE;i++) /* initialize */
    flag[i]=FALSE;
   clrscr();
   do
    { flushall();
   printf("\n\n1)Insert\n2)Search\n3)Print\n4)Quit");
```

```
    printf("\nEnter Your Choice : ");
    scanf("%d",&op);
    switch(op)
     { case 1: printf("\n Enter a number to be inserted:");
             scanf("%d",&x);
             insert(data,flag,x);
             break;
        case 2: printf("\n Enter a number to be searched :");
             scanf("%d",&x);
             if((loc=search(data,flag,x))==-1)
               printf("\n****Element not found****");
             else
               printf("\n***Found at the location=%d",loc);
             break;
        case 3:  print(data,flag);
             break;
     }
    }while(op!=4);
 }
void insert( int data[],int flag[],int x)
{int i=0,j;
 j=h(x); /*hashed location*/
 do
   { if(!flag[j])
      { data[j]=x;
     flag[j]=TRUE;
     return;
      }
     else
```

```
    { i++;
   j=(h(x)+i)%SIZE;
     }
  }while(i<SIZE);
printf("\n*****hash table is full");
}
int search(int data[],int flag[],int x)
 {int i=0,j;
 j=h(x); /*hashed location*/
 do
  { if(data[j]==x)
     return(j);
    i++;
    j=(h(x)+i)%SIZE;
  }while(i<SIZE && flag[j]);
 return(-1);
}

void print(int data[],int flag[])
 { int i;
   for(i=0;i<SIZE;i++)
   if(flag[i])
    printf("\n(%d) %d",i,data[i]);
    else
    printf("\n(%d) ---",i);
 }
```

Output

```
1)Insert
2)Search
```

3)Print
4)Quit
Enter Your Choice : 1

 Enter a number to be inserted:5

1)Insert
2)Search
3)Print
4)Quit
Enter Your Choice : 1

 Enter a number to be inserted:9

1)Insert
2)Search
3)Print
4)Quit
Enter Your Choice : 1

 Enter a number to be inserted:6

1)Insert
2)Search
3)Print
4)Quit
Enter Your Choice : 3

(0) ---
(1) ---

(2) ---

(3) ---

(4) ---

(5) 5

(6) 6

(7) ---

(8) ---

(9) 9

1)Insert

2)Search

3)Print

4)Quit

Enter Your Choice :2

 Enter a number to be searched :6

***Found at the location=6

1)Insert

2)Search

3)Print

4)Quit

Enter Your Choice : 4

□□□